101

Great Ways
to Compete in
Today's Job Market

Selected and Introduced by

Michelle A. Riklan
and David Riklan

A Product of

SelfGrowth.com

101 Great Ways to Compete in Today's Job Market
By Michelle A. Riklan and David Riklan

Published by
Self Improvement Online, Inc.
http://www.SelfGrowth.com
1130 Campus Drive West, Morganville, NJ 07751

This book is dedicated in memory of

Natalie Landy

who always wanted to know "What's cooking?"

ACKNOWLEDGEMENTS

I am so fortunate to belong to many professional organizations that provide support, resources, and valuable tools that I use in my day-to-day business. At this past year's National Resume Writer's Association[1] (NRWA) Conference, I sat next to Loretta Peters, an author from *101 Great Ways to Enhance your Career*. Loretta wanted to know when the next book was coming out. I hadn't really thought about it at the time, but with some collaborative brainstorming in between speakers, the concept for *101 Great Ways to Compete in Today's Job Market* was formed.

My goal with this new project was to provide a resource for individuals to help them get ahead of the competition or to maintain a competitive edge. With 101 authors providing insights on developing leadership attributes, creating marketing materials for job-search, utilizing social media to network and develop a positive online presence/brand-identity, moving up the corporate ladder, self-promotion, and so much more, I believe we have achieved our goal.

It goes without question that this project could not come to fruition without the talented authors, colleagues, and staff who have contributed.

- Thank you to our featured authors, William Arruda, Lewis Howes, Harvey McKay, Brian Tracy, Denis Waitley, Martin Yate, and Tom Hopkins, and to all of our 101 experts.
- Without the support of the entire SelfGrowth.com team, this book could not have been created. To Sam Etkin, Adriene Hayes, Kristina Kanaley, Joe DePalma, and Nimrod Grinvald, your efforts have been invaluable.
- Special thanks to my Office Manager, Robin Kugler, who keeps me organized, on task, and sane.

As always, thanks to my husband David and three incredible children; Joshua, Jonathan, and Rachel.

---

[1] The mission of The NRWA, a nonprofit trade association for professional resume writers, is to increase the visibility of the industry, encourage ethical practices, promote excellence, and raise industry standards through peer marketing and training.

The NRWA offers education, resources, and networking opportunities for career industry writers, including professionals from:

workforce and community centers
college and university career services
military transition and career centers
independent businesses

TABLE OF CONTENTS

INTRODUCTION

By Michelle A. Riklan and David Riklan

"Anytime you find someone more successful than you are, especially when you're both engaged in the same business - you know they're doing something that you aren't." — Malcolm X

What does it take to compete in a challenging job market? For those just starting out, it may mean getting a foot in the door, any door. For the seasoned professional, it may mean staying updated with current knowledge and skills to ensure job security or to advance to the next level. For others, it may be about taking a risk, starting a business, going back to school, or making a career transition. However you define it, in today's job market it is real.

Our collaborative authors have generously offered their expertise, each offering a fresh perspective and unique strategies to help arm our readers with tools that they need to not only be in the game, but to get ahead of the competition. *101 Great Ways to Compete in Today's Job Market* is a comprehensive collection of 101 unique chapters from some of the industry's leading experts. Our experts are passionate about their messages, highly credentialed, and dedicated to helping individuals navigate the job market waves.

Our mission in bringing to you *101 Great Ways to Compete in Today's Job Market* is that you will find chapters that speak to you on a personal level and find valuable tools that will give you a competitive edge in your career.

What You Can Learn From this Book

- You *can* brand yourself and recession-proof your career.
- You *can* self-promote without losing your self-respect.
- You *can* effectively handle challenging interviews and win the job.

1

- You *can* ensure your résumé lands on the top of the pile.
- You *can* overcome job search obstacles such as poor credit or being fired from a previous position.
- You *can* develop skills that will rapidly improve your marketability.
- You *can* land a job using social media.

And so much more! Whether you are seeking answers for yourself or working with a client, this book offers solutions, suggestions, advice, and support on a wide range of topics including: LinkedIn, Twitter, career branding, networking, interviewing, job hunting, turning down a job offer / promotion, leadership development, contracting…

This book is a perfect tool for anyone who is looking to start a career, get ahead in their current position, return to the workforce, start their own business or is in a role that assists others with career development.

How the Book is Organized

We have organized this book by topic to simplify the information-gathering process. If you are looking for information on *LinkedIn,* just go to the table of contents, locate the corresponding page numbers and start reading! If you are seeking tips on how to develop your *leadership skills,* it's all right there. We tried to make it simple and hope you find this book easy to navigate.

Although not every chapter will relate to each individual's interests and needs, it is designed like a buffet. There is plenty to choose from. Some chapters will appeal to you and some may not. If one chapter isn't what you want, the next one might be. You can always go back for more.

Who Should Read This Book

101 Great Ways to Compete in Today's Job Market is designed for a broad audience ranging from the CEO of a major corporation to the return to work individual or recent college graduate. It is a clear, concise smorgasbord of information to choose from, featuring many of the industry's top experts.

1

A Guide to Appearance

❧

Anuraag Awasthi, PhD

Two people appear for a job interview. One is dressed professionally—neat clothes, well groomed—and the other is dressed in casual clothes and has unkempt hair. As an interviewer, who would you be more inclined to consider for the job, irrespective of the role? The answer is obvious. Research has shown that even before we have opened our mouth and the formal communication has begun, our visual communication has already taken place.

We live in a visual world where appearances matter. People form impressions based on how we look. Our first personal impact on others is always visual. People evaluate us during the first 30 seconds, when the brain unconsciously observes our appearance based on:

- Appropriateness of clothes and shoes
- State of the face
- State of the hair
- State of the nails and hands
- Body odor

Based on this subconscious assessment, we form impression about the other person in terms of his or her:

- Economic level
- Education level

- Trustworthiness
- Social position
- Intelligence
- Level of sophistication
- Moral character
- Success

First impression is the last impression. This, unfortunately, is true, and it requires a huge effort and lots of time to change this impression. In job situations or professional engagements, nine out of ten times this opportunity to change the image does not arise as the person is rejected in the first meeting itself.

Research has also shown that attractive, tall, well-groomed people find jobs easily, make more money, and get ahead faster. Professor Chris Warhurst, an expert in employment studies from the University of Sydney, said that people "perceived to be better looking" were up to five times more likely to be hired over others. They had better careers and could earn up to 16 percent more than others doing the same job. The physical appearance also influences perceptions of job competence and performance.

A picture is worth more than a thousand words. A new study has revealed that employers give more importance to looks than to qualifications and job experience when hiring a candidate for a job. This includes a candidate's looks, dress, and communication style. Considering qualifications, experience being equal, appearance becomes the clinching factor.

The Beauty Premium

Today there is an advantage being beautiful. Handsome men earn, on average, 5 percent more than their less-attractive counterparts earn. Pretty people get more attention from teachers, bosses, and mentors; even babies stare longer at good-looking faces.

Stronger Brand Image

Research conducted in Australia and the United Kingdom has revealed that employers favor appearance and personality over previous job experience and qualifications. The main reason given for such a practice is a desire to conform to a company's brand image.

For those who are already working, and aspire for higher positions, it is advised to dress up for the role you aspire to. The idea is that when the time comes to promote from among a pool of hopefuls, the person who already looks the part gets the nod.

Appearance consists of such elements as clothes, grooming, hygiene, and a pleasing demeanor. Grooming and hygiene are important in both our personal and professional life. A great toned body makes no impact if accompanied by dirty, lifeless hair. An expensive designer suit loses its power if accessorized by body odor.

Enhance Your AQ

Following are given some tips on enhancing the Appearance Quotient (AQ):

Hair: Hair is your crowning glory. Keep it at a length and style you can maintain. Wash your hair at least once a week. For men, the hair should not fall over the ears or eyebrows or even touch the back of the collar. Facial hair should be neatly trimmed. Moustaches, sideburns, and beards are not recommended. For women, hair should be well groomed with a neat appearance at all times. Tie your hair in a neat hairstyle with hair pulled back from your face. Hair that falls below the jaw line should be tied into a bun. Hair-holding devices should be plain and of natural colors. If using hair color, it should not be more than one or two shades darker or lighter than your natural hair color. Avoid unnatural colors (burgundy, green, red).

Nails: Keep nails clean and clipped short along their shape. Don't chew your nails under any circumstance. For women who use nail polish, make it a sober color and not too distracting.

Teeth: Clean teeth and fresh breath are essential for self-confidence. Uneven or stained teeth can make you look dirty. Brush your teeth twice a day, and rinse well after every meal. Smokers should rinse their mouth after every smoke and use a breath freshener.

Body odor: Use an antiperspirant/deodorant and a mildly scented aftershave or cologne.

Accessories: Men should limit accessories/jewelry to three pieces. These include a watch, ring, and handkerchief. Wear a dress watch; avoid athletic styles. Avoid bracelets, necklaces, and visible piercing. Women should keep jewelry to the minimum and be conservative. Remove all facial piercing except earrings. Adopt the five-piece rule: wear a maximum of five accessories. Earrings count as two, a watch as one, allowing two additional accessories.

Hats and head coverings: Hats and caps are not appropriate in the office. Head covers required for religious purposes or to honor a cultural tradition are allowed.

Make-up: This primarily applies to women. Keep your make-up light and natural when in the office. Choose a natural look for an elegant appearance. Use colors that complement your complexion; not all make-up shades work with all skin tones. Enhance either your eyes or your lips, not both at the same time.

Footwear: Shoes should be of good-quality leather, in good condition, and polished. Their color should match your trousers or be of a darker color. For men, lace-up conservative shoes are the most appropriate. Choose black, brown, or burgundy shoes. Socks should match the color of your suit and cover your calves. For women, shoes should be pumps or sling backs. Don't wear shoes with open toes, open heel, or ankle straps. Heels should not be more than two inches. Classic athletic shoes are appropriate. Loud colors (florescent) and prints on shoes are distracting.

Clothes: Dress appropriately for the occasion. For men, the basic business wardrobe should consist of:

- Navy blue and gray suits
- White cotton, blue solid, or pinstriped shirts (Avoid short-sleeved shirts, even if you're doing business in a hot country.)
- Solid, striped, or patterned silk ties
- Black or tan shoes
- Belt in good condition matching the color of your shoes

- Leather briefcase or laptop case to create a professional appearance, even if it's old

Women's basic business wardrobe should consist of:

- Plain-color skirt suits in black, gray, or navy (Pantsuits are best avoided.)
- Solid-color blouses
- One- or two-piece dresses (jacket optional)
- Matching accessories
- No overpowering jewelry

It's not easy to compete in today's job market, with shrinking jobs and competition getting global. For one position, there are hundreds, if not thousands, of claimants. In such a clutter, what makes a job applicant stand out is personality and appearance. Try to project the best image you can, because *you never get a second chance to make a good first impression.*

Bio

Dr. Anuraag Awasthi is a keynote speaker, trainer, and consultant in people and process excellence. With a double doctorate (in computer science and management) and 25 years of successful corporate, academic, training, and consulting experience across countries, he has a passion for excellence in all spheres of life. During his corporate career, he has led functions such as HR, software development, quality assurance, information security, and customer service. Winner of several excellence awards, he is passionate about employee engagement and believes that a happy employee means a happy customer. He can be reached at Anuraag_awasthi@hotmail.com; +91- 9810068709; and http://www.campcorp.in.

2

APPEARANCE MATTERS

The Importance of Appearance

❧

Angelique Clark-Lawson

"Mom, why can't I wear this shirt?" asks my oldest son one day when he was in middle school.

"Because, sweetie, it has a hole in it, and it's starting to look kind of ratty. You can wear it to bum around in at home," says his mother, who simply exasperates him.

"But it doesn't *really* matter, Mom," he volleys back. "No one cares."

"I care. And I am sure your teachers would notice," I counter. "I would not show up to work with a stained shirt, so you won't go to school looking like you just rolled out of a dumpster." I can tell I'm quickly becoming his nemesis.

"Well, that's your job. It's different, Mom. This is just school," Andrew states with apparent authority.

As I slowly inhale, I realize this child is indeed an apple from my tree.

"Your job is to go to school. It doesn't make money like my job does, but it is still what you do. When you are older, you can choose to dress any way you'd like, but it may be harder to get a job if you haven't had any practice at having a job. And I know you love money." This seems to stop him dead in his tracks.

"Oh."

My darling boy ponders this for a few seconds while he watches me complete my morning routine.

"So if I change my shirt now," he says, "I will get a good job later?" I sense a wee bit of sarcasm from my precocious one.

"Essentially, yes. And you will get money for lunch. And probably that game you've been wanting."

I also realize I'm entering into a thinly veiled bribe because I want to get him out the door without an argument. But I also want him to tuck the message away: You can get what you want, but a level of responsibility— and sometimes sacrifice—is required. On some level, it is about "the system." But if you play by the rules to start, you can blaze your own path later.

"All right, Mom. You win. But that means you should probably take me shopping so I can get some new shirts."

BAM! Yes, definitely my kid.

How We Look Truly Matters

Never to be underestimated, appearance in anything is never missed. Visual judgments usually come first before we apply the other senses. It's all driven by how we see each other that cuts across all countries and all cultures. Each society has a standard, a hierarchy as it were, for what is considered acceptable attire for different societal environments. Appearance has a history for all of us. Typically, we don't seem to make it a high priority unless we are going out on a first date or heading into a job interview. Then we run to the nearest clothing store and try on various articles of clothing that make us look and feel attractive and confident. This is not an inane vanity but rather an acute awareness that how we look matters. If we already feel good about ourselves, what could be better than a well-dressed version of that? We're not trying to be something we are not just to make that impression, but we can always bump up the amperage and still be who we are.

As a speech-language pathologist, I address social skills within the scope of my practice. Appearance is a projection of oneself and a lens through which the world sees a finished product. This form of nonverbal communication tells the world, "Hey, I got this." Why would you want to project any less?

The rules for social niceties envelope appearance. And appearance is not limited to clothes. Sensory input creates an imprint, and it's a natural process to attach meaning to what that system presents us. The next step in that process is to determine what value it has and incorporate it or let it go. Our society has agreed that there is a look to success; and though there may be variations to this, we seem to all know it when we see it. If you waltz into any situation already even slightly above the base for acceptable appearance, you feel more attractive, more intelligent, confident, happier, funnier. And others see you the same way. You stand out. Just raise the bar and you'll exceed it—because that is what we do.

Pop quiz: Do I imply that you have to go out and spend a fortune for that bar to be considered elevated enough to get people to do a double take? I sure don't. However, I know that if you have something that may either look expensive or is expensive, but you got an amazing deal on it, you project this feeling of power. The level of mystique is highly intriguing when you have a secret. This is in no way being elusive. That's very different. Bonus points if this piece is unique enough to catch another person's attention so much so that that person needs to comment on it. Then you can gush a little bit about how you came to possess this treasure. This is you demonstrating savvy. This can be a way to keep you in the mind of the person you really hope remembers you. Hey, Cinderella is proof that an article of clothing can alter you life.

Your Appearance Is Your Brand

Let me be clear, I do not advocate cookie-cutter clones! I am definitely not saying that xyz is the only way to look/be/act. I'm all about being an individual. And part of being who you are is making the best of yourself. Whether it's your stance or your handshake, your clothing choices or your facial expressions, it becomes your brand. When you show up for anything, how do you present? What has your feedback been from others about how they see you? If you are ready to hear it, have some friends tell you what they see, and take in all the information and decide if this is the way you want to be received. If not, change it.

"As human beings, our greatness lies not so much in being able to remake the world—that is the myth of the atomic age—as in being able to remake ourselves." —Mahatma Gandhi

This is absolutely one of my favorite quotes of all time, one I have used as a personal mantra whenever I move into something unfamiliar yet desired. If we don't push ourselves outside our comfort zone, we may never experience a deep satisfaction from having done so. This will put a smile on your face that will be hard to miss. And it will complement anything you wear.

Bio

Angelique (Angela) Clark-Lawson has been a speech-language pathologist in the health care field for 16 years, with interest in traumatic brain injury and autism. Currently, she is working toward her doctorate in health psychology through Walden University. Additionally, she is a certified professional life coach with a planned specialization in recovery. Originally from the southern California area, she has made Springfield, Missouri, her home for the past 20 years with her husband, Ben Lawson, a fine-arts photographer, and their four boys, Andrew, 24; Erich, 21; Parker, 14; and Kiefer, 9. An animal lover with a special affinity for cats, she has an even greater love in meeting new people and being able to inspire them to a happier and more fulfilling life. Angelique believes that you can always remake yourself no matter what has happened in your past because it's all about the future. To contact Angelique or for more information, go to http://www.newleaf-lifecoaching.com;
http://www.facebook.com/NewLeafLifeCoaching; or
http://www.linkedin.com/in/drangelique.

3

Escape the Résumé Black Hole: Use Applicant Tracking Systems to Your Advantage

Robin Schlinger

If you are a job seeker, you may hate Applicant Tracking Systems (ATS) or see them as a black hole because they seem to reject their applications and seem not human. However, by ignoring the systems, you have eliminated yourself from consideration from 70 percent of the jobs out there, even if you network into a job.

As a job seeker, you will want to keep up with the latest news in these areas. You may think you do not want to work for a company that uses an applicant tracking system because any company that screens résumés mechanically is not a company you want to work for. However, that may be self-defeating because companies have been forced, in many cases, to use the ATS because of the volume of applicants or governmental regulations. Here are the reasons many companies use an ATS.

Number of Applicants

Companies that post jobs online receive hundreds, if not thousands, of applicants per job. Many of these résumés are from applicants who apply to many jobs on the Internet, whether or not they are qualified for the job.

Let's say for every opening, a company decides to read the thousand résumés it receives for the announcement. If you have a thousand résumés, and a reviewer spends three minutes reading every résumé (which is what many job seekers hope a reviewer would spend on their résumé), it would take a reviewer 3,000 minutes—the equivalent of 40 hours—just to review the initial number of résumés the company receives. Companies do not have the personnel to spend 40 hours just to review résumés without doing other work.

As the number of applicants to jobs increased because of the Internet, companies began to use ATSs. By using algorithms to search for keywords indicating possession of the key skills required for a job, this substantially reduced the number of résumés people needed to review and allowed them time to review the résumés thoroughly. Even if the method eliminated qualified candidates, as long as the company could find a qualified candidate for the job, it increased efficiency without impacting its ability to fill the position.

Government Reporting Requirements

Over the years, the U.S. government has increased reporting requirements on job applicants, including information on race and disabilities, to ensure conformance to Equal Employment Opportunity (EEO) requirements. By using an ATS, companies can easily comply with these reporting requirements. In addition, by selecting to interview only job applicants selected by the impartial ATS, companies protect themselves from suits from job applicants who claim discrimination.

Applicant Tracking

By using an ATS, companies gain efficiencies. The status of hiring for each person and each job now can be accessed immediately online. This saves companies time, reduces errors, and ensures proper tracking of each person's application.

How to Use an ATS for Your Advantage

Not all ATSs are the same. Many of these systems use computer algorithms to read your résumé and then search for relevant keywords and phrases, based on the job announcement and company, keywords entered in by a user, and algorithms in the program itself. You can use the job announcement and knowledge of the right format and information to help your résumé be selected to be read by an actual person after it is scanned into the ATS and then for you to be selected for the interview for the job.

ATS Résumé Formats

For your résumé to be selected, the ATS must be able to read your résumé. Many systems cannot read PDF files or newer Word (.docx) files, so you may need to use Word (.doc) or plain text files for your résumé. Many ATSs will not read headers, footers, text boxes, graphs, or tables in Word files. Special characters cannot be read by an ATS.

ATSs look for specific information. This includes contact information, including name, address, phone numbers, and email address and typical résumé information using traditional headers, such as "Profile Summary," "Professional Experience," "Education," and "Certifications." You will want to add company name and date, position, and job description on separate lines for each position held.

Keywords/Phrases

To be selected, your résumé must have the right keywords. You can find the right keywords and phrases to use by looking at the announcement to create phrases in your résumé (if you have done the items) in *each* job you have used that skill. Include the phrase in context in your summary if you have done that skill.

If there is something you have not done, but it is not a job requirement, you may want to state in your summary you are capable of learning that skill. However, if there are too many items you have to do this with, this is *not* the job you want to apply for. Once a reviewer reads your résumé, he or she will reject you.

Job Requirements

The federal government now requires all applicants to jobs from companies accepting federal contacts to meet all job requirements listed in job announcements. Some ATSs can check applications to be sure the applicants meet these requirements. Even if not, once the ATS selects your résumé, a reviewer will read it to be sure you really qualify for the job. Your résumé must clearly show this. If you don't meet the job requirements, do not apply for the job.

Accomplishments

You must show the reviewer why she or he should hire you! Others will qualify for the job, but you need to stand out to be selected. You can do this with quantifiable accomplishments.

Judiciously Applying for Jobs

Applicant Tracking Systems keep track of *each* job you apply for in a company. Generally, you can apply only once for each job. Companies reject additional applications. In addition, if you apply for too many jobs (could be even just two) within a company, you may be rejected for future jobs. If a company accepts you for more job applications, you may have to use the first one for all the jobs you apply for with the company. If you submit more than one résumé, the hiring manager may compare the résumés, and if they are not consistent, reject it.

Final Words

Remember, you can use this information to your advantage. Because most applicants do not follow these guidelines, if you follow them, you are more likely to be selected for the job. Of course, ATSs do not replace the need to network to find jobs. By networking and having a strong résumé formatted properly to be read by an ATS (for example, do not use a functional résumé), you will have a much better chance to get the job. If your résumé passes the ATS filter and you have networked to get noticed, you have increased your chances of being selected.

B<small>IO</small>

Robin Schlinger, as a recognized résumé writing expert, is a Master Career Director, Certified Professional Résumé Writer, Certified Master Résumé Writer, Certified Federal Résumé Writer, Certified Electronic Career Coach, and Job and Career Transition Coach. Robin adds value to résumés and other career marketing documents as the owner of Robin's Resumes® (http://robinresumes.com). Robin often speaks at job-seeker and career industry conferences. Robin uses her previous experience as a senior engineer and planning analyst to help her clients. Robin earned a BSChE with a concentration in writing from MIT.

4

Successfully Transitioning into the Workplace as a Working Mom

Denise Reilly

Even though motherhood is one of the most rewarding and wonderful experiences a woman can have, raising a happy, healthy, and successful family is a formidable task. Be encouraged by the fact that you are in very good company. More than 70 percent of moms with children under the age of 18 have joined the workforce (U.S. Bureau of Labor Statistics). Deciding to go back to work adds an entirely new level of complexity to your life and that of your family's. Your life has undoubtedly changed in a profound way.

Given the new demands in your life, the plans you may have had in place may no longer seem ideal. Fortunately, it's often said, with great change comes great opportunity. This is an ideal time for self-reflection and to evaluate how these new changes have impacted your needs. This is also an opportune time to consider new careers and investigate new possibilities. There are more options than ever to accommodate working mothers: flexible schedules, part-time opportunities, work-from-home opportunities, and starting your own business.

Before reentering the work force, analyze your situation carefully. Prioritize your needs, identify potential options, seek advice from experts, and create both short-term and long-term plans to meet your goals. These key steps will ensure that you make a choice that is conducive to both you and your family.

Begin with a thorough analysis of what your needs are, as well as the needs of your family. It is critical that you realize this is a two-step process. The No. 1 mistake working moms make as they attempt to balance their family and their career is that they leave themselves out of the equation. It's important to truly understand that a mom who feels unfulfilled is not her best self. In fact, it's not uncommon for this self-sacrificing approach to jeopardize the very thing moms are trying to protect—their relationship with spouse and children. When someone is unhappy in any given situation, it bleeds into every area of her life. Working moms are no exception to this; they are, in fact, more vulnerable than most. Happy moms lead happy families.

Analyze Your Situation

As you analyze your particular situation, determine your flexibility in terms of income needs. It's important to get clear on both the minimum and the ideal income you will need to ensure the financial well-being of your family.

Consider the cost of day care, commuting, clothing, lunches, and tax implications as you assess the costs and benefits of working. Also consider the routine expenses you will now incur for each child such as added health insurance premiums, doctors' appointments, prescriptions, dental bills, clothing, food, formula, diapers, and activities.

While you are looking at your financial needs, think about what your work/ life balance needs are. Would it be worthwhile or even feasible to consider a reduction in pay in exchange for reduced hours or flexible scheduling? Work/ life balance is critical. You can't put a price on a stress-free environment for your family.

Some additional points to consider when analyzing your personal situation are your family's needs such as schedules, a spouse who travels, external support systems for emergencies, childhood illnesses, and aging parents. Outline the parameters that you have to work with as you evaluate your current or potential careers.

Determine Your Values and Goals

What are the most important things in your life? In addition to being a mother, what is it that makes you feel happy and fulfilled? It is OK for a mom to find fulfillment in activities outside the family. In fact, it's important to engage in these types of activities.

I suggest you start by doing a quick free-writing exercise. Sit in a quiet space and just write for 5 to 10 minutes about what is important to you. Write sentences, words, phrases, whatever comes to mind. As you review this list, you will probably be able to group or combine some items into common themes. Rank your priorities in order of importance. In addition to your baby's well-being and your personal relationships, you will see a variety of things such as creativity, personal fitness, financial fitness, spirituality, and faith. Whatever it is, it's important to you. Therefore, it should be considered as you make life decisions.

Investigate Options

Once you have clearly identified your income requirements and your priorities, you are well positioned to identify potential fits for you and your family. Be certain to conduct research and seek the advice of both experienced working mothers and career counseling professionals.

You are fortunate that in the technological age in which we live, many resources are available to you right at your fingertips. Begin with searches for the top careers for working moms; include the top companies as well. Do not limit your search to companies in your area. Many of today's more progressive companies offer telecommuting or work-from-home positions. These positions include work in customer service, sales, IT support in addition to consulting and freelance writing. You will find a surprising number of family-friendly careers. Some require additional training or education; others do not.

Give some thought to your entrepreneurial side as well. What home-based businesses might suit your financial and personal needs? You can look for things such as Web design, social media management, or something more conventional such as interior design, in-home day care, housekeeping, selling

Mary Kay, personal shopping, or even pet sitting. Think of the things you like to do. Starting a business doing something you are passionate about is a labor of love. And it has the added beauty of enabling you to work when it is most convenient for you.

As you begin to think about what is best for you and your family, I encourage you to think creatively and keep an open mind to the many possibilities available to you. These are also very personal choices. It doesn't mean you shouldn't seek the advice of others. In fact, I highly recommend you do so. However, what works for one family or friend may not work for you. And don't feel as though you need to keep up with the Joneses or the super stay-at-home mom or even the working mothers you know. Do what works for you.

Before you make a final decision, consult a professional: a life coach, a recruiter, or a career counselor. It's simply unwise to make a life-changing decision such as this without the benefit and guidance of a professional.

Planning and Preparation

Regardless of whether you decide to look at alternative careers or return to your previous occupation, careful planning will facilitate your transition. Quality child care is, of course, a high priority. You can apply a host of tips and strategies here. Do your research and consult experienced working moms in your area. You may find a number of helpful options. More and more companies offer on-site day care. In some instances, privately managed day cares are conveniently located in office parks. You may find a home-based day care close to home, or you might find an au pair situation works best. Begin searching as early as possible. Good day cares generally have long waiting lists. Remember, fellow working moms will be one of your best resources.

It's also wise to develop a "Plan B" for emergencies. Consider things such as childhood illnesses and unanticipated work travel. What support system do you have? What is the sick time policy for the job you will be taking? If you do not have immediate family close by, mommy groups are a wonderful source of support and expertise.

If you will be breast-feeding, you will need to find a private location on the job. It's also critical to ensure you have an adequate supply stored up prior to your start date.

Finally, take a few practice dry runs before your first day. You don't want to get off to a chaotic start on your first day. In preparation for this, I recommend you take steps to prepare your child for the transition as well. These steps will differ, depending on the age of the child. If you have a newborn, you may want to bring him or her to the day care for a week or so for short periods. If you have an older child, do the same and explain what the new routine will be. In transitioning my daughter to this phase of our lives, I worked to make this exciting. I told her stories of how much fun she would have and socialized her to the group before the big first day. I also took her shopping for a stuffed animal to be her special friend at school. It's so important to ensure that your prework jitters are not passed along to your child. Children are extremely sensitive to your moods and feelings.

Emotions

Although preparation will ease the transition for you and your family, it does not fully address the emotions you will experience as you enter this new phase of your life. New working moms commonly feel a sense of loss and even guilt at this time. It's important to realize this is normal and over time should ease. Keep in mind that you are serving as a role model to your child and setting a good example for her or him. It's also helpful to understand that any changes you make do not have to be permanent. If your income is a must, consider work-from-home opportunities or part-time activities, or start your own business. Be creative in your problem solving and you will find something that works.

Always remember that working mothers are strong, capable, talented women. They not only set a great example for our children but also contribute significantly to the workforce and economic growth.

References

Blades, Joan, and Kristin Rowe-Finkbeiner. 2006. *The Motherhood Manifesto: What America's Moms Want—And What to Do About It*. New York: Nation Books.

Reilly, Denise. 2012. *The Balancing Act: Time Management Solutions for the Working Mom*, WorkingMomsAdvisor LLC.

Wright, Judith. 2006. *The Soft Addiction Solution: Break Free of the Seemingly Harmless Habits That Keep You from the Life You Want*. New York: Jeremy P. Tarcher.

Bio

Denise Reilly is the mother of two and lives in the Tampa Bay area with her children and husband of 20 years. She has spent more than 15 years in leadership and personal development, serving as a consultant for Fortune 500 companies such as Capital One, Aetna Healthcare, and Wells Fargo Bank. An accomplished author and speaker, Denise is also the editor-in-chief of *Inbox Magazine* and the Web site WorkingMomsAdvisor. com. This publication is dedicated to empowering working moms to achieve success, well-being, and balance in their lives. You can contact Denise at denisereilly@WorkingMomsAdvisor.com.

5

Is Bad Credit Stopping You from Getting the Job You Want?

Alan Akina

Imagine that you finally get the chance to apply for the job you've always wanted, a job that will further your career while earning more than you ever have. You spend hours getting ready then head out to get that job. You submit your résumé and have an introductory interview with the HR manager. It lasts just minutes, but you think it went well. And you're hoping you'll be called back for a second interview. You know you're qualified for the position. And you have a good work history, which that company should be pleased to see. You would make a good addition to their team. And you're excited!

Then a week goes by, and you don't hear from anyone. So you wait another week. You still don't get that call you've been anxiously waiting for. After two weeks, you decide to call the HR manager and check on your status. And that's when your hopes and dreams vanish before your eyes.

The HR manager tells you, "Sorry, we went with someone else. There was a problem with your credit check. You did not pass our requirements."

Whether this is new to you or you have already experienced this before, what do you do now?

Well before you decide to settle for an average job that's easier to get, that you know is beneath you and you really don't want, here's how to get the job you want, even if you have bad credit now.

23

Credit Check

Because of the Fair Credit Reporting Act, employers have the right to access your credit report. They need your permission, but saying no could be as bad as saying no to your bride or groom on the big day. What is considered a good credit score differs from employer to employer, but this is a good general rule of thumb: Most credit scores fall between 300 and 850. A score of 720 or above suggests that you've been managing your credit in an acceptable way. This is not set in stone and does not necessarily mean you have great credit, but you can use it to get a good idea of your first improved credit score goal.

So why do employers check your credit? For many reasons. They might be looking for money management habits, past lawsuits, judgments, or bankruptcies. One common scenario is when two people have applied for the same position, and the company uses their credit reports to determine which one to choose, especially if one has significant debt obligations that could affect performance and focus on the job. As you can imagine, an employer would much rather have someone working with the company who doesn't have the burden of financial stress affecting him or her every day.

Boost Your Credit Score

Here are five simple steps you can follow to boost your credit score and help you get your dream job.

Step 1: know your starting line. I suggest you download your free credit report from AnnualCreditReport.com. You can get a free report from each of the three major credit bureaus. Your credit report is like your financial report card. It tracks all of your past financial activity. This helps lenders and employers determine your money-management skills and financial responsibility.

Step 2: check your credit score. I suggest either of these two free sites: CreditKarma.com gives you your score from TransUnion; CreditSesame.com gives you your score from Experian. Your credit score is like a letter grade you would receive on your report card at school. The three major credit bureaus call this a FICO score. The higher your score, the more trustworthy you are considered to be.

Step 3: identify and fix any errors found on your credit report. Start with checking your personal information—social security number, address, correct spelling of your name, and the like—to make sure this is your credit report, not someone else's. Next, look for any credit accounts that do not belong to you. Then check that your payment history is correct. If you find errors, start by contacting the credit-reporting agencies for each item. They are responsible for correcting inaccurate or incomplete information in your report under the Fair Credit Reporting Act. Tell them about your issues in writing. Include your name and address. Then clearly explain each entry in your credit report that you are disputing. Provide copies of any supporting material that backs up your case (do not send the originals). And request that they correct the error or delete it from your report. Including a copy of the credit report that shows the items in error is always a good idea too. Next, do the same for each creditor connected with an error you are disputing. Include all the information you provided to the credit bureaus. You can expect this entire process to take from 30 to 90 days.

Step 4: get all of your accounts up to date. If you're behind and think you need help getting current, contact the creditor to work out a payment plan. Creditors love it when you talk to them and make an effort to get it right.

Step 5: understand your credit score. The best way to improve your score is to understand how your credit score is calculated. This chart shows you what is most important to you.

How a FICO Score breaks down

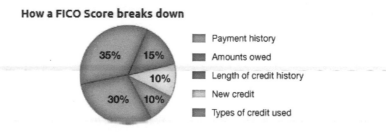

This begins with making your credit payments on time, which is the biggest factor, and accounts for 35 percent of your credit score. If you know you have trouble paying on time, you may want to consider setting up automatic payments that are deducted from your bank account on the same day each month. The amount of debt you have is worth 30 percent of your credit score. It's imperative that you make a plan to start paying down your debt today—and stick with it. Identify your credit accounts that charge you the highest interest rates, and work to pay off those accounts first while still making the minimum payments on your other accounts.

Once your debt with the highest interest rate is paid off, roll the entire amount that was going to that debt to the next highest interest debt. To find out how you can get the help you need to make a better credit score a reality in your life, you can get your free copy of my *Super Duper Simple Book on Money* at www.101Financial.com/book.

Bio

Alan Akina—founder of the financial education company 101 Financial, Amazon No. 1 best-selling author, and financial fitness reporter for FOX affiliate *KHON2 News*—has a passion for helping average people take control of their personal finances by empowering them with the personal financial education they need. After searching for a way to eliminate his own financial problems, Alan was able to achieve financial peace of mind. His mission is to help others do what he has done so they can experience a life of financial peace of mind and prosperity too. Find out more about Alan Akina at http://www.101Financial.com; Alan@101Financial.com; or @AlanAkina101.

6

BALANCE & CLARITY

Questions to Ask as You Read This Book

❧ ～ ❧

Anne Merkel, PhD

- Why am I reading this book? What do I hope to gain from it now? What puts me in the position to want or need this information? What are my intentions or goals?

When you are totally clear about your intentions and goals, you are able to more easily attract the results to yourself. In a job search or within the job market today, personal balance and clarity are both of absolute importance.

- Why do I need or want the contents of this book? What opportunities do I hope to attract via the information here? What will I be willing and able to implement to benefit myself?

Again, clarity is important. Is this just another self-help book that you will read and then place on the bookshelf to gather dust? What is your commitment level as you read through the various chapters?

- Why did I choose this book over others? What makes this special? What is contained here that is not found elsewhere?

Did you buy this on a whim or as a favor to a friend or because it "spoke to you" or because it really may have some value?

- Why am I reading this chapter right now? What do I hope to gain here reading what a former career counselor, executive marketing consultant, director of training and development, and present energy psychologist has to say?

Based on thousands of client cases, I've found that clarity of mind and balance of body, mind, and spirit make all the difference in the world in how you present yourself to others. And in this market, it is imperative that you project a positive image that exudes confidence, focus, and expertise.

If your actions and intentions are driven by fears or other negative emotions, then these will weaken you and naturally tarnish the image you want to project. Self-sabotage? We call this *stuck emotions.*

• Why does this matter?

To position yourself best in today's job market, you must provide value to any prospective employer based on who you are, the persona that you project, the training you've had to prepare you for the position, the experience that you bring to the new position, and the emotional clarity that surrounds you. A prospective employer's first impression of you will speak volumes and may determine the outcome of an interview. Your present employer, colleagues, customers, vendors all subconsciously read your energy, and if you're not congruent and end up "wearing a mask," then you may expect a short career there. The more awareness you have about your own strengths, weaknesses, opportunities, and threats, (SWOT analysis), the better your outcome will be in the long run.

• Why am I evaluating my place in the job market now?

Were you laid off? Are you bored with your present job? Do you feel as though you need a positive change? Have you had problems in your present job? Do you harbor fears about your abilities? Did you go after the job for the pay rather than your passion for the work to be done?

Choose from the following questions those that most closely relate to your situation:

• Why do I feel uncomfortable in this job? Is this because of a person, the place, a thing, or me? Am I being pressured by an outside source to start looking around? Can this discomfort be remedied to make my present situation more tolerable?

- Why do I want to leave this job? Do I really want to leave? Am I being forced out, or is this my true desire and personal choice? Is there something I can change to shift this opinion so that I may stay here? Do I fear failure in this position? If so, what will be different in any other job?

- Why is X job a better fit for me? If I'm looking to make a move, then am I totally clear on why the other position seems better? Does every position I consider seem better when compared to the one I am now in? Why? Am I looking for more money? If so, am I also balancing my search for the more important day-to-day details of the job for a more enjoyable tenure?

- Why was I laid off? Was this about me or was it a companywide change? Could I have predicted that this would happen? If so, then why am I so surprised and hurt? Did I choose a bad fit or vulnerable position or wrong company in the first place? What can I do differently next time?

- Why do I want to search for a (another) job? Clarity, clarity, clarity is needed here. If I'm running away, still harboring negative emotions, a bad fit for the present position, underutilized or underexperienced, then I need to know this and face it directly because potential employers will read through my facade. Masks hide only so much. And they cause lots of stress to me, the wearer.

- Why do I want to work for myself? Have I burned my bridges with others too often? Am I running away? Do I have problems with authority figures? Do I have what it takes to be a self-starter? Am I cut out to be a self-disciplined entrepreneur? Can I get the job done on my own? Do I have the right skills for my focus area? What more do I need to get started?

- Why am I searching for work or currently living in this geographic location? Is this my long-term home? Do I truly love and desire to live here? Am I choosing to move to this new location to be with someone special? What are my motives for searching or working here? Will being here make me happy if a job fails?

- Why am I searching in or working in this industry? Is this the industry where my training and expertise can best shine? Will I or do I excel in this industry? Have I worked here before? Do I desire to learn new techniques and information so I can fit into this industry next? Do I have high regard for this industry? Does it pay sufficiently well to meet my financial needs and desires? Do I feel confident here? Is there upward mobility? What must I learn to best position myself here?

- Why do I feel blocked or uncomfortable? What past or present work issues may be affecting me?

When you harbor hidden negative emotions, they always come out to sabotage you at some point. If your feelings are positive, on the other hand, these can empower you to do well and succeed in any position. You must know *what* you feel. Then, if you can't discover *why*, wonderful energy-therapy tools are available to help you discover and clear all inner resistance and blockage to your success.

- Why do I feel this emotion?

Identify what emotions you feel now about your current situation. Why do you think you feel this way? Do you know what could help you feel better so that you can get back to performing steadily and positively in your position?

When you become familiar with your inner self, then you'll be able to better balance your mind, body, and spirit to attract and keep the best in your life—both personally and professionally.

Getting into balance by first gaining clarity and then by clearing emotional blocks and resistance can be the most profound work you will ever do—and the most rewarding in all areas of your life.

Bio

Dr. Anne Merkel is a certified whole-person coach and energy psychologist and a doctoral student of classical naturopathy and energy medicine. She has extensive experience as a career counselor, executive marketing consultant, and director of training and development from her many years in corporate America. Anne utilizes a variety of energy-therapy modalities to support clients and other health and wellness practitioners worldwide. She certifies energy-therapy practitioners and hosts weeklong personal healing retreats via The Ariela Group of Wholistic Services. You can learn more about her whole-person approach at http://arielagroup.com or http://myeftcoach.com. You can call (706) 374-6460 for more information.

7

BALANCE & CONSISTENCY

Balance Your Workload with a Generous Number of Minivacations for Maximum Productivity

❧

Denis Waitley

By reenergizing and renewing yourself frequently, you will avoid burnout and become much more motivated and productive. Don't keep your nose to the grindstone for years and wait for retirement to travel. Balance and consistency are the keys. Enjoy the process, not just the result. Don't fight the passing of time. Don't fear it, squander it, or try to hide from it under a superficial cosmetic veil of fads and indulgences. Life and time go together. Do enjoy each phase of life. Do make the most of each day, and draw maximum joy from each moment.

Many people today are concerned with quality time, time generally defined in part as that spent on recreation, personal pursuits, time with children, spouses and friends. While I certainly believe quality time is important, I believe two other aspects of time are equally important.

First, one must also spend quantity time. The average father spends less than 30 minutes each week in direct one-on-one communication with each of his children. How can we possibly expect good family relationships with so little communication?

Second, one must spend regular time. Many supervisors and company presidents go for weeks, even months, without seeing many of their employees.

There's no substitute for regular meetings and open forums in which managers and team members can share ideas.

Time has a dual structure. On one hand, we live our daily routines meeting present contingencies as they arise. On the other hand, our most ambitious goals and desires need time so that they can be assembled and cemented. A long-term goal connects pieces of time into one block. These blocks can be imagined and projected into the future as we do when we set goals for ourselves. Or these blocks of time can be created in retrospect as we do when we look back at what we've accomplished.

It's not in the image of our big dreams that we run the risk of losing our focus and motivation. It's the drudgery and routine of our daily lives that present the greatest danger to our hopes for achievement. Good time management means that you maximize the daily return on the energy and mental effort you expend.

Ways to maximize your time productivity:

- Write down in one place all the important contacts you have and all of your goals and priorities. Make a back up copy, preferably on CD, DVD or Zip disc. Write down every commitment you make at the time you make it.
- Stop wasting the first hour of your workday. Having the chat and first cup of coffee, reading the paper, and socializing are the three costliest opening exercises that lower productivity.
- Do one thing well at a time. It takes time to start and stop work on each activity. Stay with a task until it is completed.
- Don't open unimportant mail. More than a fourth of the mail you receive can be tossed before you open or read it, and that includes email.
- Handle each piece of paper only once and never more than twice. Don't set aside anything without taking action. Carry work, reading material, audiotapes, and your laptop computer with you everywhere you go. Convert down time into uplink time.
- Spend 20 minutes at the beginning of each week and 10 minutes at the beginning of each day planning your to-do list.
- Set aside personal relaxation time during the day. Don't work during lunch. It's neither noble nor nutritional to skip important energy input and stress-relieving time. Throughout the day, ask yourself, "What's the

best use of my time right now?" As the day grows short, focus on projects you can least afford to leave undone.

• And as we said at the beginning of this message, take vacations often, minivacations of two or three days, and leave your work at home. The harder you work, the more you need to balance your exercise and leisure time.

Action idea: Plan a relaxing three-day vacation within the next three months without taking any business work with you. Reserve it on your calendar this week.

Reproduced with permission from Denis Waitley's Weekly Ezine. To subscribe to Denis Waitley's Weekly Ezine, go to http://deniswaitley.com or send an email with "Join" in the subject to subscribe@deniswaitley.com.

Bio

Denis Waitley is one of America's most respected authors, keynote lecturers, and productivity consultants on high-performance human achievement. He has inspired, informed, challenged, and entertained audiences for over 25 years from the boardrooms of multinational corporations to the control rooms of NASA's space program. Denis has been voted business speaker of the year by the Sales and Marketing Executives Association and by Toastmasters International and has been inducted into the International Speakers Hall of Fame. With more than 10 million audio programs sold in 14 languages, Denis Waitley's CD album, "The Psychology of Winning," is still the all-time best selling program on self-mastery. To order this bestseller or his newest release, "The Platinum Collection" and save 30 percent, go to Denis Waitley Featured Products or call (800) 929-0434. To subscribe to the free Denis Waitley's Weekly E-zine, send a blank email to subscribe@deniswaitley.com.

8

BE NICE

Why Being Nice Leads to Success

≈≈≈≈≈

Cynthia W. Lett

It's commonly understood that we want to do business with people we like. Think about it. If you have bids from two companies that offer basically the same options, but one of the vendors is represented by a nice, respectful professional who has shown that he likes you, which company would you hire? Most likely, you would choose the "nice guy." So how can you be sure you are the nice guy? Knowledge and practice of proper business etiquette will help.

In business today, complaints about others' behavior outweigh the delight in working with them. We encounter cursing, ignoring conversations, neglecting to make introductions, weak handshakes, not wearing name badges so we can read them, cell phone conversations that interrupt face-to-face communication, texting during meetings and conversations, pathetic voice mails, having to listen to others' iPods at their desks, being interrupted while concentrating on work, and a myriad of other rude pet peeves. No wonder we are stressed out by our work and workplaces.

I know you don't want to be "that guy." Avoiding a bad reputation is easy if you pay more attention to the relationship you have with others than to your own needs. "But," you ask, "how do I get what I want?" You'll be amazed how much more recognition and opportunity for success you'll have when you pay attention to others' needs. It's so unique in today's workplace that being even a "little nicer" can reap great benefits.

Useful Practices

Here are some practices that will set you apart from others, especially your competition in the workplace. As a bonus, if you practice these skills everywhere with everyone, your social life will improve.

- Smile at everyone whenever you can.
- Listen to whoever is speaking to you and acknowledge that person.
- Validate others' points whether you agree with them or not. Everyone has a right to an opinion.
- Greet everyone you meet. Even if you said hello yesterday, today is a new day. Say hello again. If you say hello, say good-bye when you leave.
- Shake hands firmly but not with bone-crushing strength. Three seconds is the time of the typical handshake in the United States.
- Don't use foul language with anyone for any reason. You *will* offend someone, but you may never know whom you will offend. People won't tell you; they will just leave you alone.
- Speak up; don't mumble. If you believe you have something to say, say it so the person with whom you are speaking can hear you.
- Always try to make a great impression on everyone you meet. Wear clean clothes appropriate to the situation. Stand up straight. Brush your teeth, comb your hair, and wash your face. Avoid body odor. Use deodorant, and don't overdue the fragrance. Look as though you were happy with yourself. If you do, others will be happy too.
- Don't make your cell phone more important than the person standing in front of you. If you must check who is calling, ask permission by saying, "Do you mind if I take a quick look?" Don't answer it and talk to the caller; just see who has called. Let it go to voice mail for retrieval when others are not right in front of you. The exception to this is if you are expecting an important call. In that case, ask permission in advance from those with you to answer it.
- If you need to check your messages, excuse yourself from present company for no more than three minutes. Check and return the calls necessary, and get back to your company quickly. Then apologize for stepping away once you return.
- If you are going to get something for yourself—such as a drink at the bar, dessert at the cafeteria, or more paper from the supply closet—and other people are standing with you, offer to retrieve something for them

as well. Think about them and show that their time and comfort are important to you.

- Don't gossip. Gossip is sharing anything that you personally didn't witness. You will most likely get details wrong and could put someone in an unflattering position if you take what someone else has said happened as truth. If someone asks you about it, just say you weren't there, so you can't comment.
- Don't take items from others' desks without permission.
- Don't use a speakerphone if you can see that anyone else can hear the conversation.
- If you want to use a speakerphone, always ask permission of the others on the other end. When using it with more than one other listener, identify yourself each time you speak.
- Always be on time. When we are late, we waste other people's time—there is no excuse for this. If the unforeseen happens and you must be late, call and make sure it will be convenient for the others to wait for you.
- Make requests, not demands. This basic etiquette rule is ignored constantly. Use words such as *may I* and *do you mind* and *if you can* rather than barking orders. We all believe we should choose to act, not be demeaned to react.
- Always speak to people with respect and concern. No matter the position you hold, you are no better than others; nor are they better than you. If they don't know it, show them with your actions, not snide remarks.
- Learn how to introduce yourself and others. Consider the order of precedence (where one's position falls on the list of importance). Always remember that the client or guest, if one is present, has the most important position.

This is a relatively short list. There are many more considerations to developing respectful and professional relationships that will help you get ahead in your career/business. Start here, master this list, and practice these skills every day, and you will undoubtedly be considered the "nice guy" among your competition. Then find out what more you can do to make the other person's life easier. This will reap its own benefit for you.

Bio

Cynthia has been teaching professionals for over thirty years how to set themselves apart from their competition and advance their careers and social lives. She is an international speaker, consultant, and coach to Fortune 1000 executives, government agencies in thirty countries, and savvy professionals worldwide. She is the director of The Lett Group and executive director of the International Society of Protocol & Etiquette Professionals. Cynthia is the author of *That's So Annoying: An Etiquette Expert on the World's Most Irritating Habits and What to Do About Them* and *Lett's Talk ... Real Etiquette Dilemmas and How to Solve Them.* As a recognized media expert, her commentary on workplace/career issues is regularly featured on TV and radio and in newspapers and magazines. Visit her online at http://www.cynthialett.com or at http://www.lettgroup.com.

9

Developing Your Personal Brand for Career Success

Marshall Brown

The world of work has changed. In the past, as long as you did your job and met expectations, you were paid. According to William Bridges, author of *Creating You and Co* and *Jobshift*, "Jobs were slots, boxes and pigeonholes. Jobs demanded performance in a script that was already written."

Those days are over. Today, whether you are working in a for-profit or not-for-profit business, employers pay for results and what you can produce for them. And those who are succeeding are the ones who know what they have to offer and what they are capable of doing better than some of their competition does. It's also about taking charge of your own career and knowing your marketable and transferable skills.

It is imperative in today's competitive job market to know *you*. Knowing what you have to offer and then marketing and branding yourself as the person with that information will help to separate you from your competition. It's what makes you unique! Your marketability will depend on your ability to demonstrate, on paper and verbally, your skills (even if within the same organization).

Whether you are thinking about making a career change or are satisfied in your current position, it's time to discover your skills, your strengths, and your personal brand.

Any marketing professional will tell you that one of the first things you have to know about a product before you put a marketing plan together is the benefits. What makes this product different? Why should I buy it? How will it benefit me (and maybe my team)? Translating this to your job or career means knowing what *you* have to offer. What makes *you* different? Why should Mr. or Ms. HR person hire *you*?

- Large companies understand the power of branding a product. They spend a lot of time, money, and energy to create a brand that is eye-catching and appealing enough to sell their product through to market. They want to make sure that the buyer has a strong connection with that brand.
- Now, think of yourself as a company with one employee—you. How much time, money, and energy have you spent in developing a personal brand unique enough to sell to your market? An individual who has a well-defined personal brand has more status and a tremendous advantage over the competition in the marketplace. With a great personal brand, you are already half sold and far above the competition.

If you don't know what skills you offer (and, therefore, not sure how to market your brand), *find out*! You can take various types of assessments, some available online such as checklists, card sorts, and experience stories. If you need some help preparing your list, hire a career coach or counselor. Don't forget to include the soft skills as well as the hard skills when putting your list together. They can be just as important when marketing you.

And if you think you know what you have to offer and how to brand yourself, *great*! I encourage you to look beyond your current skill set and look at developing additional benefits of "brand you." By asking yourself the following questions (and discussing with your peers, friends, family or "board of advisers"), you should be able to come up with specific ways you might want to work on improving your brand in the next six months.

- I am known among my peers or coworkers for these projects or skills.
- My current project is challenging and provocative to me in these ways.
- In the past three months, I have learned the following new things that will help me to move forward.
- Three important people whom I have added to my Rolodex (or contact list) in the last three months.

- By next year at this time, I would like to be known for these skills or projects.

In addition to knowing your skills, abilities, and experience when developing your marketing plan, I also encourage you to:

- Determine the needs of your target market;
- Develop *your* personal brand statement that says why you are the best candidate;
- Tailor your brand statement to the specific job; and
- Let people know about your brand—Network! Network! Get the visibility that your brand needs (and deserves).

Developing your brand takes time and energy. And it's well worth it!

"The days of the mammoth corporations are coming to an end. People are going to have to create their own lives, their own careers, and their own successes. Some people may go kicking and screaming into this new world, but there is only one message there. You're now in business for yourself." — Robert Schaen, former controller, Ameritech

Bio

Marshall Brown is a career and executive coach with a passion for encouraging individuals and organizations to reach exceptional levels of performance. He is founder and CEO of Marshall Brown & Associates, an international coaching, training, and leadership development company. His mantra is simple: "Get clear, get focused, get ahead." As a personal brand strategist, Marshall is committed to helping people identify their unique promise of value. He encourages people to discover and use their true talents and passions in life to achieve their goals and stand apart from their competition. Additional information can be found at http://www.mbrownassociates.com.

10

BRAND DISTINCTION

Building Your Brand: Setting Yourself Apart from the Crowd

Maria Matarelli

When you are competing in the job market today, it is essential to stand out from the crowd. To set yourself apart, you have to build your brand. You can do this by developing your portfolio of experience, defining your brand, and setting a plan for continuous growth.

Build Your Portfolio

It is important to be proactive in building your portfolio of experience and add to your portfolio while things are going well and not when you're up against a deadline or looking for a new opportunity. As you build your portfolio, identify which elements enhance your body of work. For example, what could you learn more about that would demonstrate your knowledge or skill level? What could you add to your experience, whether it's learning a new skill, mentoring others, or any leadership roles you could take on?

Find opportunities to gain that experience and then add them to your résumé and portfolio. If there are certifications in your industry or desired field, begin working toward them or find training classes to enhance your knowledge and reach those achievements. Certifications can provide an indicator of your knowledge level and show initiative for having taken the time to achieve them.

As you build your portfolio, look for opportunities to contribute to online discussion forums, articles to publish online, or other ways to demonstrate your expertise. Create a profile on a professional networking site such as LinkedIn. You can connect with other professionals, list your work experience and samples of your work, and even request recommendations from people you have worked with. Having a professional profile picture and a well-written description of your expertise and work experience really helps to pull together your portfolio of your abilities.

Define Your Brand

Define your three Ws:

1. Who you are
2. What you do
3. Why you do it

It is important to define your three Ws. Getting clear on who you are, what you do, and why you do it will help other people get to know you better, making it easier for them to refer you to others. As you become clear on your areas of focus and expertise, look at what sets you apart from other people in your industry.

As you build your portfolio, think about your market differentiator. What sets you apart? Adding those extra bells and whistles can be the differentiator in your brand. If you aren't sure, ask the people around you what gives you a competitive edge. Is it your technical knowledge and ability to translate ideas into business terms? Is it your ability to relate to people of all backgrounds, building effective relationships and excellent communication? Is it your attention to detail and the quality of your work?

Focus on the combination of skills that composes your expertise and unique skill set offering. That's your brand. What are your areas of expertise? What's your tagline? For example:

Maria Matarelli, Professional Speaker, Certified
Professional Coach, Business Consultant

*Inspiring people to leverage their strengths and push past
limiting beliefs to achieve unparalleled results.*

As you develop your brand and begin to build an online presence, everything you share on social media should be branded with your social media name or Web site directing people to information on who you are and what you do. For example, there is an app called Show and Tell (www.showandtellmobile. com) with which you can add your personal logo or Web site to pictures or video that you post online. It is easy to do from the palm of your hand using your smartphone, and you can direct people to your profile page that talks about your expertise.

Set a Plan for Continuous Growth

As you become clear on your areas of expertise, develop a brand marketing plan and keep track of what you are doing to grow your brand. Where do you want to be in a year? In five years? What can you do now to get there? Creating a skills-development strategy will help you identify what skills you want to add to your skill set. Doing the same thing each year, you may stay in the same place. Adding to your expertise can open up new opportunities. What will give you a competitive edge over others with similar skills? Differentiate yourself.

As you continue to grow, expand your network by stepping out of your daily routine and find events aligned with your interests. There are many social interest groups and professional organizations across many industries. Connecting with like-minded professionals can expand your knowledge and network beyond your current organization.

Attend events in your area—and bring your business cards. If you do not have business cards at your job, you can create your own online for a reasonable cost. Include your contact information and links to your online portfolio, Web site, or professional networking accounts. As you meet people, share your three Ws, but more important, show interest in what they do and ask how you could create value for them. As you network, if you can provide value for other people, they will likely tell other people about your skills and how great you have been to work with. Create value for others without expecting anything in return.

Standing out from the Crowd

As you determine your direction and career ambitions, don't just have a résumé—build your brand. Build your portfolio of work, define your brand, and set a plan for continuous growth. Find your differentiator; share what sets you apart and expand your network. Remember, don't seek what other people can do for you; build value for others and know where you want to go, and doors will open.

B<small>IO</small>

Maria Matarelli is a certified professional coach, professional speaker, and business consultant. She travels to consult organizations and speak at conferences around the world. Maria is passionate about inspiring people to enjoy what they do while working toward achieving a state of higher performance. Consultant turned entrepreneur, Maria has achieved many industry certifications and has held leadership positions with several not-for-profit professional development organizations. For more tips on how to build your brand, reach your next goal, or to have Maria speak at an event near you, visit http://www.mariamatarelli.com. Also connect with Maria at http://www.linkedin.com/in/mariamatarelli; https://twitter.com/mariamatarelli; https://facebook.com/mariamatarelli or http://www.youtube.com/mariamatarelli.

11

Why You? The Power of Personal Branding

❧

Royston Guest

We live in the age of the brand. From the technology we use for work and play to the clothes we wear, the car we drive, the restaurants we frequent, and the stores where we shop, we make conscious and subconscious choices. These choices are determined not only by cost, style, and build quality but also by the brand values that underpin those products and organizations.

In today's fast moving and ever-changing world, we're increasingly seeing the concept of brand extending to people. With more competition for jobs than ever before, and challenging global unemployment statistics, the days when people held one job for life are long gone.

Suppose you go for an interview, and the interviewer asks you, "Why should I choose you?" How good would you be at answering that question with confidence, clarity, and purpose?

In today's job market, you *must* be able to stand out from the crowd with a compelling personal brand proposition. Having a compelling personal brand proposition and being able to communicate it in a simple, clear, and concise way presents you with more choices in life—both personally and professionally.

At its simplest, your personal brand is how others perceive you. In a professional context, that perception can affect your promotion chances, the type of work that you're given, or the likelihood of your job application standing out. Your brand is the sum total of a lot of professional and personal factors. It is not only what you are in terms of qualifications, experience, and your skill set but also who you are. You cannot just leave it to chance. It must be a conscious process to design, build, and constantly develop your own personal brand proposition.

Having worked with hundreds of thousands of people over the last 15 years from all walks of life, across 27 countries, I've created a five-step process for creating your compelling personal brand proposition.

Step 1: Take Ownership

It's about conscious awareness and being proactive in designing and building your personal brand proposition. It's about taking personal ownership.

Step 2: Identify Key Traits in the Makeup of a Strong Personal Brand Proposition

Think about those individuals in your personal or professional life whom you really admire and respect. What is it about their personal brand that you really admire? What is it that makes them stand out? Mind map on a piece of paper their key traits, and as you think about other people from different areas of your life, add their traits to the list. Then carry the list around with you for a week and add the traits you admire of anyone you meet.

Also think about great leaders or individuals living today or from the past. If I said to you Nelson Mandela, what brand traits would spring to mind? Empathy, courage, resilience, humility? "Hey you locked me up for 27 years; however, let's lead the country together!" It takes a huge amount of humility from deep down as a human being to adopt this mind-set and way of being.

In addition to this exercise, two others are critical in creating your compelling personal brand proposition. Firstly, think back to your childhood and some of your family values and the way you were brought up. What are those values? How important are they to you today? Are they the foundation and filter through which you drive your decision making and determine what is right and what is wrong?

47

At the core of your personal brand are your personal values. Take time to capture these in black and white, clearly articulating why they are important to you and how you live your personal values daily. More and more companies today ask about your personal values in an interview. They are looking for alignment between your personal values and the company's values.

Secondly, be clear on what your purpose is, what you enjoy doing, and where you feel you can make a difference and add value. I always say to people, "If you can turn your passion into your career, then every day you have the opportunity to truly enrich the lives of others doing work that you love doing."

Once you've completed these exercises, identify the seven brand traits that you already do well. And, because life is a journey of never ending development and improvement, also capture the seven areas/traits where you feel you have further development to do in creating your compelling personal brand proposition.

Step 3: Sense Checking Perception Versus Reality

They say feedback is the food of champions. You can get feedback in the form of mystery shops, 360 feedback, personal brand insights, and other such tools. Armed with the seven traits you think you do well and your seven developmental areas, ask six people to help you with this step—three personal and three professional contacts. Explain to them what you are doing (but don't share your traits with them yet!), and ask them for seven traits they think are already strong in your personal brand and seven traits they think you need to develop. How aligned are their traits with yours? Do perception (your interpretation) and reality (their view) match?

Step 4: Hone, Polish, and Refine Your Personal Brand Proposition

This step is simple and aligns to *kaizen*, the principle of continuous improvement. Every day you meet new people, you're put into unique situations, and you experience different challenges. You're constantly adapting to the changing environment; therefore, your personal brand is constantly evolving. At the end of each day, ask yourself these two questions:

1. Have I been true to my personal brand today, living with authenticity, purpose, and focus?
2. What one thing have I done today to enhance my personal brand?

Step 5: Be the Real Deal

Finally, and perhaps most important, is Step 5, your brand in action. The key to personal branding is to ensure that the face you show to your friends and colleagues chimes with your ambitions. The key element in developing your personal brand is authenticity. The core of your personal brand should reflect your personality, who you are, and what you stand for.

In a world that has created so much uncertainty and where trust is broken between nations and individuals, the one thing people are all looking for more than ever is connection. A connection to individuals who are the real deal: authentic, integral, and values driven. With these traits as the cornerstones of your compelling brand, you can create a personal brand proposition that will serve you in realizing your personal and professional goals.

I wish you every success in creating your compelling personal brand proposition. If you have any questions, simply email me or my team at enquiries@ pti-worldwide.com.

Bio

Royston Guest is CEO of Pti Worldwide, a global consultancy and training organization with a proven track record in delivering business growth, people transformation, and peak performance. As an accomplished business strategist, Royston has worked with thousands of companies in more than 27 countries, helping them to grow their businesses and unlock their people potential. He is also an acclaimed speaker and respected author, inspiring individuals around the world at conferences, events, and coaching sessions, and through his books and articles. Royston's fresh, passionate, and results-driven style leaves people inspired, motivated, and energized with real-world ideas, strategies, and methods to achieve their personal and professional goals.

12

Do You Secretly Hate Going to Work?

Donald Burns

On October 12, 1989, en route to a meeting with a top customer, I finally realized I had a problem. As my train rolled to a stop in Grand Central Station, something inside me just snapped. I'd already made this trip at least a dozen times, but today the very idea of negotiating another presales agreement made me sick.

A year earlier, age 38, I felt successful, even unstoppable. I had just earned my dream job—significantly more money and prestige—a big promotion into senior sales management. But within a year, I was restless and bored and could not stomach the idea of another year of sales management or, God forbid, another 30 years.

I stepped off the train, walked halfway across the glorious lobby of Grand Central, and stopped in front of the famous clock tower. I stood there paralyzed for five minutes, just watching all the other commuters run rings around me, eager to get where they were going.

Happy on the outside but miserable on the inside, I was trapped in a dream job I was starting to hate. And the more I hated that job, the more the money kept rolling in. My worst fear was that I'd be exposed as flaky and quickly replaced by somebody who really wanted the job. I was wasting everybody's time, especially my own, unlike those commuters hustling and bustling around me—all of them obviously happy and productive at work. Or so I thought at the time.

Ever felt trapped in an awful job?

A bad employment situation is like a bad marriage. Every waking minute feels like wasted time. You are trapped, the clock is ticking, and paranoia and fear interfere with normal life. Will you run out of time and get pushed out before leaving on your own terms? Why would anybody hire you?

Can you imagine running out of money?

According to an article in the *Washington Times* in August 2006, "Many women fear they'll lose their income and end up a bag lady, forgotten and destitute."

How did you get into this mess in the first place?

- Maybe it's your own fault—my story, for example—so be careful what you wish for.
- Maybe you were just minding your own business but the world around you changed—or blew up—due to circumstances beyond your control.
- Maybe you're making a natural transition, a separation from the military or a planned retirement.
- Or maybe some combination of the above. Doesn't matter how or why you're trapped at work. As soon as you hear that clock ticking, start planning your exit!

Here is your three-step action plan to break free.

Since the great crash of 2008, I've advised at least 1,200 people on their job transitions. All of my success stories—several hundred among the 1,200— are doing some variation of this three-step plan:

- *Feel the heat.* Find a job target that turns you on, that ignites a burning desire. Don't leave home without it! This is the master step—and the No. 1 prerequisite—that drives a successful job search. When you're passionate about your goal, you'll blow past all of the inevitable indifference and rejection. In my experience, weak desire is the No. 1 reason that job searches crash. This is the most important piece of advice that you can glean from this chapter. If you can find your personal ignition button, all the rest is just mechanics.
- *Share your vision.* People can't help you if they don't know what you want. Show them a compelling bio, résumé, CV, LinkedIn profile, brand,

tagline, Twitter stream, Web site, portfolio, or whatever else it takes to transfigure the dream inside your head onto a computer screen or the printed page. Potential employers, networking contacts, recruiters all need a crystal-clear idea of what you're trying to do. Forget the 90-second "elevator" speech. Can you write a compelling pitch on the back of a business card? When you approach people who don't know you, assume you've got 5 to 10 seconds to make your case.

- *Ask people to help you.* Many people recoil from this step, including me, so break through any reluctance to reach out. Eventually, you'll reach real people who reside in or near your job target (real people, not some pixels on Facebook). Another name for this is targeted networking. Most people I know say they hate networking, which they confuse with time-wasting meetings ("Let's exchange business cards"). If you hate networking, just call it connecting. Master two tools, LinkedIn.com and Switchboard.com, great resources for finding and connecting with people.

If you persist with this process, I promise you'll eventually achieve great results. Maybe not the results you originally intended because each search takes on a life of its own. Surprises and serendipities are inevitable. Happen all the time.

Don't do what I did!

Unfortunately for me in 1989, standing at the clock tower in Grand Central Station, watching "happy" people rushing to work, I was clueless about the art and science of career transitions. I had a vague idea that I wanted to jump-start myself into a writing career but had no idea how to do it. I did not even have the prerequisite burning desire described earlier. Instead of a burning desire, I was feeling those white-hot flames of employment hell. Eventually, I took a flying leap of faith into the unknown world of writing and advertising. It all worked out, but I didn't know what I was doing.

I guarantee your own transition story will be much better than mine because resources are available that did not exist even 10 years ago. You need not reinvent the wheel and take a flying leap of faith as I did. You might decide that you don't want to work in another job at all. Maybe you'd rather be working for yourself in your own business. This is a realistic option if you can package up a marketable skill or talent that people will pay for. (This is the topic of a different chapter, but, Step 1, go searching on the Internet and find success stories who navigated situations similar to yours.) Or maybe you're approaching retirement age and—like my own father 20 years ago—you are fearful and clueless about cutting the corporate umbilical cord. About 10,000 baby boomers are retiring every day, so you're not alone. Again, information on this topic is all over the Internet. My Web site (CareerDefense.com), for instance, focuses on what's working now in career transitions. Each week I email a three-minute video with useful, real-time information and tips from the front lines of the job war.

Leaving my dream job in 1989 was one of the best decisions of my life, even though the transition took five years and nearly bankrupted me. But if you can imagine a better life, a better career, or a better job, you can succeed by following the three-step plan in this chapter.

Start by finding your ignition button. Find your passion, and I promise that all the rest is just working out the mechanics. If I could do it—totally clueless—I'd bet money that you can do it.

Just don't waste time as I did. Do your research, seek advice from experts, and take the shortcuts. I've enjoyed each of my five careers and don't regret a single choice. But I do regret having wasted so much time on each transition. I figured it all out on my own—trial and error—but you need not do that. Just tell me where you want to go, and I'll show you the shortcuts to get you there.

I sincerely wish you the very best of good luck in your search.

BIO

Donald Burns, an executive career coach, has helped several hundred people transition into better jobs and more fulfilling careers. Recently he launched Career Defense TV, a Web-TV channel that reports on what's working now in the current employment market. Donald calls himself the "poster child for job changers." Visit his Web site, http://www.CareerDefense.com.

13

To Compete in Today's Job Market, You Have to Break Some Rules

Tawn Holstra

Choose

You and I are always making choices. Every moment of every day we choose what to wear, how fast to drive, coffee or no coffee, to stay on our diets, to save or spend, to reach for the stars or go for security.

Now for the big choice—what career? What is the right job for you? If any job will do, no problem, plenty of generic jobs are available that will help you pay the bills. However, if you are looking for that one special job, a unique place for you to show up every day and give your best, then you have to make some choices. Choosing what you really want is extremely powerful and gives you focus. When you know what you want, a big chunk of the work is done. Make that bold choice! Once you have your choice, the real fun begins!

For well over 100 years, we have been conditioned that if we do well in school, we will get a good job that will eventually pay off our mortgages and put our kids through college. We even lull ourselves with thoughts of our "someday" retirement. Unfortunately, that American Dream we have been so wholeheartedly immersed in is not only gone but quite dead and buried, as long gone as the gold watch and the pension. The job market is just not that kind of secure anymore.

It is not news that the job market has changed dramatically in the last 20 years. Today's college graduates will hold so many jobs in their work life that research firms are overwhelmed with the data fluctuations. The numbers range from seven careers in a lifetime to as many as 100 jobs per individual. At the same time, four out of five workers today have been at their job for less than a year. This means that people are moving from job to job so fast that we cannot count the data before they change.

In today's market, the truth be told, if you are worth anything, you are probably unemployable! For the most part, jobs are about fitting in and following rules. Companies need workers who follow instructions and do not diverge from the manual/system/policies. If you are creative, full of hope, and ambitious with great ideas, then you probably won't fit in, or not for long.

Building a Cathedral

Even more likely is that you don't actually want a job. You want a career—a series of projects and jobs (paid or not) that inspire you, get you much needed experience, give you direct access to express your ideas, and make a difference in your chosen field. Some of the best training I ever received in my chosen career was as a volunteer. If you're working inside your career, then every project or job will help you in some way toward your goal. Each project will also assist you to develop your network, a high standard of excellence, and a reputation. Some workers are breaking rocks and some are building a cathedral, the same activities with completely different attitudes and outcomes.

As you prepare to compete in the job market, then, the real question is, "What are you *competing* for?" When you choose to apply to a company, the question is not only are you qualified for the job but also can you see your contribution at that company? If the answer is no, then don't bother; if the answer is yes, then you *must* prepare!

Preparation Is King (or Queen)

The most important thing you can do to put yourself above the pack is to know what you are talking about. Even with little to no experience, you can prepare for your interview as you would prepare for any presentation that you might make once you have the job. From the interviewer's point of view, *how* you interview is as important as what you talk about. Most applicants expect to immerse themselves in the company after they have the job. Don't make this mistake. That you made the effort to learn about the company speaks volumes about your commitment, your work ethic, and how serious you are about wanting the position. Do your homework on the company. Learn everything you can before you get to the interview. Look at not only what the company needs but also what you need. Are your values aligned? Can you make a valuable contribution to the company? Where do you see yourself in three years? Five years? If you are still planning on being in that position, how will you have developed? Get on Google; take the time to learn the leaderships' names. You may learn more than you need, but you cannot sound equipped to handle a job if you don't know anything about the employer.

There are *no* unimportant jobs in a company. Everything you do as an employee affects the whole, and literally every position in a company impacts the bottom line. The lowest wage earner in any company can make a mistake that could cost vast amounts of money, or thoughtlessly be abrupt with a customer on the phone and leave a bad taste in a customer's mouth thus damaging the whole company's reputation. Whatever position you are applying for, you should know what impact it has on the other departments and to the company's mission overall. Remember to look at the big picture, and speak to that in your interview.

Your Internal Dialogue Is Running the Show

In working with some of the best human performance experts in the world, it has become profoundly clear that what you say to yourself turns into your beliefs and then your actions and then your reality. So watch what you think. The great Usain Bolt has been heard many times saying, "I can't be beat because I am the fastest man in the world!" He does not wonder if it's true or if it's appropriate to say it. Nor does he say it after the race. He declares it before the race, before his moment of truth. In fact, he says it as if it were already true. With his words, he creates a reality.

What do you say before your moment of truth? Do you boldly own your new job? Or are you hoping and wondering if you are going to get it? Your inner dialogue shapes everything and tells you what you can and can't do. Most people never take on mastering their internal chatter. Masters will tell you that it is the first and maybe the hardest thing to get a handle on.

Take the time to create your own bold statement. Create a phrase that when you can say it, you want to jump out of your seat and start doing your work. This statement is what you *know* more than anything else. It is a promise, a declaration of you. If you are the one for the job, then damn well be it.

Bio

Best-selling author, speaker, and business owner, Tawn Holstra is a masterful business manager with 35+ years of hands-on experience in building businesses with her clients. She specializes in human performance, mastering your internal dialogue, communication, developing trust, and all aspects of producing breakthrough results. She holds a masters certification in ontological design, is a Department of Defense contractor for SEAL team families, a segment host on *Conscious Talk Radio*, and a popular international columnist and blogger. Clients include Microsoft, Intel, and SEAL Team 7. She is the author of *The Rule Breaker's Manifesto: Direct Access to Power, Creativity, and Joy* and of *Savoring Seattle*, a cookbook to benefit FareStart's homeless job training program Designing Your Child's Education. For more info, log on to http://tawnholstra.com or http://tawnholstra.com/business101.

14

Building Motivation to Reach the Summit

☙ ~ ❧

Joe Brodnicki

Have you ever wondered why traditional motivational activities are like energy drinks? Once the high wears off, you crash and find yourself at the bottom of the roller coaster. Pep talks and motivational seminars don't really work. Motivation is about having the energy and focus over the long haul.

Lasting motivation is more like climbing Mount Everest. Before you're ready to make the final ascent, you need to take care of the basics. Once you've laid this foundation, you're ready to unleash your energy and passion to reach the summit.

Whatever your personal summit, living out your highest dreams, values, and potentials takes a firm foundation of your basic human needs. If you're interested in building this type of motivation, read on. You will identify your basic motivational needs and learn a strategy for meeting them effectively.

Basic Needs

Your most basic needs are for survival. They include air, water, and food. You are motivated to meet the need when you don't have enough of it. When you meet the deficiency, you're ready to continue. You can't climb Mount Everest without oxygen, food, and water. You might go on for a while based on will-power, but how long can you last if you're hungry, thirsty, or struggling for

58

air? Unless you meet those basic needs, you won't be able to continue for long.

How well are you coping with your survival needs? Are you healthy, feeling good, well rested, full of energy, and mentally alert? If you are, you're coping with your survival needs well. If you're not, or you feel unneeded tension and stress, then it's time to look at your coping strategies for meeting these needs. (We'll look at this later in this chapter.)

The next level of basic needs is for safety and security. If you have placed too much value on these needs, you may be experiencing a need to control everything or find yourself unable to take reasonable risks or try new things. If safety means too much to you, it's a bit like having a fear of drowning in a bathtub. You may feel frustrated and stuck. Your motivation is drained from you. With these needs met, you have a healthy appetite for the unknown and can relax your guard enough to grow and deal with new experiences.

The third level of basic needs include things such as love, inclusion, belonging, and affection. You should have little trouble knowing how well you're coping with these needs. Feelings of loneliness, isolation, alienation, and rejection are good indicators of deficiencies in this area. The ability to meet these needs affects more than your personal life. It can have a profound impact on how well you communicate and connect with people. If you've ever gone into a meeting, a job interview, or a sales call feeling as though you didn't belong there or were desperate to make an impression, you know how a lack of inclusion, belonging, or even the ability to show affection in an appropriate way can affect the conversation.

The final level is self-esteem. You may resist the idea that self-esteem is important. Consider how you build confidence. You don't do it by feelings of self-loathing, self-contempt, or self-doubt. You know someone who has some great skills but who is plagued by a lack of self-regard. Self-esteem means unconditionally accepting yourself as you are. To live in the moment and to recognize and solve problems, you must accept things the way they are. This acceptance helps us see the past, present, and future more clearly and doesn't waste a lot of energy on "ifs" or "buts." When you've met these needs, you have the energy and focus to live out your highest and best values and potential.

Meeting Foundational Motivational Needs

Books, training, an action plan, a great network of people, and a good coach are all helpful in meeting foundational motivational needs. First, though, you need to use your ability to create powerful and useful meanings for these basic needs. We are driven or inhibited by our meanings. For instance, if reaching your high sales target has come to mean, "If I don't meet it I'm a failure" and exercise means torture (no pain, no gain), then your motivation to meet these needs is going to be misdirected, and your motivation is going to meet some serious roadblocks: ("Why should I want to punish myself by exercising?" "Mondays are hell!")

To create meanings to unleash and do your best to get what you want and live fully, first, be aware of the needs mentioned earlier. This doesn't sound like a big deal, but you can't act on things that you're not aware of. All the basic needs must be met to realize our full humanity. All this takes some practice and reflection. The more you stick with it, the more you'll recognize your needs and put yourself in a position to have the motivation to do the things that really matter.

Next, just accept these foundational needs. We all have them. We all need to have them met in ways that are good for us. If you don't accept the need, it affects your behavior and motivation. When people don't get their need for self-esteem met, they might act out in unproductive ways with outbursts of anger or violence just to get noticed. Or they might seek to meet that need through relationships that don't support them (think "Looking for Love in All the Wrong Places."). Accept the need for what it is: something everyone has and a means to help you live your best life.

Become aware of what the need means to you. What do affection and security mean to you? You might be surprised what they answers are. For someone with a substance abuse problem, alcohol may mean acceptance. In your career, boss may mean a threat to your security or self-esteem. What needs do your career or business fill? And what are the meanings you've attached to them?

Now, quality control your meanings. How does that meaning work for you? If security means taking no risks, it might tell you of a need to change your meaning. How well does the meaning that work is a necessary evil or drudgery work for you? What would be a healthier way of thinking about security? Is taking small risks proactive and healthy for your development? You may need to give yourself permission to change your meanings—you weren't born with them remember!

Finally, you're ready for action. Make your action plans, develop new ways of meeting the needs, and watch how the quality and quantity of your motivation changes. Keep revisiting this basic needs process and note the changes, both large and small.

References

Hall, M. 2010. *Unleashing Your Real Self.* Retrieved from http://www.neuro-semantics.com/meta-states/unleashing-your-real-self.

Maslow, A. 1968. *Toward a Psychology of Being.* New York: John Wiley and Sons.

B<small>IO</small>

Joe Brodnicki is a transformational coach, trainer, and consultant who helps leaders, individuals, and teams unleash their highest potential. Joe helps his clients at the fundamental levels of developing the beliefs, attitudes, and structures that support excellence and the specific change clients are looking for. His best clients welcome change and seek to create excellence. He holds a diploma in self-actualizing psychology and is a licensed neuro-semantics/neuro-linguistics trainer (International Institute of Neuro-Semantics) and meta-coach (Meta-coach Foundation). When you're ready to realize your full potential as a leader, individual, or your team, contact Joe at joeb2665@mindspring.com or at (615) 830-9355 or through http://JoeBrodnicki.com.

15

Business Networking for Career Success

～

Loretta Peters

Whatever employment situation you are in, you must network for career success. Because it is likely you already know many people, leveraging and expanding your network today will make searching for your next career opportunity much easier.

What Is Business Networking?

If you're still not clear what business networking is, let's just say that when you engage groups of like-minded people, business and employment opportunities have a tendency to be found, whether it's for your benefit or someone else's.

Getting Started

Family, friends, clients, prospects, your dentist and accountant, your boss, and the people in your office are part of your network. Being aware of who is in your network will help you when you have a specific need.

Organizing Your Network

Keep an active list of people in your network with phone numbers and emails so you can touch base regularly. Enter your list in a contact management tool.

Then create categories or groups (e.g., clients, prospects, chamber members) that make it easy for searching and sending targeted communications such as e-newsletters. Manage your network by tracking how often you are in communication with each group.

Where to Build Your Business Network

Reaching your network through social media, blogs, and Skype, where messages can be sent to anyone around the world, is a way to stay connected daily. That said, combining Internet networking methodologies with face-to-face business networking is a win-win strategy for business networking success.

Develop Your Strategy

Business networking is often strategic and involves a personal commitment. Having a strategy or plan will help you generate better results, for example:

- Do you want to meet decision makers?
- Do you need resources in a vertical market'?
- Are you looking for a new job?
- Do you need feedback on a new idea?

Knowing why you want to build your business network will help you stay focused on accomplishing your goals. This includes choosing events that make the most sense for you to attend or sponsor.

Networking at Chamber Events, Business Journal Events, Charitable Events, Trade Shows, and National and International Events

Being prepared before attending any business event is highly encouraged. Knowing what the event is about and researching the industry beforehand will prepare you for successful encounters with others. Expect industry experts to be in attendance, and invest some time learning about current hot topics so that you feel comfortable conversing with them.

Arrive early so you can see the name tags of those who are expected to attend. Whenever possible, ask to see the attendee list. If you or your company is sponsoring an event, the attendee list is usually included. Look for people who may know the people you want to meet. Then ask for an introduction.

Building Dialogue

Whether your introduction lasts for a few minutes or longer, asking questions that will engage the other person will help in developing rapport. Business topics are an easy way to establish mutual trust without getting too personal.

Your goal is to establish a connection, collect a business card, and move on to the next person. This is a courtesy to the person you just met. Then it is your responsibility to follow up within a few days and invest in building the relationship. This is an important step to growing and sustaining your network that will pay off over time.

Networking in Global, National, and Regional Organizations

Where can you find valuable connections? In your own organization! As you find opportunities in other departments at your company, how will you get in front of the executive team who will hire you?

If you need to learn how a department in which you are interested operates, ask some team members to lunch (this is networking). Listen for challenges that you could help solve if you were part of the team. The more knowledge you have about the department before meeting with the executive team, the better position for the job you will be in.

Next, understanding how your talents, skills, and experience contribute to solving problems in the department for which you are applying is good information for your résumé. If you need help with this, email me at the address given in the following bio. Also, as you grow your network internally, think whom you can ask for a reference.

Now think of how you will introduce yourself to the executive team. Email, interoffice mail, phone, through another colleague, or while attending an event is acceptable. In your conversation, mention a few ways you could help the team with your background. Then send your résumé and cover letter and follow up weekly with another idea of how you could help the department. Whether you land the job, you will have established some credibility for yourself, and this could lead to another job referral from an executive.

Networking Using Social Media

Are you using social media regularly to build your business network? If not, you are missing out. LinkedIn is the preferred social media platform for business and is a great way to reach your network daily. I've scheduled several business meetings using LinkedIn and Facebook at 10 P.M., and you could too. You can learn everything about LinkedIn through its help center online. However, if you need help using these tools, email me.

LinkedIn Groups for Business Networking

Much like organizing groups into a database, you can use LinkedIn groups to do the same. The only difference is that you invite LinkedIn members already within your network to join. Once members join your group, you can engage with them about specific business matters any time. You can also share links to specific information that demonstrates your thought leadership in a particular area of expertise. This is great for building your personal brand and replacing traditional email.

Your Résumé as a Network Tool

Because employers and recruiters will most likely Google you after you send them your résumé, using key words from your résumé in your LinkedIn profile and other social media is a way to use your résumé as a networking tool. If you are using more than one social media site, it is important that your message be consistent across platforms, or it could affect your chances of getting hired. Thinking about your online networking strategy so that it is consistent and generates the results you are expecting is the way to go.

Building a Business Network for Life: 10 Tips for Building and Sustaining Your Business Network

1. Network outside of your organization by attending or sponsoring local events.
2. Have a clear brand message that communicates what you do in 10 seconds.
3. Reconnect with those from past jobs.
4. Stay in touch regularly.
5. Use a contact management system.
6. Find ways to help your network.
7. Be a thought leader in your industry.
8. Give more than you get.
9. Keep growing your network.
10. Always carry business cards.

Bio

Loretta leads personal brand marketing programs for businesses and professionals that include social media, networking, personal brand development, online identity management, and online brand awareness used for today's talent management, marketing, and advertising. Loretta graduated with a BA in business administration, with a minor in English. She maintains several certifications in personal branding, online identity management, and social media. Loretta is one of 24 master résumé writers in the United States through the Resume Writing Academy and is a member of several associations. To learn more, visit http://www.EnterprisingCareers.com/.

16

Athletes on the Field and in the Boardroom Conquering the Competition

Mickey Matthews

"Sport has the power to change the world. It has the power to inspire. It has the power to unite people in a way that little else does. Sport can awaken hope where there was previously only despair." —Nelson Mandela

For us as executives and leaders, what we have learned from sports; what we take way from the practices, wins, and losses; and how we transfer and utilize that to beat our competition in the employment market as we do on the field will best define us.

Corporations and their shareholders, to quote Charlie Sheen, are all about "winning." Executives want to do more than compete; they need to conquer. Therein lies the pot of gold at the end of the rainbow. How do we conquer our competition in the labor market to assist our current or future employers in achieving their goals?

You are a CEO, senior executive, hiring manager. What attributes do you want in your team?

- Leadership
- Followership
- Flexibility
- Decisiveness
- Intelligence

- Resiliency
- Discipline

Where do we learn these skills? Sports.

Each game, each practice, each chalk talk, each ride home with your parents "back in the day" involved lessons learned that you can translate into success in your career. In the words of basketball legend Michael Jordan, "Talent wins games, but teamwork and intelligence wins championships." This applies in sports and in business.

How do you make this leap and, as we say, "conquer the competition"? In working with our global clients such as Aramark, Kohler, Novartis, and others, our advice is that to differentiate from competition *by competing*, it must be attitudinal first. Remember (and live by) the attributes mentioned earlier evidencing those in your personal and professional demeanor. Lead where appropriate, follow when required, and be solution oriented. Take the lessons you have learned from the playing field and activate those in your everyday life by overcoming obstacles (defeat), being humble (in victory), and inspiring others through example (Cal Ripen, Hall of Fame baseball player), or through sheer "in your face" tenacity (Michael Jordan)—whichever method you are comfortable with.

Reflect your athletic accomplishments, involvement, and learnings also in your personal career-marketing tools. Your résumé, your LinkedIn profile, your Website, all of your social media tools must integrate and incorporate your individual or team sports achievements. These not only show your personality and depth but also are icebreakers or networking "introducers" to create linkages. Through bonding about teams, sports, championships, or common alumni athletic interests, you can articulate the discipline, resiliency, and decisiveness that employers demand. Hiring managers will have confidence in how you would handle stress, a new situation, or a challenge because they are not hiring to be anyone's training ground and want experienced and savvy hires who will make them look good. If you can show a track record—professionally and personally—of being a winner, you will conquer the competition in the business world.

So you have added your athletic and sports-related achievements to your résumé and online profiles. You have gone back in your memory bank to your days on the field, recalling the lessons learned of the hard work, the grind, the comradery, the ups, the downs. Likely, you have even teased out the learnings that preparation, perfect practice, and desire can combine as one into achieving goals and objectives. You are living this mantra and realizing that Jim Collins in *Great by Choice* was right when he said, "High achievers and great leaders possess ambition, a purpose, personal humility and a will to succeed all that you learned on the playing field."

To conquer the competition in today's employment market, understand what hiring executives are seeking in their teams. Walk the walk and talk the talk in blending intensity, discipline, personal accountability, and drive as you have learned through sports. And highlight your athletic competitive lessons as the foundation of your passion for excellence.

Bio

Mickey Matthews serves as Vice Chairman, Practice Groups, which places him on the Global Board for Stanton Chase International, a top ten ranked global executive search firm (http://www.stantonchase.com). Previously, he served as Vice President, North America, and as Global Director of marketing for the firm. Mickey has successfully executed numerous executive search assignments for clients such as ADM, Aramark, Tyco, Deloitte Touche, Kohler, DuPont, and others. An All-America and All-Ivy League lacrosse player at Brown University, he was Captain when the team achieved a final No. 6 national ranking. Mickey received a BA in business and economics, with distinction, from Brown University and graduated Beta Sigma Gamma from the Fellows Executive MBA program, Loyola University. Contact info: m.matthews@stantonchase.com.

17

What Do You Want to Do with the Rest of Your Life?

Harvey Feldman, MBA, CEC

What is the first thing most people do after deciding to look for a new job? That's right, they usually write an updated résumé. What's wrong with that? For starters, if you hate your current job or don't like the field you are in or are tired of doing the same thing you've done for the past 5, 10, or more years, looking for a new job or position based solely on your history is likely to get you more of the same. Yet so many new job seekers continue to pursue "opportunities" in a field that they derive little or no satisfaction from.

If you could plan your business or career around something you actually enjoyed doing, and find a job that made every day an exciting and rewarding new adventure, wouldn't that give you a more satisfying long-term result? As a business and executive coach, I often begin a career/business coaching engagement by asking this simple question: "If you could do anything at all, if you had complete control of your life and job, without limits, what would you *choose* to do?"

This is not an easy question to answer; it often requires a level of thought and introspection that most of us are unaccustomed to applying. It begins with "thinking outside the box" and not being restricted by what you've done before, the limits of your training and education, and the "gremlins" that tell you "you can't" or "you aren't good enough" and keep you from stretching and truly excelling. But once you have come up with a satisfactory answer, you have taken the first major and important step in establishing your ultimate goal, defining a positive new future, and creating a realistic target to aim for.

If you could do anything at all that you wanted to do, and knew you could not fail, what would it be? Your starting point takes you beyond risk and lets you begin with a dream. Without the dream, your goals remain mired in the past, and your new job reality will simply mirror the past. Once you have identified this dream (and you might have more than one objective), it is time to flesh out the image. What specifically would you be doing? Whom would you be doing it with? Where would you be doing it (at home on your own, large company, small company, with a group of associates, online)? What about it would you find most satisfying? How much would you earn? How would you get paid? How would you dress each day? Would it be nearby or far away? Whom would you serve, and how would they benefit? What would be the best path for growth? Now write a specific and detailed job description that incorporates everything you know about this position, its responsibilities, reporting structure, and so on. The more details of your ideal job you can come up with, the easier it will be to define exactly what you are looking for (although nothing about this is easy).

Now it's time for a skills assessment. Do you have the necessary skills to do this job successfully? If not, what is missing? Where can you get those skills? How important is it? How committed are you to achieving this and being successful? Do you have any personal traits or particular characteristics that will help you (dedication, perseverance, special interests, prior experience, hobbies, burning desire)? Continue to fine-tune both your skills assessment and your job description until you are confident that they are aligned.

Looking back to your definition of who would be most likely to want/need your services, identify specific markets or sectors. Depending on the type of company you most want to work for, identify the "Top 10" in each sector. The goal here is to develop a short list of companies that will become your targets for marketing the new you. Within each of these companies, what is the title or titles of the individuals you would need to speak to? What types of skills or personal characteristics would they be looking for in a new employee and want to hire? Again, it is important to be as specific and exhaustive as you can in determining this information. You may want to spend a fair amount of time doing your own research; finding the answers that are right for you is a valuable exercise. Remember, the greater the level of detail you can develop in identifying targets, the more effective your pinpoint targeted marketing efforts will be.

Once you know what work you want to do, where you can do it, the companies most likely to need it, and the title and specific needs of the person you need to speak with, you *now* can begin thinking about putting together a résumé, or more specifically, a compelling sales document (*you* are the product!) for achieving your goals. If your ideal job means starting a new business on your own, your next step is developing a comprehensive business plan. But that's a topic for another chapter.

Your résumé needs to focus on actual achievements, with quantified results wherever possible. It should be action based. For example, not "I was involved with ...," but rather, "As a direct result of my planning and leadership, customer complaints declined by 42 percent, and an additional 15 percent gross profit was added to the bottom line." If you are changing careers, also talk about your passion as it relates to your newly defined job description and how it helps (or will help) you to make a significant and immediate contribution to the operation and profitability of your employer. It is difficult to generalize exactly how to write about your particular strengths and skills (that's where a good coach comes in), but this should help you in framing your arguments in a powerful and compelling way.

You don't need to be stuck and unhappy doing the same job year in and year out if you change your thinking, expand your goal setting, and extend your reach. What I hope I have given you in this short article is a new approach and positive mind-set that the job of your dreams is out there and within your grasp. By developing your goals and identifying specific objectives creatively and realistically, you can plan, create, and successfully implement a targeted marketing campaign aimed at only the specific companies and individuals most likely to want and need someone with your talents and drive. Someone once said, "If you love what you do, you will never work a day in your life." That is a goal worth achieving.

So what do *you* want to do with the rest of your life?

<u>B<small>IO</small></u>

Harvey Feldman, MBA, CEC, has over 35 years of experience in business and consulting. After operating his own successful marketing consulting practice for over 20 years, Harvey studied to become an executive/business/life coach. He works primarily with business owners and corporate executives to maximize revenues, productivity, profitability, and satisfaction. His unique background and experience have enabled him to help his clients achieve amazing breakthroughs and outstanding results. For more information, or to schedule a complimentary Business Breakthrough Coaching Session, call Harvey at (201) 962-8462; email him at harveyfnj@optonline.net; or log on to http://www.harveyfeldman.com.

18

Moving on Up

❧

Jim M. Allen

"I love my job and the company I work for," Barb told me during our first career-coaching session. "But I've been there a long time, and I'd really like to move up in the organization. Is that reasonable, or should I just look for another job someplace else?"

Her question is reasonable—and one that I get regularly (not surprisingly, given the rather tumultuous job market we find ourselves in these days). Although it's impossible for an outsider to say that you should or should not look for a job with a different employer, I can share some ideas to help you— just as I helped Barb—evaluate whether it's possible to create a positive job change with your current employer and how you might go about that.

Before making a move to make a move, I encourage you to focus on a few important steps, which, I believe, will give you a solid foundation to move forward.

Step 1: Know Your Job Inside and Out

Seriously. I mean, really, *really* know your job. Be the best at what you do or, at the very least, be among the best of those who do your job in your company. Understand all aspects about how your position interacts with every other section, division, and employee of your company. Take every training class that's offered, and keep up to date with necessary certifications and licenses.

Step 2: Learn Your Boss's Job

Understanding what your boss does and the challenges she or he faces will help you assist her or him more readily while showing that, should the possibility arise, you can help fill the void when your boss moves up. Of course, it's not a guarantee that you'll get that job should it go vacant, but it improves your chances and gives you a greater understanding of how the company operates. Do this in such a way that you don't come across as trying to give your boss the bum's rush out the door. Always view this as a way of helping a co-worker help the company succeed, not as a way of helping yourself succeed.

Step 3: Develop a Power Personality

Over the years, I've noticed that people who are the most successful at moving within any company and holding multiple positions of increasing responsibility are those who have similar personality traits while still being unique individuals. These people are:

- *Outspoken*: These successful personalities don't pull punches. They speak their minds when they have strong ideas, opinions, and concerns.
- *Confident*: When they present ideas, they believe in them and do not worry excessively about being wrong or making mistakes. They present their thoughts in a concise and straightforward manner so that they are easily understood.
- *Passionate and rational*: They fight passionately in support of their ideas, but they do so from a rational basis, looking closely at how an idea or discussion affects their company and its customers. Although not unemotional, they do not allow emotional reactions to situations to cloud their judgment. They develop thought-out plans of action for implementing ideas and pursuing creative solutions.
- *Well-spoken and well-read*: Developing ideas is how businesses stay in business for a long time. Power personalities know that to develop ideas. They read a lot in many different areas, not just their own technical realm. They also understand that being able to speak easily about ideas—theirs or their organization's—is vital to helping their companies grow. The more ideas you see, the more you'll have. The better able you are to speak about your ideas, the more of them others will put into practice.
- *Honest*: If they make a mistake, they own up to it, without excuses and with appropriate apologies.

- *Humble*: Although technically expert in their field, these folk share the praise and reward that comes their way. Indeed, they are eager to recognize how others on their team and organization contribute to any success at hand.

You could use a number of other terms to describe a power personality, but these core traits account for the successes that power personalities achieve. Each of these can be improved upon, or learned in many cases, if you find a particular trait lacking in your personality. Becoming well-spoken, for example, is largely a matter of training and practice, which you can get from a good public speaking course or by participating in a local Toastmaster's group. You can develop confidence by taking classes in various subjects through a local college or a local Dale Carnegie vendor or by working with a therapist or coach. Work on those areas where you're weak. When you're confident you've developed them to a point of mastery, you're ready to make your move.

Step 4: Make Your Move

It's time to get a sense of what potential there is with your current employer. The easiest way to do this is to simply ask. Schedule a meeting with your supervisor or human resources representative if you're not within a few weeks of a scheduled review period. If you are close to a performance review, wait until then to discuss this with your boss.

Once you have the meeting, explain that you're interested in moving up in the company and would like to know how likely such a move is, from the company's perspective. If there is a possibility, in what time frame could such a move take place? If not, what obstacles are involved? Either way, what additional skills, training, and experience does your boss believe you need to be successful with such a job change? The answers—combined with your knowledge of the company, its history, and operations—will give you an indicator about your chances to successfully make the move you seek.

If your boss indicates that there's little or no possibility, you will want to decide if you're willing to continue working your current job with minimal potential for a job change or whether it's more important to make the job change, even if that means changing employers.

If the potential is there, how quickly can you meet the requirements to make that change? What education, training, or coaching do you need to rise to the challenge? What is your time frame and plan for completing these items so that you can prepare yourself?

Either way, be sure to follow up with your employer after the meeting, in either an email or a memo, thanking everyone involved for the meeting and summarizing your understanding of what they told you. This ensures that you heard them correctly and took down all the correct information, information that is vital to helping you decide what to do next.

Whether they say yes or no to your making a big change, the skills you learned in the steps I've outlined will help you. These skills will help you master a new position anywhere. Whether you're simply moving over or moving up or moving on—you'll be moving toward success. Enjoy!

Bio

Jim M. Allen, "the Big Idea Coach," is a professional life coach and speaker who works with motivated individuals ready to achieve their biggest life goals. For more information, visit him at http://www.coachjim.com, or contact him via email at JimAllen@CoachJim.com.

19

Compete in Today's Job Market with a Career Coach in Your Corner

Moe Vara

The Job Market

If I had to compare finding a job to anything, I would compare it to a firewalk. As in the case of a firewalk, a job search in the current job market can, if you're unprepared, involve a lot of pain and feel as if it is impossible to find the job you truly want. You may feel that far too many capable professionals are searching for a job; hence making it impossible for you to successfully secure the job you love. Generally, these types of thoughts and fears stop us in our tracks. They paralyze our ambitions, hopes, and dreams.

A firewalk is an extreme example of overcoming your fears and creating the empowered mind-set that allows you to accomplish what may seem impossible to achieve.

A word of warning: *Never* try a firewalk without full training and support. This is not something you want to do by yourself without training and a qualified support system. The same applies to competing in today's job market. You need training and a professional support system—hence a career coach.

A lot has been written by other career coaches about the importance of the mind-set. So this chapter will not focus on the mind-set of the individual. But before moving on to other topics, it must be acknowledged that it is crucial

78

that you work with your career coach to create the mind-set necessary to believe your goals are doable. Because if you don't believe they are doable, you will not be able to do them.

I suggest you start the strategy session with your career coach when the mind-set is addressed.

The Key Topics for the Career Strategy Session

A career coach can help you focus on your CV and produce an impressive portfolio to impress the reviewer. But the first item on the agenda is not the CV or the portfolio. The first item on the agenda must be your *vision*. Do you have a clear vision? Do you really want it? Can you taste it? Having a clear vision is one of the traits of successful people.

Next on the agenda is goal setting based on the vision. Do you have *goals*? Where do you want to be in one, three, five years? Do you have the necessary focus? Laser-sharp focus on the desired outcome is another trait of successful people.

In the process of arriving at your vision and setting your goals, you must determine why you want the stated results. Why do you want that particular job? The more reasons you can come up with for wanting an outcome, the more fuel you will have to get it done.

The next item on the agenda is the development of a detailed *action plan* to meet the desired goals. Without a specific and detailed action plan, it will be difficult to get the desired result within the time frame you imagine.

Your action plan must include the CV and the portfolio, which are tools for finding the desired job. However, a great CV and an impressive portfolio are not going to cut it. You need *market intelligence*. A critical topic that must be included in your action plan is *news and media*. With the help of a career coach, you can explore the type of press or media you should monitor and the sort of things you should now notice. This process will help you identify where you should be searching for a job and, when you identify and reach out to potential employers, what to talk about and how to impress them by your overall and in-depth understanding of your market.

Networking is another vital element that will assist you in gathering market intelligence and building rapport with potential employers. Hence you need to identify where you should be networking and include that in your action plan. Would you network online—on LinkedIn and LinkedIn groups? Or offline—in seminars, conferences, and training events? I recommend both. I encourage all job seekers to be actively involved on LinkedIn and associated groups. This is a great way to extend your reach, obtain endorsements, and build rapport with potential friends, colleagues, and employers.

Another item in your action plan must pertain to *training*. In addition to technical expertise, what other skills would your boss be looking for in you? Would he or she be looking for a problem solver, a go-getter, and an energetic employee? Or one who always brings problems but never solutions? I think the answer is clear.

The next item in your action plan must be to dig deeper and talk about *communication*. How do you communicate to your potential employer that you are, in fact, the right person for the job? As you may know, research has shown that 55 percent of our communication is done through our body postures and only a shocking 7 percent is done through our words. So it is not so much what you say to potential employers—it is about your body language. Again, this is an area that a career coach can help you perfect for the desired outcome.

Imagine if potential employers filmed you at the interview or at a networking event and then watched you on the television with the sound muted. What would they think? Would they see a desperate person who is overwhelmed with problems? Or would they see a person who is confident, focused, and professional in his or her demeanor? What are you communicating?

How will you sit, stand, walk, or shake hands with a potential employer to convey confidence? What body postures should you adopt? What about eye contact? A career coach can help you in this regard. A coach can also help you identify the gestures necessary to communicate your message in the most efficient way. The goal should be to develop or rediscover natural body postures and gestures that convey the intended message. A career coach can also help you see the impact of your facial expressions and tone of voice on others.

Hence nonverbal communication should definitely be on the agenda for the career strategy session.

The Professional Career Coach

There is nothing worse than not knowing what to do and giving up on your ambitions, hopes, and dreams. To compete in today's job market, you need a coach in your corner to help you get clarity on your vision and goals. A coach will help you to strategically target and go after what you want.

A career coach occupies a unique place in your life. A coach is not your manager who will almost definitely have her or his own agenda. Nor is a coach a friend or a family member who will jump to conclusions based on your emotional ties. A career coach is a professional who is trained to be in your corner to bridge the gap between where you are right now and where you want to be.

You can be successful on your own, but with a career coach in your corner, your chances of success are a thousand fold higher. The choice is yours.

Bio

Moe Vara is the founder of Global Empowering Solutions and a career-empowerment coach. He is also a chartered civil engineer with 25 years of work experience. So he fully understands the challenges professionals and businesses face on a daily basis. He has been trained by Robbins Madanes Training Institute as a strategic intervention coach. His ambition is to help people strategically take their careers or businesses to a whole new level. His client base includes individuals from all over the world. He works one on one and in groups. He works in person and online. You can reach Moe at moe@globalempoweringsolutions.com or by logging on to http://www.globalempoweringsolutions.com/contact-us/.

20

Career Coaching for Your Competitive Edge

❧

Trinise L. Kennedy

Competing in today's job market relies heavily on your ability to do two crucial things. First, you must *figure out* exactly what you want from your work. Second, you must boldly *ask* for what you need from a job. Such simple instructions may be easy to take lightly or even skip over. Yet your future job satisfaction and livelihood rest greatly on your mastery of these twin elements.

Would you recognize your dream job if it actually showed up? Have you thought about the kind of office setting you would thrive in? Ideally, how many hours a week would you like to work? Should you be searching for an existing job posting? Or is it more advantageous for you to create a job or career more suited to *your* lifestyle?

Although it is wise to capitalize on your strengths to develop your competitive edge in the quest for your dream job, you must also be able to evaluate and choose the most rewarding career path for yourself. One thing to consider is whether you will truly enjoy working a particular job. What would it take for you to feel totally satisfied with your work?

According to NBC's Brian Mooar, "A research group reported that job satisfaction is the lowest it's been since the group began studying it 22 years ago." The Associated Press reported that only 45 percent of Americans are satisfied with their work, which leaves the remaining 55 percent unhappy with their current job.

Job Satisfaction Factors

Taking time to carefully consider what you want from a job, before seeking one, can surely help to safeguard you from job dissatisfaction. Sure, it is important to choose a job or career that will allow you to earn sufficient money to support yourself. Yet many other vital factors contribute to overall job satisfaction.

Other career elements to ponder include:

- *Your work style*: Do you work better on your own or within a team environment?
- *Type of work*: Are you genuinely interested in the kind of work required for the job, or are you considering the job for other reasons?
- *Creative input*: Do you prefer a job in which your creativity can flourish, or do you prefer to be given a set of specific tasks for completion?
- *Recognition*: Is it important for you to feel rewarded for a job well done, or do you simply receive fulfillment from knowing you did the job well?
- *Benefits package*: Does your job offer health, dental, and life insurance and retirement plan options, or do you have to find and pay for your own benefits?
- *Job location*: How close is it to your home, and how long is your commute?
- *Office structure*: Will you be working in a tiny cubicle, or will you be set up with a spacious office of your own?
- *Work attire*: Do you already have the proper wardrobe for your job, or will you need to purchase new clothes for work?
- *Non-negotiables*: What are the perks or benefits that you absolutely must have to accept the job?

Jobs with Benefits

Make a list of the job benefits that you absolutely must have. These will most likely be essentials such as health, dental, disability, and life insurance; stock options; and retirement plans. Some companies offer benefits for child care, relocation, or travel expenses. While you are at it, check into the number of vacation days and personal days that come along with the position. All of these elements combined contribute to your overall benefits package.

Top 10 Companies to Work for in 2013

What makes a company a top company depends on what strikes your fancy. The most coveted job positions come with highly attractive perks, benefits, and incentives.

One gracious company—in the state with the highest number of Fortune 500 companies—rewarded 400 employees with $50,000 toward a new car for helping it reach its goal. A top company in Texas built bigger benefits into the mix by offering discounted apartment rentals to its employees, along with a 50 percent match of 401K contributions up to 7 percent of a worker's salary. Another top-rated company—with customers that include Google, Quicken Loans, and the New York Yankees—paid a whopping 100 percent of health care premiums for employees and their dependents. Plus this same benefit-boasting company threw in a free vacation for its staff every two years. (For the list, "Top Companies to Work for in 2013," go to http://www.TRINISE.com.)

Be knowledgeable on common benefits package offerings, and ask for exactly what you want. Skip the lengthy benefits discussion during your interview. A good time to discuss benefits is when you have a firm job offer. At that time, you will have more authority to negotiate and get the benefits that you require.

Are You Interested in the Job?

The more interested you are in your job, the higher your chances for enjoying your work. Studies have shown that only 51 percent of workers now find their jobs interesting. This is a significant drop from the 70 percent who found their work interesting as noted in a 1987 survey.

Now more than ever, workers are impacted by job interest. What are you into? What do you like? Ponder these questions before you start job hunting. Is there a job that closely matches your interests? Or will you have to create a job or business that allows you to do what you enjoy most?

I recommend that you take a personality assessment before embarking on any new job or career. It is vital to know yourself intimately so that you become familiar with the way you function as a person, as well as on a job.

A personality assessment will give you a straightforward analysis of your interests and tendencies. You can use these results to find the jobs or careers that are best suited to you. Then you'll have a solid basis from which to start your career search. (For a list of top career personality tests, go to http://www.TRINISE.com.)

Next, take out a piece of paper and begin to brainstorm job and career ideas that most resonate with you. For now, just allow your ideas to flow freely without ruling anything out. You can always go back over this list later and decide what makes sense for you.

As a final point, you are now adequately armed with the tools and information to determine what you want from a job. For the highest possibility of job satisfaction, choose your career path based on your interests and strengths. Select a job that most closely fits in with your lifestyle. Unabashedly ask for what you want from your job—and get it.

Bɪᴏ

Trinise L. Kennedy, "Law of Attraction Goddess," is one of the world's most conscious leaders in personal empowerment. Trinise guides her private business clients as well as celebrity clients with powerful tools and processes to effectively and permanently transform their lives.

Trinise's dynamic background encompasses success in real estate investing through creative finance, network marketing, entrepreneurship, authorship, and embodying consciousness.

Trinise's most recent celebrity clients include Australian Recording Artist and Producer Traffik connected with the labels Funkonditionalove and Chosen Warrior Music, as well as hip hop Rapper Kokane who is most notably known for his co-appearances on Dr. Dre's critically-acclaimed album "2001" which debuted at number two on the U.S. Billboard 200 chart boasting 516,000 copies sold within its first week.

International transformational leader, author, and business strategist, Trinise L. Kennedy leads individuals in applying the Law of Attraction to achieve their desired results. Trinise specializes in teaching others techniques to consciously attract more money into their lives. Additionally, she teaches practical strategies for making money at home building an online business.

Discover more about Trinise and get access to her daily wealth and success tips at http://www.TRINISE.com.

21

Staying in the Game on Your Terms

Kim Petry

In today's economy, many employees and business owners remain in positions in which they are dissatisfied because of economic uncertainty. Even though the competitive environment remains fierce, you can take simple steps to ensure that you are in control of your career destiny.

The first step is to develop your vision and define your career trajectory. A powerful technique toward attaining your optimal goal is the Minimum at Dream, or MAD, matrix. To develop your MAD matrix, divide a sheet of paper into four columns. In the first column, outline categories of importance to you; for example, compensation, work environment, colleagues, job satisfaction, location, industry, self-fulfillment. Label each of the remaining three columns as follows: "Minimum" (second column), "At" (third column), "Dream" (fourth column). For the "Minimum" column, list the minimum you would require for each category. For example, if your minimum compensation is $60,000, list it. Do the same for each of your categories. For the "At" column, record for each category what would make you comfortable, content, and fulfilled. For the "Dream" column, list your dream expectations. Outline what your dream role/business would look like. The key to this matrix is believing that your dream categories are attainable. Review this page daily with a focus on your dream category. This will help to set the foundation of your expectations and help to focus your energy.

Once you have outlined your expectations, make and commit to annual networking goals. These goals should include four components:

1.   Recruiters and headhunters
2.   Organizations, conferences, seminars
3.   References and contacts
4.   Online presence

The recruiter and headhunter landscape is extremely fragmented. The players in this industry range from large firms down to independent headhunters. It is important to continually maintain a current list of recruiters and set a goal for meeting new recruiters to add to your list. You can meet recruiters through friends, colleagues, research online, and LinkedIn. Use these different venues to expand your circle. Regularly make sure your list is up-to-date. Send an updated résumé with a cover letter outlining your major requirements for your next role, even if you are not currently in the market for a new position. This important step helps to set your expectations while keeping you on that contact's radar. Additionally, once or twice a year, call your recruiting contacts or reach out with an email. At a minimum, this regular contact will keep you apprised of the current employment market.

Participate in at least one (preferably more) industry, trade, networking, or special interest organization. If you are not aware of any in your area, search the Internet or check with colleagues. Organizations and groups present great opportunities to meet new individuals, broaden your network, and expand your reach. Do not limit yourself to a specific industry or area of expertise. For example, Toastmasters is a great organization to belong to if you are seeking to improve your public speaking skills; it can also serve to meet new contacts. Set a goal each year as to the number of meetings and conferences that you plan on attending, and make it happen. In addition, set a minimum goal as to the number of new contacts you would like to make at each event. You would be surprised where a simple introduction can go.

References and contacts are critical for successful networking. Keep a running updated list of people you have worked for, people you admire, and people you want to stay in touch with. Make a point to update the list regularly, and keep in touch with each individual via email, letter, or calls, depending upon your relationship with that individual. Gauge your communication on each of your contact's preferences. For your key contacts, initiate a lunch, dinner, or coffee at least twice a year. This serves as an opportunity to stay in touch and allows for valuable mentoring and feedback. If you are open to it, constructive feedback serves as one of the most powerful tools. Ask your contacts for their opinions, advice, and feedback whenever possible.

Online presence and résumé building are critical. Sites such as LinkedIn are great tools for getting exposure and making new contacts. Make sure your profile is up-to-date and outlines your major strengths and accomplishments. Include a condensed summary of your experience and areas of expertise. Although you do not want to list your entire résumé, for each role listed be sure to include your scope, areas of responsibility, and key accomplishments. Your accomplishments should outline variables that set you apart from the crowd. For example, if you improved a process, be sure to include the quantitative impact. Did you reduce processing time by 50 percent? Did the change have an impact on the number or cost of employees? You would be surprised how many recruiters, colleagues, and industry experts will reach out to you based upon your experience and accomplishments. Make sure any information you have online presents you in the best manner possible. Many employers perform Internet searches on prospective employees. Your employment opportunities decline significantly if you have a great professional LinkedIn page yet a compromising Facebook page.

By having a vision and going for it, you can create your future and not leave it to chance or to others. It is critical to maintain your network, contacts, online presence, and relationships, even when you are satisfied in your current role. New opportunities are always available. And performing the work up front will ensure the next opportunity is the right one for you.

Bio

Kim Petry is a CPA and senior finance executive with 20+ years' experience in strategically leading large global finance teams for premier organizations, including American Express, TIAA-CREF, US Trust/Schwab, and PriceWaterhouseCoopers. Kim recently joined Spend Smart as EVP and CFO. Additionally, she is founder of Your Empowered Self (YES), a successful coaching organization aimed at empowering individuals to attain their full potential. Kim received her MBA in finance from NYU and her BBA in accounting from Adelphi University, graduating first in her class. Kim participates on several boards and resides with her family in Garden City, New York. Contact her at kimpetry22@gmail.com.

22

CAREER DEVELOPMENT

Career Development Takes Work

✤～✤

Carol Davies, MA

Let me ask you a question. Do you feel that you have your absolutely perfect career or, even more important, the career that you have always envisioned? If so, this will be the result of a lot of sustained effort and hard work on your part. This personal achievement and success didn't happen overnight in your career development. Planning and subsequent execution is the key.

Career development is important because it is important that people spend their lives doing things they love and feel as though they can excel at. This will mean doing the things you have to do to get the career you really want. Use smart goal setting to get to your final career destination.

How to Create a Career Development Plan

1. The first step in positive career development is to decide on the career you want to have. Know yourself, know what you're good at, and know what excites you. Perhaps you will have to see a career counselor and take tests that will help you to determine your personality and jobs that will fit it well.

2. Be practical by learning what needs to occur for you to meet the criteria for the career you want. Career advancement does not happen immediately. Careful planning is necessary to get to where you want to be. Be sensible about your aspirations and about the route to get there. Do you

perhaps need more education or extra training courses relevant to your field or your career development? Find these things out and then be realistic about pursuing your goals.

3. Know where you are now. Think about your professional and educational training, work experience, work skills, interests, and hobbies. Ask yourself some pertinent questions such as:

    *   What motivates you?
    *   What has shaped your career choices?
    *   How did you get to your current career position?

4. Know where your end goal is or where your final career destination will be. Again, ask yourself some tough questions:

    *   How have your skills, experience, qualifications, and values served you at work?
    *   If you had the time, money, and connections to find your perfect career, what would it be?
    *   Where would you like to see yourself in the future—1 year, 5 years, 10 years?

5. Know what it will take to get to your goal. This involves some serious reality testing. You have to do research and then make balanced and informed decisions about the practicality of what you find out. Determine how much time and money you are prepared to spend. Have you got sufficient funds to support your search, or is your money source limited?

    *   Are you prepared to make changes and sacrifices if you have to?

6. Write your plan down. Once you've got 1 to 5 in place, it's time to sum up your career development plan and crystalize it by writing it down.

    *   Set out all the detailed action steps that will take you to your ultimate career goal. Break it down into tiny steps. Take one step, then the next, and the next. Keep on going. A positive result stems from doing steps in an orderly fashion.
    *   It is easier to commit to your goals if you can look at them in written form every day. The printed word is a powerful motivator.
    *   You will also want to keep an eye on the outcome of your actions to make sure they are actually helping you to move toward your

ultimate goal. Remember—take proactive steps, and put yourself in charge of your career.

- Aristotle said: "First, have a definite, clear practical ideal; a goal, an objective. Second, have the necessary means to achieve your ends; wisdom, money, materials, and methods. Third, adjust all your means to that end."

7. Just Do it. Career development is important because—I am convinced— that it is important that people spend their lives on things they care about and feel as though they can do well at. Enjoy the rest of your working life in a satisfying career.

Bio

Carol Davies, MA, is a certified professional business and career success coach and owner of The Passion Motivator Coaching. She helps entrepreneurs find their passion, get focused, and achieve success. She coaches holistically with EFT, NLP, the passion test, among other tools. She is also a speaker, trainer, and contributing author to the book *Ready, Aim, Captivate* and several books on gratitude. She has worked in the United Nations for more than 20 years and has helped people of many different backgrounds, beliefs, and goals to deal with transition and culture shock. Carol's guiding principle is "Happiness is a choice." Carol's Web site is http://www.thepassionmotivator.com; her email is carol@thepassionmotivator.com; her phone number is (519) 686-2691.

23

How to Get What You Want out of Life

❦

Martin Yate, CPC

Times of change are unsettling, and the less you understand about how to secure your future, the more unsettling they are. I know you are thinking that there must be a better way to change your life's trajectory. There is. I have been dealing with these issues for 30 years; it is how I have spent my entire professional career.

If you want to make this change, there are some essentials truths you must face:

- You are somewhere along the path of what will likely be a 50-year work life.
- The statistics say you will change jobs (not always by choice) about every four years.
- You will probably have three or more distinct careers over the span of your professional life.
- During this time, you can expect economic recessions to swing by every seven to 10 years.
- By age 50, both age and wage discrimination will further complicate your course.

This adds up to 12 or more job changes over 50 years, with 3 of them likely to involve the much greater challenges and financial dislocation associated with changing, not just your job but also your entire career. This makes job-search

94

and career-management skills the most important survival skills you can ever develop. But no one ever told you this.

It's Time for Change

You are ready for a radical shift in your career-management strategy because the advice you've been given—get an education, choose a career, settle down and do a good job; patience and loyalty will be rewarded with job security and life success—doesn't make sense in a world where corporate greed all too often turns your life into a disposable commodity that will be used and discarded, unless you *take control and change the trajectory of your life*. If you hope to achieve financial stability and get what you want out of life, you *must* take responsibility for your destiny.

Change Is Constant

A successful career is no longer a given that came as a gift with your college diploma. It's a critical aspect of your life, and it needs management. To survive and succeed in a professional world where there is no certainty, but perhaps more opportunity, you need to adapt.

Recognize that change is constant, and by taking responsibility for the trajectory of your life going forward, you can learn how to get what you want out of life.

Your Most Important Professional Skills

Corporations have no loyalty to you; they have loyalty only to the shareholders and are almost solely concerned with profit *now*, this quarter. You are just another cog in the moneymaking machine, and if an employer can find a way to make or save money by automating or exporting your job, then your means of putting food on the table and a roof over your head are gone. So cast off any mistaken notions of thick-and-thin fidelity to your employer, and focus your attention with laserlike precision on you: What's best for your career and for your life?

Change Your Trajectory

When a company dispenses with your services, it's nothing personal. The company is doing what it must do to survive and satisfy the shareholders. You need to do the same thing. Take control of your economic survival and your success by acting with the same forethought, objectivity, and self-interest as a corporation.

Let's take that a step further: Start thinking of yourself as a corporation—as MeInc, a financial entity that must survive and prosper over the long haul. *You are MeInc,* a small company with a successful future to be won.

As MeInc, you have products and services to sell: the skills and experience you've accumulated over the course of your working life. These products and services that embody the professional you have to consistently fulfill the needs of your customers, employers.

This means that MeInc needs to organize and structure its activities just as a corporation with departments would, each with a specific set of responsibilities focused on the overall success of MeInc. You will need:

- *Research and development*: to identify and develop products with the maximum marketplace appeal. In other words, you have to monitor market demand and develop the skills that employers want.
- *Marketing and public relations*: to establish credibility for the professional services you deliver, and to ensure that this credibility becomes visible to an ever-widening circle, starting with your current department and expanding outwards through the company, your local professional community, and beyond, as your strategic career plans dictate.
- *Sales*: to constantly develop new strategies to sell your products and services, including development of the primary tools of professional survival: résumé creation, networking and network-integrated job-search strategy, interviewing, negotiation, and all the tools of effective career management.
- *Strategic planning*: to plan strategies for growth within the company, time strategic career moves that take you to new employers, monitor the health of your profession, and make plans for career change—and all on your timetable. Working with R&D and marketing, strategic planning will also constantly monitor opportunities and strategies for the pursuit

of completely new revenue streams—alternate entrepreneurial endeavors that minimize disruption of MeInc's cash flow and maximize the odds of success for these endeavors.

- *Finance*: to ensure you invest wisely in initiatives that will deliver a return on investment. You must invest in your future, in your success, rather than fritter away your income on the instant gratification drummed into your head by 24/7 media.

Enlightened Self-Interest

You have been raised to be a good consumer and to live in debt. We all typically absorb around 3,000 advertising messages every day. To make your dreams come true, you have to break free of senseless loyalty in the belief that a corporation will take care of you, and instead invest yourself, your time, and your income in the activities that will help you get what you want out of life, that will make MeInc successful and give you the opportunity for a fulfilling life.

Bɪᴏ

Martin Yate, CPC, *New York Times* bestseller, is the author of K*nock 'Em Dead—The Ultimate Job Search Guide,* now in its 27th edition. It is the keystone of a 15-book career management series, collectively published in some 63 foreign language editions. Martin has been in career management for 35 year years and has established a global reputation as a thought leader of his profession. As Dun & Bradstreet says, "He's just about the best in the business." At http://www.KnockEmDead.com, Martin offers résumé & LinkedIn profile writing and career coaching services.

24

How to Become a Must-Have Employee

❦

Fredrik Lyhagen

Career management is not an isolated exercise every couple of years when changing employer. It's a continual process to make you attractive for promotion with your current and future potential employer. And there's no secret sauce to it. With an idea of your desired career direction, a bit of research, and a structured approach, you can go from a "good-enough" to a "must-have" employee.

The Only Constant Is Change

"The only constant is change," as stated by Greek philosopher Heraclitus, is ever so true now. Especially in the job market.

Don't be fooled into thinking that you're competing for only your next job; you're also competing for your current job. Most companies are "right sizing" on a continual basis, letting people go, and moving people around, optimizing the organization for maximum return for the stockholders.

The increased pressure on productivity applies to your manager as well. So even with the best intentions, the yearly performance review and career development talks slips down on the priority list and often becomes a task of completing HR requirements rather than a development talk. So without enough time for your manager to engage, he or she will rely on the stories about you floating around in the organization—your reputation. How do you

98

make your reputation a vehicle that carries your professional career in the direction you want?

Which Emotions Do You Evoke?

Marketers of this world know that people choose based on emotions and only afterward rationalize their choice by looking at the available facts. And you know what? Recruiters are people too. The deciding factor for being promoted or hired is not your achievement in your latest position, your excellent degree, or your reference letters. The deciding factor is how you make the recruiters feel.

Recruiters look for easy ways to choose, so all available facts will never be evaluated. But samples will be taken, and the recruiter will then decide whether to proceed with a candidate based on the feelings these samples evoke. Do you give them the feeling of being an achiever? A feeling of fitting into the team? Of being honest, of being likable, of being rewarding to be around?

You need to actively build your reputation—your personal brand. And the feeling your brand instills has to be consistent and congruent with reality. You can never jeopardize your entire brand by letting one aspect of it be inconsistent with your brand values.

The Three Cs of Personal Brand Management

To help your personal branding journey, I suggest you base it on the three Cs of brand management. It's a simple method to help you take a structured approach and thus significantly increase your chances of keeping to the process and getting the results you want.

For brevity of this article, I assume that you are clear about the direction you want to take your career over the next few years.

Step 1: Collect Continually

The first step is about how you *see* people reacting to your personal brand. Your brand is based on other people's perception of you. What you think of your self is irrelevant. So make a habit of collecting feedback on how you are perceived. You can easily create a brief survey using free Web-based tools and send it to your target audience. Remember to keep it clear, concise, and anonymous to increase response rates. Example of a questions are:

- Name three of my best qualities.
- Name three adjectives you associate with me.
- If I were able improve one personal quality significantly, which one would you recommend me to pick and why?
- Name one quality that sets me apart from my peers.

Don't worry too much about defining your target audience. Personal branding is a continual process. You gain more knowledge about your brand perception and audience with every repetition, allowing you to become more targeted and more relevant with time. The key is to start; the rest will follow. A good way to complement the information you get from the survey is to Google yourself. Do the results support the direction you want to take your personal brand?

Step 2: Craft Consistently

The second step is about what you *say* about your personal brand. Based on the previous step, you can now start to craft your brand and your branding journey. The journey is as important as the goal, if not more important, for two reasons:

1. Building a brand takes time, and ruining one takes seconds, so respect the time it takes to build a consistent and credible brand and enjoy the journey.
2. As you evolve as a person, so does your brand; therefore, be very clear about the direction you want to go, but don't worry too much about a specific goal.

Start by extracting the positives of the survey, overlay your desired direction, and then craft your brand statement to support your direction. Then focus on how you add value to your target audience in a two-step reiterative process. Start listing the extrinsic values and consider associated intrinsic values. Refine your extrinsic and intrinsic value until you have extracted a handful of words or phrases of each that represents the direction you want to take and stay grounded in your current personal brand.

The key question in this step is to ask yourself, "Why would my target care?"

Step 3: Communicate Confidently

The third step is about what you *do* to evolve your personal brand. Understanding how your personal brand is perceived and having a strong brand statement is good, but stopping there does little to evolve your brand to support your direction.

Identify activities that help build your personal brand. These activities must both allow you to communicate your brand statement with relevance and confidence and be an example of what your personal brand stands for. One of the two is not good enough. Example of activities:

- Participate in the local chapter of a relevant association.
- Contribute to trade magazines.
- Speak at conferences.
- Write and publish white papers.
- Organize online events.
- Start a blog on a relevant topic.
- Start an online newsletter.

To break through the media noise, I recommend that you niche yourself and be bold in your communication. Take a stand for something. As an example, if you have set out a career direction in corporate finance, first try to narrow it down to a niche such as brand valuation, sales finance, ethics, compliance, or explaining finance to nonfinance people. Secondly, find an angle to your chosen niche that is a "pattern interrupt"; in other words, when your target audience glances over available content in the niche, your messaging stands out from the mass and triggers curiosity.

To draw on the words of Søren Kiekegarrd: "To dare is to lose your foothold for a moment; not to dare is to lose yourself."

The Pitfall

The most common pitfall is the fear of taking a stand for something. To take a stand, you must be clear on your vision and your goals. It can be beneficial to seek support from a coach to facilitate your inner journey toward a clear and

101

confident view of who you are and where you want to go. Only then can you build a genuine sustainable personal brand.

Today is the first day of the rest of your career. How will you take your personal brand from "good enough" to "must have"?

Bio

Fredrik Lyhagen is an executive coach who draws his experience from an international career in sales and management and combines it with his passion for eating clean, moving freely, and living consciously to inspire and assist on the inner journey toward greatness. You can contact him at http://www.mindcorecoaching.com.

25

Follow Your Passion: Tap into Your Unlimited Potential

❧⁓❧

Bob White

For many of us, especially men, much of our lives are devoted to supporting a family via a career. All too many look upon a career as just a means of making money; however, for those who most succeed in their career, it is a passion. (Generally speaking, this can include anything related to personal development.)

What Is Your Passion?

Mark Hamilton, in his book titled *The Book* (go ahead and laugh, that really is the name of the book), describes the one quality necessary for real success in a career: "Downstream focus happens when your thoughts naturally flow back to your work, even in the evenings and weekends. ... Is watching TV or listening to a ball game or bowling or hanging out with friends hard to pull away from in your evenings? Those are indicators that you have not experienced a *downstream focus* to success. Every person has a door inside that opens to the person he or she was meant to be. ... Without discovering and opening that door, you will never soar."

A Free Resource

A free resource is available that can help you select a career precisely geared to the specific type of work you are most interested in. It is called the O'Net Career Interest Assessment. It has been incorporated in an excellent personal development and career workshop, the Personal Success & Leadership Workshop (http://www.PSLinstitute.com/workshop.html). The assessment is in the second of two sessions.

The Six Basic Career Categories

You will find in the career interest assessment six basic categories or types of work:

- Conventional
- Investigative
- Entrepreneurial
- Social
- Artistic
- Realistic

Most careers are a combination of two or more of these types. This assessment describes each of these categories and allows you to select your top three preferences. Then it displays those careers that most closely represent the combination of your top preferences.

It Takes Thought and Preparation

As part of the workshop, you will also find an article, "The Ten Steps for Choosing a Career." The ten steps are:

1. Begin with your values.
2. Identify your skills and talents.
3. Identify your preferences.
4. Experiment.
5. Become broadly literate.
6. In your first job, opt for experience first, money second.
7. Aim for a job in which you can become 100 percent committed.
8. Live within your means.

9.   Invest in furthering your career.

10. Be willing to change and adapt.

The point is, it takes some serious forethought (and preparation) to select a career that most suits you. It is not a task to be taken lightly because so much of your time and life will be devoted to this work.

A Career Is Half Your Life

Why be like so many who typically use the expression "TGIF" (thank goodness it's Friday) and can't wait for the weekend or evenings when they can do *anything* but what they work on in their career? Granted, there is life after work. Definitely, you will want to spend time with your spouse and children in the evenings and on weekends; however, why dread having to return to work on Monday? Unless it is something you can look forward to, you're wasting half your life.

Be a Lifelong Learner

Besides your career, develop an interest in and knowledge of a variety of subjects/fields. The more you learn/know, the more interesting life becomes and the better able you are to help others. Set goals and learn how to use your time wisely. Life is short, and year by year opportunities slip through our fingers because we keep telling ourselves, "There's always tomorrow!"

"For of all sad words of tongue or pen, the saddest are these: 'It might have been!'" –John Greenleaf Whittier

One good example is learning first aid and CPR. Just think; you might be in a situation where a person's life is in jeopardy and you are the only one present who knows CPR. And it's not difficult to learn. Your local Red Cross offers courses on a regular basis. Learn a musical instrument. Take a foreign language. Join Toastmasters to learn public speaking and leadership skills. Nothing builds your overall self-confidence more quickly than learning to speak in front of a group of people. Join Big Brothers or Big Sisters and become a friend to a young person who is missing that parent in his or her life. There are so many exciting things to learn and do; the possibilities are endless. The more you take advantage of them, the more meaningful your life becomes. Here again, balance and priorities are important. Expand yourself, yet keep life simple by focusing on those things that have the greatest meaning in your life.

Tap into Your Unlimited Potential

We were born with unlimited potential. Each of us has self-imposed limiting beliefs, many of which we "inherited" from our parents. It is only by realizing that we have unlimited potential that we can break through these limiting beliefs. We were born with two minds: our conscious mind and our subconscious mind. Our habits and behaviors are governed by our subconscious mind, which is our self-image. Our conscious mind decides what we want and, when properly used, can program our subconscious mind. Emotion is the vehicle that effectively allows our conscious mind to communicate with (program) our subconscious mind. The process that enables this communication is called imprinting, as described in *Advanced Formula for Success* by Robert Anthony. Imprinting consists of visualization, affirmation, and feeling the associated emotion. (An affirmation is a statement in the present tense you speak out loud to yourself of your having succeeded in a goal, often starting with, "I am ... ." For example: "I am a compassionate and caring person.")

When repeated on a regular basis, imprinting changes your self-image (how you see yourself). Our self-image (subconscious mind), again, governs our habits and behaviors. Once we have decided what we want out of life (interests/dreams/goals/aspirations), a positive self-image (acquired via imprinting) causes it all to almost automatically flow unto us. We can think more clearly and see the steps we need to take. Our imagination is in gear and running at full throttle leading us there. There are no limits. Seeing is becoming, and imprinting is the vehicle. However, we must start with the desired result in mind; otherwise, there is no focus or progress

Try Imprinting

1. Set a goal for each thing you want to accomplish in your life, including career goals.
2. Convert each goal into a goal/role. For example: goal, a best-selling book; goal/role, renowned author.

3. For each goal/role, compose an affirmation. For example: "My book, *Your Passion—Your Career,* is a best-seller!"
4. Visualize in your mind your accomplished goal. For example: "See" people excitedly buying, reading, and successfully applying your book.
5. Imagine the emotion you would feel. For example: the emotion of seeing these people succeeding using your book as a guide.

Use Imprinting at least weekly for each goal: visualize it, state the affirmation, feel the emotion. The more often you do this, the more solid the impressions become in your mind, and the quicker you will progress toward your goals: becoming the person you are capable of being.

<u>Bio</u>

After graduating from the University of Tennessee, Bob White worked as an electrical engineer for the Tennessee Valley Authority (TVA). Having studied the area of self-improvement and total quality management for years, he spearheaded the creation of an employee suggestion system at work and became an examiner for the Tennessee Quality Award the year of its inception. In 2001, he started Personal Success & Leadership Institute, and in January 2004, created a personal development and career workshop. Bob and his wife have 8 grown children and 20 grandchildren. He lives in Chattanooga, Tennessee. Contact him by email at rcwhite3@bellsouth.net.

26

Recipe for Succeeding Inside Out

❧

Nancy Lee Bentley

Tips and truths from a veteran food and health entrepreneur who discovered that real success doesn't just come from cookie-cutter formulas or doing things by the book. You have to make it for yourself, out of yourself, from scratch.

If, according to the ancient Chinese, chaos and crisis equal opportunity, then times have never been better for creating your ideal livelihood. Yet most of us don't look at it this way. So, what *is* the best formula for success in today's crazy, tough, almost jobless market?

An explosion of small business entrepreneurs is doing business on the Internet. Amidst the "expert" marketing advice—such as "Secrets for Making $28.578.59 in 7 Days"—you'll find tons of pricey programs with piecemeal approaches for laser targeting your niche, strategizing social media, and leveraging yourself with info products you and your team can repurpose once you've set up the right software and systems.

You'll even find more enlightened, evolved business gurus who also integrate important spiritual realities such as the Laws of Attraction and Manifestation—whatever you focus on becomes a reality, perseverance furthers, and do what you love and the money will follow. (They don't tell you how soon.)

All good advice, for sure. But as a chef and food and health entrepreneur, I can tell you that few cookie-cutter recipes and cookbook formulas—whether they're for great food, business, or health—rarely give you all the information you need to be a success. A few important ingredients or steps—essential secrets *not spelled out* in the printed recipe—are always missing. These keys can make the difference in a scrumptious, airy soufflé or between a rising business and one that falls flat.

Although many chefs ruthlessly guard their special secrets, please help yourself to some of my hard-won insights from my own in-the-trenches food business experience:

- *It's not a step-by-step process.* Realize that things will unfold in unique, unpredictable ways. Be flexible and adapt.
- *It's more of an art than a science.* Experience, still the best teacher, can't be bought but only extracted through trial and error, living and doing.
- *Expect the unexpected.* It probably won't turn out as you've projected—'nuff said.
- *It's not just the more you know but how conscious you are that increases your chances of success.* Even if you have all your ducks in a row, so to speak, shift happens. Having it all together—with your marketing plans, website, and all—is no guarantee that you're automatically going to be successful.

Why not? Let my less-than-appetizing authentic story shed some light on this.

A love affair with food and nutrition, my life has been like a large all-you-can-eat buffet of learning experiences. Despite "following all the recipes" and what some might consider some pretty amazing successes, my professional career hasn't exactly been what you would call *The Joy of Cooking.* I'm not done yet.

My full-circle food story started at age five, making mud pies in the sandbox. Little did I know that four decades later I'd find myself "stuck in the mud" at the most critical point in my career. Yet this difficult process ultimately revealed what the true meaning of whole health and succeeding inside out really is.

Appreciating good food and nature came early from spending after school hours learning to cook and doing chores on our self-sufficient family farm. Church suppers, recipe collecting, and catering jobs all whetted my appetite, but my zest for writing on the high school paper and lousy cafeteria food gelled my move to a Cornell food, nutrition, and communications degree on the way to a professional career in it.

Then a bevy of leading-edge food/health related jobs in different sectors of industry, government, education, politics, and media gave me a huge repertoire of skills and experience. I did just about everything you can do with food, from creating healthy foods and co-op networks to creating wheat-free recipes for Cher, baking Prince's purple-topped birthday cake, and helping to organize the first Organic Trade Association.

Later, well-launched into championing healthy-food issues, writing about global health politics landed me in hot water. Then the carefully planned launch of my self-published *Truly Cultured* was trashed when the books were mysteriously "misbound" at the printers. This took me out of circulation into a dark, downward spiral, an almost seven-year cycle of working my way through what felt like a total career breaker.

Ironically, my most profound insights have come, not from my successes, but from my knockdowns. All this adversity forced me to review, face, and take responsibility for creating my own reality. Instead of resisting and recycling the same stuck issues, getting real and diving into the, gooey, messy center of myself finally exposed and helped me embrace the unsavory buried treasure within. This is where I learned that what's *in* the way, *is* the way.

So here are just a few priceless, practical, and more elusive tidbits of wisdom I've gleaned from being in hot kitchens and pressure-cooker political snafus:

- *Think income, not job.* Even though you may prefer the security of a job, you'll learn to love flying on your own.
- *Create your own but not alone.* Cooperate, get a coach, collaborate. It's just not possible to do everything yourself, even if you are a super solo entrepreneur. Do what you do best. Delegate the rest.
- *Let it happen; don't make it happen.* Part of the 12.21.12 change is a transition from right-brain, male-dominated thinking. And it's time. Women entrepreneurs will create more than half of the 10 million new jobs by 2018, according to Forbes. We're cooperating and collaborating with

open-heart and universal forces instead of insisting upon our own way. Working together works.

- *Your business is a reflection of you.* No accidents or coincidences—we all create our own reality. "As above, so below," the alchemists say. What manifests in our outer world is a reflection of what's on the inside. And though we're always happy when it's pleasurable and prosperous, we often fail to see the true gifts when so-called negative events or circumstances happen. These are simply mirrors reflecting the glitches and misaligned resistances that keep us from truly *BEing* and manifesting who we are, in business and life. Celebrate them.

- *Don't be afraid to make mistakes.* You will. But don't let that scare you. Don't let fear keep you frozen. Learn as you go. Don't get hung up in the perfectionist "paralysis of analysis" trap. You are unique; learn to listen to your own expert within. Let the expert's wisdom lead you to better health and prosperity. And spiritual growth.

- *Failure, like sour and bitter, is just one of the flavors of life.* To be healthy, we need to taste all four flavors—sweet, salty, sour, bitter—every day. Tasting unpleasant experiences doesn't have to destroy us. Viewing things through a bigger window can make us stronger. Who knows? Failing in business may even be some kind of initiation or essential ingredient for success!

- *Got lemons? Make "lesson-ade."* As I've found out, my own challenging trial turned out to be one of my biggest gifts and learning lessons. Now it's an important focus of my work, helping others who are stuck, spinning their wheels with recurring eating, health, weight, financial, relationship, or spiritual issues. It doesn't matter.

- *We're all just spiritual beings having a human experience.* Entrepreneur, employee, or executive—got a body? You've got lessons. From a higher perspective, these are not just about succeeding in business, but about succeeding as souls, as spiritual beings in the marketplace, on the playground, on the stage of life. And in the end, we each have to define what "success" personally means to us. *Remember the pearl in the oyster.* It started out as an irritating grain of sand.

Bio

Nancy Lee Bentley is a dynamic wholistic health expert, new-thought leader, speaker, author, and coach with a full-circle body, mind, heart, and soul approach to health. Author of *Truly Cultured,* she has been interviewed on all the major networks, not only because she's done "just about everything you can do with food" but also because she's a real, in-the-trenches pioneer laying the foundations for organic and natural foods, local food systems, and holistic health today. Honored for her healthy "soup-to-nuts" career, she is most fulfilled from enlightening nourishment, empowering her clients to stop spinning their wheels with recurring issues and start finding their own road map to health. Email: Nancy@WholisticHealthExpert.com; Website: http://www.WholisticHealthExpert.com; other contacts: http://www.TrulyCultured.com, http://www.YourTango.com.

27

The Two Critical Components to Effective and Fulfilling Career Transition in the 21st Century

❦

Marc de Bruin

In August 1999, I resigned from the law firm I worked at as a litigation lawyer. Loads of hard thought had gone into this decision. I did not want to practice law anymore. In fact, at that stage, I had had enough of every aspect that had to do with law. I had to quit.

The senior partner did not take my message too well. He had brought me into the firm as the rising star in real estate and criminal law. He must have felt betrayed and hurt. I felt anxious and relieved at the same time. On January 1, 2000, I would be out of law—and without good income.

Technically, I was facing a career transition. In reality, I was facing my worst demons. As much as I knew I *did not* want to be a lawyer anymore, I had *no* clue about what I *did* want to do or what I could be good at. At age 30, I was staring into an abyss. The only thing I figured I was good at—law—was the one thing I was throwing out the window. In some of the dark days I experienced, I envisioned myself applying for whatever work was available, or having no work at all—that one freaked me out big time.

Had I known then what I know now, my career transition would have been a fair bit smoother. On the other hand, the whole experience taught me the lessons I now aim to convey to you if you are faced with leaving your old career behind to start a new one.

Job culture has changed in the last couple of decades. The times that employees stuck with one employer for 45+ years until they reached retirement? Well, they are memories of the past. Most employers do not want to "hire for life" anymore either. Employee statistics show that we change jobs or careers roughly every two to five years, accounting for about 11 switches in the whole of our working life.

Generally, we change career because we *want* to (voluntary) or because we *have* to (involuntary). Either way, part of the transition is finding a new vocation. I am not necessarily talking about people changing employers within their current industry or line of work. I am focusing more on the ones that change more drastically, the people who want to or have to reinvent themselves, career-wise.

So what is the most effective and successful, least painful and least stressful way to make an about-face in your career? This book covers many factors. I would like to discuss two elements that I know to be the crucial ones to your effortless career transition. Master these, and you will pretty much always come out on top and in front of less clear-minded career changers.

Know Your Career Values

Your career, or work, values are the answer to the question: What do you consider first most important, second most important, and so on when it comes to a fulfilling career? This could be anything: receiving good pay, meeting technological challenges, being praised, working with people, making a difference, solving problems, closing a deal, working in a team, having variety, working part time, working close to home. You *must* find the most important ones for *you* to transition your career successfully.

I had *no* well-defined idea about what I wanted from my career. What I did know was that I wanted to travel (preferably overseas), do something I could do anywhere in the world, help people, and have fun in doing so. That ultimately led me to becoming a counselor/coach and Body Stress Release practitioner and immigrating to Australia. Those guiding principles ensured I was not going to settle for anything that did not comply with my value set. The clearer you are about your career values, the easier it will be to filter your options and to decide what will serve you well. Career counselors can help you properly define your career values. It will be well worth your effort.

Know Your Personality

Some people are thinkers, others feelers; some are leaders, others team players; some are conceptual, others practical. We are all different. I use personality-type profiling in my private practice to assess a person's natural stronger and weaker points when it comes to work. Not to pigeonhole people, but to make sure they stay mostly in line with what they are *naturally* good at. Your career will be so much more fulfilling when you build on your innate strengths. Make sure you have your strengths (*and* points for improvement!) assessed by a professional specializing in personality-type profiling. The Myers-Briggs Type Indicator, the Keirsey Temperament Sorter, the DISC profiler—they are all fine, as long as you use the results to your benefit. I have seen clients go through massive "a-has" when they found out what they are good at innately and choose a career based on it (rather than on mum and dad's desires).

I walked this journey in reverse. I didn't know anything about personality types. I had to learn by trial and error what profession really suited me, and only then learned about *why* that was so. I probably would not have chosen to become a litigation lawyer to begin with. A position as a lecturer at a university would have been a better option. Hindsight is a great teacher.

Neurologically, personality type and values will gear your brain to look for career opportunities matching both of them. Neuroscience teaches us that our five senses are guided by our neurology to look for people, situations, circumstances, and events that are in line with what we believe and want to experience. In other words, you will be more open to more fitting opportunities, ones you might have missed before!

Practically, your personality and values will allow you to focus more specifically in desired career directions. A well-known adage states: "If the 'what' and the 'why' are clear, the 'how' becomes easier." And that definitely is true with this topic. The "what" element is largely defined by your personality; the "why" element by your values; the "how" element—meaning your actions—will be guided by both.

Whether you call it Law of Attraction, Law of Deliberate Intent, Pull Principle, hard work, or something else doesn't matter. What does matter is that your personality and values will give you a toolbox with which you can forge or

115

find a new career, one that will actually fit you like a glove and will fulfill the values you deem important in your work life.

There will be some (hard) work involved; this book gives you loads of guidance around that. What's more important is that opportunities will come your way without much work on your behalf as well, purely because you are focused on them. And that's the fun part, the path of least resistance.

Obviously, the proof of the pudding will be in the eating. So go ahead, assess your personality type, and define your values. You will be glad you did; I can promise you that.

BIO

Marc de Bruin is a counselor, coach, master NLP practitioner, and personality-types facilitator in Queensland, Australia. Working as trainer and mentor with many high profile companies globally and in his own private practice, Marc is an expert at career development and career and life transition. He mentors using universal principles in business and private settings. Marc teaches his clients to create "knowareness," a powerful state of presence that allows clients to make the right decisions at the right time, all the time. Email Marc at marc@landmarc.com.au to arrange an introductory 30-minute session. His Web site is http://www.landmarc.com.au.

28

Find Work, Flexibility, and Freedom: 5 Tips for Securing Opportunities as a Contractor

꙳ ～ ꙳

Philip Lowit

In today's economy, where there are fewer full-time positions than there have been in the past, abundant opportunities are available for job seekers willing to consider contract or contingent workforce positions. Firms in the fast growing information-technology sector often engage a significant percentage of their teams as contractors or outside consultants. This practice is not a short-term trend or fad. Filling project roles with contingent workers is an emerging reality representing a significant segment of today's job market.

While securing full-time employment is likely to remain the ultimate goal of most job seekers, contract work provides many benefits, with flexibility at the top of the list. Contract or project-based jobs may lack traditional full-time job perks such as health insurance, paid vacation, and 401K plans. However, they often compensate for this with a slightly higher wage (per hour) than a comparable salaried position, allowing you to pursue benefits on your own. Taking on project-based contract work can open the door to new opportunities and help you expand and diversify your skills in new areas. It can also help you hone your skills and expertise in a particular area. Either way, you do so while bringing in income, growing your network, and building up work history on your résumé. More important, the choice is yours. Contract work lets you pursue exciting opportunities to practice new skills, work with new people, or even live in a new place—all with the flexibility of a limited time commitment. If you are continuing to seek full-time status, there is no better way to get a foot in the door and showcase your skills, work ethic, and personality than by joining a company as a contractor.

The techniques and process to specifically pursue project-based contract work are similar to seeking traditional employment opportunities. Prioritizing the following tips can impact your value as a project-based contractor and help you differentiate yourself from the crowd.

Tip 1: Think Like an Entrepreneur

As a contractor, you are your own business and your own business development manager. Don't think of yourself as simply a potential employee. Instead, think of yourself as your own company and of your prospective employers as clients. Consider what you need to do to sell yourself and what your value proposition is to these clients. Write out your talking points or an "elevator pitch." Print your own business cards with your key information; they are inexpensive to create and can assist in presenting yourself as a polished professional. Whether on LinkedIn or other social media platforms, your online profile should reflect your personal brand. What does it say about you? What makes you stand out? How will you provide value to paying clients? How will you perform to ensure they give you an excellent reference? Last, remember that not all business is good business. In contract-work opportunities, consider what is best for you. Don't be afraid to be turn someone down if you don't feel the project is a good fit for you or you feel that it will be challenging to provide excellent value for your potential customer.

Tip 2: Invest in Yourself

It may sound cliché, but there is no better time than the present to invest in you. Whether pursuing an educational degree, a professional certification, advanced training, or working on a project that enhances your skills, your credentials are what set you apart from the competition. Joining the right professional associations can add to your credentials and provide important networking opportunities. Don't sit by and wait for opportunities to come to you. Demonstrating initiative is a differentiator. Bet on yourself.

Tip 3: Market Yourself

Most contractors are hired not for their general background, but rather for their specialized experience in a particular skill, area of expertise, or project history. When targeting contract-work opportunities, highlight in your résumé or CV the details of your specialized technical background, core competencies, professional certifications, and any past project performance that make you the ideal contractor to hire for that particular opportunity. Besides your education and work experience, think about what else you can use to market yourself as an expert at what you do. How do you share your expertise with others? Do you have a blog? Or perhaps an active professional social media profile? Publishing your own content can expand your network and get you noticed by other thought leaders and even prospective employers. Finally, speaking well about yourself is one thing, but having someone else say good things about you is more effective. A glowing endorsement or recommendation from an employer, client, or other thought leader in your profession provides the third-party validation essential to position *you* as a talented expert.

Tip 4: Network, Network, Network

Despite what you may think, your search for contract work—or any job for that matter—does not always require your computer. Spend time getting to know the firms and the individuals that hire for project-based or contract work. Online research is a start, but there is no substitute for a strong in-person encounter. Career fairs can also be a good place to begin, but trade association events (remember Tip 2?), industry meetups or conferences, technology user groups, and other professional gatherings are great places to meet the people and companies that drive job opportunities in your profession. As a contractor, you need to always be building your network and your pipeline of opportunities, even as you are working. Whether you take a project that lasts six weeks or six months, always keep an eye on the opportunities ahead. Stay in touch with your contacts and hiring managers as you move on to new projects, keeping those in your network aware of your availability to take on work.

Tip 5: Take Care of Your Needs

As previously mentioned, project-based contract work often does not include the full benefits packages offered by full-time employment, so it is important to know some of the ways to secure these perks on your own. Start with health insurance. Changing regulations should make it possible to secure a policy on your own; however, in some cases, you may be able to secure a group health plan through a professional association. No 401K? Study up on IRAs. And as for your tax status, know the ins and outs of the various tax forms required for contractors, and make sure you consult with a good accountant on these issues. If you are an incorporated independent consultant, you will most likely need to secure business liability and other often required insurances. Check with your attorney to make sure you have covered any legal or contract issues.

Whether you use it as a stepping-stone to build work history on the path to full-time employment or as a way to remain flexible and opportunistic, project-based contract work is an increasingly common arrangement between job seekers and employers. Knowing how to build your value as a contractor will help you differentiate yourself from the crowd.

Bio

Philip Lowit is cofounder and CEO of TSymmetry, a nationally recognized information technology consulting firm and systems integrator. He has more than 20 years of leadership, entrepreneurship, and business development experience in the information technology and human capital industries. Philip was recognized as a 2012 SmartCEO Future 50 Award winner. He is an active member of Young Presidents' Organization (YPO), Business Executives for National Security (BENS), AFCEA, and the TechServe Alliance. Philip holds an MBA with a focus in Marketing from Fordham University and a Bachelor of Science business degree from Rider University.

His Web site is http://www.tsymmetry.com; his email address is Philip.lowit@tsymmetry.com.

29

3 Core Values for Succeeding in Today's Job Market

Rob White

Forty-five years ago, I finished college and moved to Boston with $60 in cash. Today, my real estate portfolio is valued in the tens of millions. Along the way, I learned a lot about getting jobs and creating jobs. And much of what I learned boils down to simple core values. At first blush, these values may seem quaint or old-fashioned, nostrums from another era that don't belong in a fast-paced, technological world. It's true that I never used the Internet, social networking, or collaborative tools to make a dime. Personal technology didn't exist when I made my fortune. But the core values I'm about to relay are timeless and apply to any field. They've enabled countless people, past and present, to achieve their financial and lifestyle dreams. Let's take a look at each one.

1. Value a Winning Attitude

When I first got to college, I felt out of place, having grown up in a mill town where most men stayed on to work in the factories after high school. Rather than making new friends, I hung out with the dorm janitor, Peter, because his socioeconomic background was close to my own. After three weeks, Peter showed a great act of kindness by telling me to stop hiding and start honing my natural talents. "If you don't believe in yourself, Bobby, you'll be pushing a mop for the rest of your life rather than using this [pointing to my head]."

With that, he booted me from his office and into the world of college that I'd gone there to experience

When the door to Peter's office shut, a new reality opened. I gave myself permission to trust that I was in college for a purpose. Eventually, I came up with a pet phrase that I still often utter: "If it is to be, it's up to me." Those nine words inspired me, and they can inspire you too. If you take the time to absorb them deep in your mind, you'll radiate incredible confidence that motivates you to try things different and new. This refreshing attitude makes others want to be in your company.

I'm not talking about hocus-pocus magical thinking that enables you to will the winning numbers on your lottery ticket. I'm referring to a "WOW factor" that lies within your DNA. Great industrialists such as Andrew Carnegie and Henry Ford had it. Sheryl Sandberg and Marissa Mayer have it too. The good news is that like physical DNA, which is locked in at birth, the WOW factor, an unrelenting belief in yourself, is always there to support you when you learn the truth about yourself. "If it is to be, it is up to thee." Take this from affirmation to actualization, and the world will clamor for your employ.

Tip: Imagine your title is "triumphant victor." Though you wouldn't put that on a job application or business card, carry it in your head; if you believe it to be true, others will too.

2. Value Self-Growth

After college, I became a teacher in an urban school. I enjoyed the profession and loved shaping young minds. But after 17 years, I longed for a new career, one that would put me in the driver's seat. And one that had no financial ceiling. The catalyst for change was actually a piece of advice I gave to one of my math students, Debbie. Debbie wanted to attend an elite private high school. Her grades were borderline, but the real hurdle was her own conviction that she wasn't smart enough to get admitted. I told her that it was time to decide that she was smarter than she thought she was and to adopt the behavior of a winning student. In six months, she became a model student and a different person. She was accepted to the high school with a full scholarship. I then knew it was time for me to become a different person too. At the end of the year, I turned in my resignation and ventured into the world of business with nothing but my savings account and a book on how to make a million in real estate.

When job candidates approach me about working in my organization, the first thing I ask is this: "Can you think of a failure that has helped shape you into a better person than you were five years ago? Ten years ago?" I want to know about the most powerful life-changing experiences they've had. After that, we get into more mundane inquiries about the education, skills, and on-the-job experience listed on their résumés.

Tip: Be enthusiastic about communicating your life as an unfolding journey. Speak proudly of the stops, wrong turns, and the course corrections you've made along the way.

3. Value the Power of Continual Improvement

The history of humanity and the history of business are replete with stories of once mighty people and once mighty companies that have faded into oblivion because they failed to continually improve themselves or their products and services. When it comes to improvements in your personal life and your business, you never arrive—you're always in process, always becoming.

The same holds true when it comes to launching or bolstering a career. Don't think of yourself as just a designer, software engineer, writer, chef, or salesperson—those are just titles. Put the word *evolving* in front, as in *evolving designer* or *evolving chef.* I'm not suggesting that you belittle yourself in any way—you've probably honed a powerful skill set and can proudly point to wonderful accomplishments in your life. But the point is this: never rest on your laurels! Employers want to know not only what you can do for them today but also what you may be able to do for them tomorrow. Will you be able to solve problems and help the organization grow in tough times as well as good times? Will you add value to the company by the very fact that continual improvement is a way of life for you?

You'll always get my attention when you demonstrate your commitment to continual improvement in everything you do. This is a make-or-break issue for me when I'm hiring. If you've never had a job, tell me how you raised the bar in school or in a personal or community project. You don't have to report earth-shaking achievements; continual improvement is about refining little things that make a difference. If you're looking to change jobs, tell me how you added value to the job you are leaving. I want to hear that you value excellence, that mediocrity is not acceptable to you.

Tip: When you present yourself, focus on what you plan to do for the company, not on what the company can do for you. Doing is about continually improving, which includes the mind-set that just good enough is never good enough. Doers are winners in today's competitive job market because they stop talking about what they are going to do and go out there and do it.

Finally, always remember that you are the chief architect of your life. No, you won't win at every job interview you have, and, no, you won't advance up every rung of every ladder in the business world. But you maximize your chances of winning again and again if you value the feeling of being a winner, value the thrill of self-growth, and value the pleasure that comes with continual improvement.

Bio

Rob White is a philosopher, a storyteller, and an author. Rob taught school for 17 years then became an entrepreneur and restaurateur. Through his determination and passion, Rob has made millions and now dedicates his life to inspiring others to accomplish their life goals. Rob created RobWhiteMedia. com to provide individuals with the resources they need to wake up to the power of WOW! A featured columnist for the *Huffington Post*, Rob is the author of *180, A Second Chance at Success* and *And Then I Met Margaret,* a collection of paradigm-shifting stories. Learn more at http://www.robwhitemedia.com.

30

How It Effects an Organization and Its Corporate Citizens and the Ongoing Saga of How a Person on the Job Search Overlooks This Serious and Critical Component

Jean Mulrine DeMange

Corporate culture is defined as "values, customs, traditions that make an organization unique." It is the character of an organization and embodies the vision of its founders or leaders. It is clearly stated in the company's mission statement. Those values are executed through an organization's managerial behavior. The culture of an organization won't change for you; you have to be sure you can fit within it, as it exists, not as you would like it to be.

At one time, companies and organizations consciously created an ideal environment or aura around their organization to draw future employees to their doors. But that was yesterday. In today's job market, companies/organization/groups are looking for a "rock star." They need results in a particular time frame, if not sooner, and expect results to continue in times of adversity, market changes, or other environmental situations. In today's competitive job market, they want people who are results oriented and outcomes based. In this article, I hope to introduce you to a process that will help you to evaluate a prospective job and to ascertain how well the position and the company fit with your experience and ethos.

First, you must know what motivates you. Take off the rose-colored glasses and take a realistic look at the company itself. This is easier to do today with Google and other Internet search tools than it once was. Look for any written statements, interviews, and discussions about the company. After you have gathered some material, consider your own work style and ask yourself if this environment would enhance your ability to advance your career. If so, how might you contribute to the organization? The answers to those questions will help you decide whether to pursue an opportunity.

During the interview process, the company is evaluating you too. Hiring managers are looking at your skills, your work/business style, your experiences, and how you evaluate your past experiences to see if you fit into their corporate or organizational culture. They will discuss their company culture, the position, and what they expect you to achieve. Listen to what they say so you can decide whether there is a good fit between you and the company as a whole—not just within the department or division in which you'd be working. This is usually the point when you will decide if you will continue the interview process.

If you like the company and the position, and you have been invited back for another interview, it is important at this juncture to make sure it is a fit for you. Take a critical look at this opportunity and a hard look at yourself, or the marriage will most likely fail. The fit will be short-lived and riddled with job dissatisfaction, frustration, and minimal accomplishments or career fulfillment. When you go on future job interviews, hiring managers will question your ability to assess a situation if you have a short-term position listed on your résumé. They'll ask you outright why you decided to work with that company, and you should be able to give them a reasonable explanation.

You should be able to explain—to yourself, at least—why you're interested in the position and if you have anything to contribute to the company. What would make you stand out in a crowd of others vying for this opportunity? From your own experience, are the company's goals reasonable or achievable in the time line that's been set out? Lastly, consider what might happen if a company changed management while you were there and took the company on a different path. Would you be able to adapt and be flexible enough to see how the new organization fits you? Or would you leave before it was clear whether you could work in that environment?

Individuals desire a position for many reasons. Sometimes job seekers have been unemployed for a while and are desperate to get back to work. Some individuals want to take their career to the next step. Sometimes they may have to relocate for their spouse's job or an ill parent. When they're anxious to get a particular position, they often create a fiction in their mind about it, which is divorced from the reality of the position in its day-to-day responsibilities and outcomes.

After you've had time to get some basic information about a company and have interviewed, I suggest you go back to your computer and check out the Internet chat boards—job, financial, and others. See if any disenchanted employees have offered their own views of the company. This might clarify some issues for you. Next, read annual reports. Is the company's stock traded? Have news releases been issued about the company? Are there newsletters that might discuss the company? Sometimes just looking at a company's advertising can tell you a lot about a company. Look to see if there are too many openings in all levels within the organization or just in certain areas. This may indicate a problem in the company or show you its growth potentials. Look at its growth in the past year or so. Look at the executive leadership team. What is the educational background and work history of the company leaders? Is your educational or professional background similar to any of theirs? This indicates that the company might view diversity in your career as healthy and appreciate your potential growth.

Many job seekers who have been out of work for some time gladly consider a position that may not be well suited to their skill set or a match with the corporate culture. It is even a bigger mistake to avidly pursue a position that you are unsuited for because your ego is urging you to seek some upper-level position. Be honest with yourself. Do you have the skills needed for this position? If not, do you meet 50 percent or less of the requirements for this position, including skills and background/experience? Have you ever worked with this type of management style or organization? Are you listening to your own intuition about pursuing this opportunity?

People work best with people in groups whose style is similar to theirs. Determine whether a company and a position are a good fit for you before pursing it. The job search is a process, and, in these changing and challenging times, you need to take an introspective review of your own skill set/abilities to see if you have been consistent in your professional style and attitudes.

Don't give up! Pursue what you feel will work for you and the organization. Show value in your work and outcomes, and you will become a value-added addition to an organization or corporation that will enhance your career and future.

Bio

Jean Mulrine DeMange is president and CEO of Wellington Thomas Ltd., a national health care recruitment firm established in 1991. Jean is based in Florida and recruits and places candidates in the supervisory/management levels up to COO in a variety of health care settings: corporate, hospital, home health, hospice, postacute health care systems, and health care venture capital/equity owned firms, including managed care health care networks/ carriers. Visit the company's Web site, http://www.WellingtonThomas.com.

31

Your Organizational Personality: Finding the Right Fit Is Key to Success

Shoya Zichy

Corporate culture is the sum of an organization's goals, behaviors, and values. Fortunate individuals who find themselves in the right culture feel both energized and highly valued by their boss, peers, and subordinates. Others, in the wrong setting, will be stifled and frustrated by practices and processes that run counter to their natural style. Finding the right culture for *your* personality is a key component to job success and overall quality of life. Cultural fit is closely related to the *structured* and *adaptable* components. Please note that neither type is better or smarter than the other. Each has its success stories and failures. They key is knowing yourself and finding the right fit.

Check Your True Preference

__meet deadlines early OR __meet deadlines at the last minute

__make detailed plans before you start OR __handle problems as they arise

__are punctual and sometimes early OR __tend to be leisurely

__like to be scheduled OR __prefer to be spontaneous

__have a tidy workplace OR __have a workplace with many piles

129

More items on the left? Your inborn style is structured with more left-brain activity. You thrive in a stable work environment with well-defined job responsibilities. You prefer working with proven products and processes that have been tested in the past. You are seen as responsible, punctual, and accountable and like to be rewarded for getting the job done in an efficient and organized manner. You typically do not like change, too many surprises, or having to work with coworkers who are too flexible or easy going. You have a neat desk, closet, files, and car. You balance your checkbook on a regular basis and keep firm control over your assets. Even relaxation is organized—play comes after the work is done. Life is tidy and predictable, and you like it that way. Your special strengths include:

- Setting and pursuing long-term goals
- Organizing projects and developing efficient systems
- Meeting and enforcing deadlines
- Properly using and conserving resources
- Completing all parts of work with precision and accuracy

More choices on the right? You are an adaptable with more right-brain activity. Chances are you prefer to work in a flat hierarchy, with the opportunity to redefine your job every day. You excel at creating new products and processes and thrive on dealing with the unexpected. Variety, change, and a flexible environment without undue rules or bureaucracy is best for you. You need to be rewarded for your willingness to take risks and to get things done, often without the assistance of others. You are seen as spontaneous and adaptable. Typically casual in your clothing and irreverent in manner, you also tend not to balance your checkbook too frequently. And if work is not fun, it is not worth doing. Your special strengths are:

- Responding easily to unexpected changes and crises
- Multitasking and keeping several balls in the air at the same time
- Being flexible, accommodating, and easy to work with
- Applying skills and interests to new fields
- Solving problems in original ways

The Conflict

Conflicts exist between the two groups—both in the workplace and in families (we tend to marry our opposite). Structured types drive their opposites crazy with their need for schedules, plans, and closure. Meanwhile, adaptables may be perceived as messy and irresponsible by their structured counterparts. Understanding these inborn differences and the contributions of each increases workplace satisfaction and productivity. It also makes for a happier marriage and better parenting.

Do Companies Have Only One Culture?

Despite an overall culture, environments have different work niches for the other personality type. For instance, companies like IBM have a few departments designed to explore new markets and products. These groups may be heavily populated by adaptables who create a unique culture within their units. Similarly, a large bank, normally a bastion of structured behavior, has overseas posts filled with employees always ready to get on a plane on a moment's notice to pursue a new client. Likewise, companies like Google need operating units with more structured components. Accounting, project management, and operations are just a few that typically draw and are run by individuals with the laser-beam focus needed to carry out the responsibilities of the group. Recognizing that you are a good fit within your unit, but at odds with the company's culture at large, reduces stress. It is easier to point out your value to the company if you understand the larger framework in which you operate.

Clues to Recognizing the Organizational Culture

Sometimes you can determine the corporate culture during the interviewing process. The degree of noise, conditions of desks, and dress code provide clues. The structured environments tend to be more subdued. Employees have desks with limited and neatly organized piles. The clothing usually is more formal. Deadlines and punctuality are high priorities. In an adaptable environment, there is restrained chaos. Deadlines, clothing, and schedules are more casual, and desks have many piles.

The world divides fairly equally between the two groups. There are no gender differences. The percentages hold up across cultures worldwide, even though some cultures *seem* to express values that favor one group over the other. Differences are inborn and hold up from cradle to grave.

Finding the right corporate culture will allow you to define your unique strengths and brand yourself so others appreciate your contributions. This is one of the most important steps to career success. It will also reduce stress, free up your creativity, and improve your relationship with your coworkers, clients, families, and friends.

Bio

An internationally recognized author and speaker, Shoya Zichy is the creator of the award-winning Color Q Personality system used in seminars on team building, leadership, sales, and career development. Her clients include Merrill Lynch, Bank of America, UBS, and the U.S. Treasury, among others. She is the author of the recently released *Personality Power—Discover Your Unique Profile and Unlock Your Potential for Breakthrough Success* and the earlier *Career Match* and *Women and The Leadership Q.* Former president of the Myers-Briggs Association of New York, Shoya had a 15-year career in private banking at Citibank, Merrill Lynch, and American Express. Log on to http://colorqpersonalities.com.

32

Cover Letters

Killer Cover Letters

❦

Tina Guillot

I remember 30 years ago buying the Sunday paper, circling the ads that seemed promising, and then getting my typewriter out of the closet, typing up cover letters for each of the ads, attaching copies of my résumé that I'd printed at the local Kinko's, addressing, stuffing, and stamping the envelopes, and then driving to the post office to mail everything. On a good weekend, I probably applied for four or five jobs. Today's technology has really made it easy for job hunters to apply for multiple positions in a matter of minutes. Sometimes, as easy as it seems, we skip the step we've always known is critical, the one that helps us land the interview: writing a killer cover letter.

Because the common practice is for one's résumé to be simple and easy to follow, it doesn't allow for a lot of detail. The cover letter provides the detail, the important specifics to the job for which you are applying. You may think, "That takes too much time!" but the truth is, technology makes it a snap, and you don't have to be a Microsoft Word expert to pull it off. As long as you have basic writing and computer skills, you can do it! Here are some steps you can take to make a useful cover letter template.

- *Set up your file* by formatting the letter according to business standards. You can find many sample cover letters on the Internet.
- *Add a date field* so that your letter will be current at all times. Make sure the field is formatted properly, for example, April 1, 2013.

- *Include a blank subject line,* where you'll add the job title later, and start with an opening paragraph summarizing your overall experience and making a general statement about your interest in applying for the position. For example, you might say, "I have been a corporate professional for the past 16 years, working for several major engineering firms in the local New Orleans area. I am interested in interviewing for the subject position with your firm."

- *Add a paragraph that provides the specifics* for each of your skills or abilities. Include how much experience you have and where you gained that experience. Use headings that can be deleted later, if you desire, but will help you easily spot the paragraphs you'll need to keep as you use your template for a specific application. For example, one of your paragraphs might look like this:

Technical Writing and Editing: I have a total of 5 years of experience in technical writing and editing. While working at XYZ Corporation, I was responsible for writing, editing, and publishing all of the internal policies and procedures. Additionally, while employed with ABC, I wrote and edited all desktop instructions for the staff of 35 people.

When using the template, you'll simply delete the headings (if desired) and delete any paragraphs not related to the specific job.

- *Add a paragraph about your salary requirements.* Deciding whether to add salary information is sometimes tough. Certainly if the job listing calls for this information, you should include it, but if it doesn't, you must determine its importance. Including your current salary may limit your potential offer, so you might want to specify your desired salary instead; however, if you aim too high, you may not get an interview. On the other hand, not including salary information may end up putting you in a position where you are called for lots of interviews where the salary is below your desired range. Do some research to find out if your current salary is average for the type of work you do. If you discover you're being overpaid, you may want to mention your current salary, but state that it is negotiable. If you find you're underpaid, then you'll know you can pad the number a bit. Keep in mind that if you are applying for various types of jobs, you'll have to have an idea of the average salary for each.

- *Add a closing paragraph* that expresses again your interest in interviewing (don't say you're interested in applying—you are applying) and closes with a statement that welcomes a call from the recruiter. For example: "I am looking forward to hearing from you soon and meeting with you in person."

- *Keep your letter professional.* Your salutation should include the specific person's name when available, such as "Dear Mr. Smith," or "Dear Sir or Madam," when not. In closing, use "Sincerely" instead of "Best" or "Fondly" or something else less formal.
- *Check, double-check, and check again* to ensure there are no typos in your template. Nothing makes a worse impression than a cover letter (or résumé) that contains errors or incorrect grammar. Get help from friends to ensure that every paragraph of your letter is well written.
- *Save your template as a read-only file* so that you don't accidentally over-write your master. Once your template is created, you can simply open the file, add the specific addressee information and job title, delete the paragraphs you don't need, and print or save the document. You'll want to leave only the paragraphs that are applicable to the job. If you are applying for a job online and there is no option to add a cover letter, copy and paste the entire letter into your résumé file as the first page. Trust me; it's not cheating!

The right cover letter may be the key to the door that takes you to your dream job.

Bio

Tina Guillot is a corporate professional, freelance writer, and motivational and inspirational speaker. She is an active member of Toastmasters International, currently serving as a club mentor and sponsor. She is also the immediate past president of New Orleans Toastmasters, the district's oldest club. Tina enjoys blogging about her family and life in the Big Easy at http://dishindahlin.com. Contact her (504) 338-7927 or at cwguillot@bellsouth.net.

33

Developing Skills That Will Rapidly Improve Your Marketability

❧ ～ ☙

Ray Dye

So you want or need to change your present situation. You are experiencing mixed emotions. The move from the known to the unknown is a source of anxiety or discomfort. Doubt clutches at you as you consider alternatives. All the same, you are not unique in this context.

Presumably, you are skilled enough to do a specific job. However, can you safely say that you can handle promotion? Can you convey confidence and competence to a prospective employer? Can you persuade and build a relationship with your peers or clients? Are you lacking in communication skills or an ability to present your knowledge to an audience?

The purpose of this chapter is to introduce a method to fast-track your progress by making you aware of the skills that are needed to equip you to better compete in the job market. When you gain this expertise, you will take your rightful place in your community.

From years of experience, I can state that this is not a sweeping claim. Believe me, you need to quickly address these key areas. If you do not, sadly, you may be compelled to be less selective in your job search.

It is not an understatement to say that we have experienced an explosion in knowledge in the last few decades. This information upsurge is also beyond the written word. It appears in large numbers of alternative media sources and requires a rapidly evolving technology to present it and store it. Most of us are struggling to learn the new technologies; consequently, we have little success in managing this information overload. It is argued that new skills and strategies are needed to deal with this flood. Yet the skills are already there!

Consider video and audio information as a discussion point. When we use these technologies, several challenges should be immediately apparent. The most obvious is real time. A video or an audio takes as much time as the original recording that you watched or heard. You are required to spend the same time listening or watching it to collect any data. How would you be able to process the video material and present your findings to an audience?

You can rely on your memory, and this might be useful over a short time frame. But, without a doubt, the majority of you will state that you have to take notes. In doing this, you summarize the information and, through your hard copy, will be in a position to inform others of the essential content. Your notes will serve as a memory aid later. This means that you will not have to replay the whole original video or audio, and you will have benefitted by avoiding spending the same time as you did before. In this situation, your notes are more than a memory aid. They are also a framework of the original information; as such, you can use them for a variety of purposes. Your notes, if effective, can enable you to condense information into a fraction of the original time.

Recently, I was on a course for eight weeks that was held one night a week. The presentations were content rich. When asked by the trainer to write a brief, pertinent comment of what we had learnt, I simply addressed my notes and did not have to page through the printed notes and review the videos.

It is obvious, then, that you must not understate the importance of developing the skills that enable you to process, absorb, digest, and review information. The true leader is an efficient communicator and can operate on a few key words that are memory aids for large amounts of originally raw data.

Because communication ability extends to writing skills, and the permanence of the written word cannot be contested, you need to address and groom those skills. You should be aware that your ability in this area is directly related to your ability to change, control, and redirect your present circumstances. Remember, what you write may have legal implications; consequently, you may be called accountable. Furthermore, these desirable skills include a proficiency in writing reports, emails, letters, copy, and communicating your opinions.

Another area of obligatory competence is the ability to read, remember, and comprehend large volumes of information daily. Reading is required for the Internet, advertising, contracts, reports, and instructional requirements. It is even required to function in our everyday lives. How often do we come across truly accomplished readers? How could your ability in this area be hindering your future prospects?

Other considerations compel you to prioritize your time. Can you, for example, balance the important and the urgent? How effective are you at preparing for and running a meeting? How persuasive are you in front of an audience? How about your sales and negotiation skills? The majority of us need to focus on these areas. Moreover, most of us have had little or no formal training. Yet these skills are of paramount importance!

The skills that I have mentioned are, in my opinion, life skills and are needed to operate and promote yourself in a social or job context. So much of communication is about taking chaos and the complex and taming it into a simplicity that is powerful and digestible. However, most of us are complacent about obtaining, improving, and refining such talents. It is necessary that you expel any hit-or-miss methods that are inefficient and inadequate, although endemic. Such methods actually rely on osmotic and imitation processes to obtain the skills. Of course, you might be fortunate enough to be able to wing it. But you are doing yourself a disservice and severely limiting your potential. Unfortunately, to live a life without limits requires some prerequisite foundations.

The solution is to recognize that the skills are important. Recognize that they need to be taught by gifted and competent specialists. And recognize that they are not just going to happen by accident. The practice of these skills is in everyday life and not delegated to some future event. Once you have deliberately learnt and revised your capabilities, you will be surprised by the shift in your ability to function. You will be the person in control. You will be equipped to lead. And you will make the changes you so desperately want in your life, job, or career.

"Chance only favors the prepared mind." —Louis Pasteur

I am aware, that initially acquiring these skills might attract undesired attention and even ridicule. Just break out of your comfort zone and expend energy to achieve a sustained effort. This is the fast-track to success. It is surprisingly rapid, and the return on your time investment is both unquestionable and beyond calculation.

So how serious are you about success?

Bio

Ray Dye, currently living in Brisbane, Australia, is a business trainer and coach. Ray is an experienced educator and ex-town councilor. As an entrepreneur, he has owned businesses in South Africa, Canada, and Australia. He believes that too many people sabotage their success by not addressing their communication, negotiation, and data-processing skills. Focused attention on these skills will ensure an improved self-confidence and effectively equip you to plan, realize, and control your own vision. These skills can be rapidly acquired and taught, and they will explode your influence in your business and personal life. Ray's Web site is http://www.raydye.com; his email is admin@raydye.com.

34

Using DISC Personality Assessments to Compete in Today's Job Market

※～※

Boyd Harrell

Imagine landing the job that is a perfect fit for you, one with maximum gratification and minimal stress. A part of landing that perfect job is knowing who you are, how others perceive you, and how to best communicate and relate to bosses, teams, and team members, and using that knowledge to be the best leader you can be. That meaningful discovery process can start with a DISC personality assessment.

Whether you're in a job, between jobs, or looking for your first job, a DISC personality assessment can help to advance your career. Though DISC assessments share some similarities with other types of assessments, Myers-Briggs for example, they differ by being easier for most people to understand and apply. A critical use of the assessment is adapting your style to better communicate and relate to others in the workplace.

DISC assessments typically take 15 or 20 minutes to complete; most are done online. When the assessment is complete, a report as short as 3 pages or as long as 50+ pages is emailed to you. These reports usually show two assessment graphs, a description of each personality style, and a detailed report on your style and how your style both differs from and relates to other styles. Even the mini-reports when studied closely can be insightful. Your greatest benefit, though, will be realized when one or more follow-up sessions are scheduled with a certified DISC professional.

There are four basic personality styles in the DISC system: *D*, *I*, *S*, and *C*, and are often associated with colors. A common association is green for *D,* red for *I*, blue for *S*, and yellow for *C* styles. No style is bad; they are all good, just different. None of us is all one type or another. We are all unique blends of green, red, blue, and yellow styles, and that blend generates for each of us a special color swatch that is ours and ours alone. Even though we are each unique, by learning how much of each color or style composes our personality makeup, we can make predictions on our behavior and become aware of how we can best adapt to interact with others. DISC can help explain the way you feel, think, and act.

Here is a summary of each style's consistent identifying characteristics:

- *D* types are dominant, drivers. They are assertive, have a need to be in control. They are doers. High-*D*-type people can be demanding, determined, strong willed, direct. They are bottom-line, goal, and task oriented, and extroverted.
- *I* types are influencers, inspiring. They are very interactive, involved, optimistic, and magnetic. High-*I*-type people like to be the center of attention and are very persuasive and fun loving. And they can be loud in an enjoyable way. They are people oriented and extroverted.
- *S* types are steady, supportive. They like a predictable environment and don't like change. They seek harmony, avoid conflict, and are calm. High-*S* types are warmhearted and soft spoken. They want to please and finish what they start. They are people oriented and introverted.
- *C types are conscientious, cautious.* They are accurate, detail oriented, and questioning and value quality. High-C types don't like confrontation, need a lot of information, want to know why, are critical thinkers, tend to be loners, and may seem aloof. They are task oriented and introverted.

A good understanding of these styles (which can only be touched upon here) will help you understand the other person's point of view. It will help you understand, or at least accept, why people respond the way they do and to know their strengths and weaknesses. You can begin to recognize when someone is in control versus out of control and gain insight to what might cause someone to be out of control. You'll be able to predict with good accuracy individuals' traits, their approach to challenges, their task or people orientation, and what type of environment they will be most productive and comfortable in. You will also learn how you can best relate and communicate with them.

These insights will help you understand people better and begin to take away the "me goggles" that you have been looking through and let you see things more from the other person's perspective. Remember, DISC is not an attempt to categorize people, but it is to help us understand them. Out of that, we can then better communicate and relate to them.

There are some other things that DISC is not. DISC is not a measure of intelligence and is not a value or belief check-off system. It is not intended to label people. It does tell us about expected behavior but does not tell us why and makes no judgment about the behavior.

About now, you may be saying to yourself, "That is all well and good. But how is that going to help me in today's job market?" That's a fair enough question, so let's take a look at some scenarios.

If you are currently employed, comprehension of DISC principles can help you work better with a team by knowing what motivates each member and how each is likely to respond to a request or a task. You'll be better equipped for conflict management and can help get someone unstuck to accelerate results. Your contributions and team leadership will impress current bosses and look good on a résumé when searching for your dream job.

If you're between jobs, DISC knowledge can be an invaluable asset to your interview success. By picking up on signals from your interviewers, you will know their dominant personality style and then be able to build quick rapport to most effectively relate to and communicate with them. This may sound to you a lot like mirroring, which has been used in sales forever, and you would be partly right. First, even if sales is not your primary occupation, to be competitive in the job market, you absolutely must sell yourself better than the next guy does. Secondly, this is a bit like mirroring on steroids. With the understanding of personality styles, your responses, gestures, and posture will be deliberate and impacting, not just mimicking.

If you're searching for your first position, understanding personality styles will give you a definite advantage during the interview stage and a huge head start to quickly set you apart from the pack once you are a part of the team.

DISC is a great tool to first create self-awareness; we cannot beware until we are aware. It is a powerful relationship, communication, and stress/conflict management tool helping us to develop tolerance for others by better understanding them. Finally, when you know who you are, what motivates you and what doesn't, you will be much better prepared to land the right position in the right company structure and culture for a long-term rewarding job.

Bio

Dr. Boyd Harrell is a business coach, author, and international speaker. He is also a certified human behavior specialist and DISC consultant helping people to understand themselves, how others tend to perceive them, and how personalities affect team building, performance, and harmony in the workplace. He can be reached through his website http://www.boydharrell.com, by email at goldswanconsulting@gmail.com, or by phone at (863) 248-3698.

35

If Your Résumé Does Not Rise to the Top, It May Fall to the Bottom

Laura DeCarlo, BS, MCD, CMRW

When you are in a job search, you face several pitfalls. One is dynamically selling yourself in your résumé. I won't waste time talking to you about the importance of hiring a professional, just as you would hire a dentist to fix your teeth or a mechanic to fix your car. Instead, I'll share with you some of the key things your résumé *must do* to stand out in a crowded and competitive job market. Then, if you can take on these challenges, more power to you!

Your Résumé Must Be Sexy

One thing résumés that get read have in common is that they frequently look good, model good. *Sexy* might seem like a funny word to use, but let's face it; they're very attractive and eye-catching, so they stand out to competition judges and employers. Ways you can make your résumé sexier:

- Insert a chart or table to visually depict results.
- Include a quote from an employer or client that pops from the text.
- Introduce a touch of subtle (and professional) color with headers or lines.
- Use simple borders or lines in the page design.
- Include a little bit of bolding and italics (be sparing).
- Increase font sizes minimally for content such as job titles and company names.
- Use text boxes and similar design elements but with restraint.

- Look at the overall page to make sure the résumé is clean and easy to read.
- Break up heavy content such as long lists of bullets with categories or titles.

Your Résumé Content Must Hook the Reader (Employer)

The second trait successful résumés have in common is that they use language with the purpose of hooking the readers and getting them excited to learn more. Many résumés have the common problem of having text and word choice that is too repetitive or simply too passive. Ways to hook the reader and make your content sing:

- Create a résumé summary/overview section that sizzles with bottom-line value. What can you do for the company that will make a big difference? If you can play up bottom-line elements that all companies seek, such as making or saving money, all the better.
- Start job descriptions with the challenge or goal of the position instead of just jumping into bulleted responsibilities and accomplishments.
- Move from passive to active word choices. Instead of *responsible for*, go with *challenged to*. Instead of *did this*, write *spearheaded this*. Get out your thesaurus and familiarize yourself with alternative words. Remember, it's not about big 50-cent words but words with power.

Your Résumé Must Avoid Common Résumé Killers to Be a Job-Search Winner

A number of definite no-nos represent common mistakes that job seekers make when writing their résumés. Here are the key errors you should work hard to avoid:

- Paragraphs masquerading as bullets: If your bullet is more than three or maybe four lines long, face it, it's a paragraph. You are going to lose your reviewer. Consider using subbullets or breaking it down into multiple bullets.
- Run on sentences: Need I say more? Probably! If a sentence has several commas or is more than two lines long, you probably need to rewrite it into a few shorter sentences.

- Inconsistent use of punctuation: If you are going to use serial commas in one place or periods at the end of bullets, be sure to use them consistently.
- Overuse of underlining, bolding, and capitalization: These make your résumé hard to read and can inhibit scannability.
- Dangling widows and orphans: If you have one word on a line by itself from a bullet or paragraph, rewrite to fix it. If you have one or two lines (only) from a job on the preceding page on the top of the next page, re-write your content or change your layout to fix this.
- Repetitive word use: This could be in one sentence or just throughout the résumé.
- Use of weak verbs and verb phrases: This includes such words as *responsible for*, *did*, and *got*.
- Incorrect capitalization: Learn the rules for capitalizing words, titles, companies, and states.
- Spelling errors: Yes, spelling errors are the No. 1 mistake in résumés.
- Inconsistent verb tense: It's always easiest to write everything in past tense so that accomplishments can be included. Never mix present tense and past tense in a résumé.
- Inconsistent sentence starts in a bullet series: One starts with a verb, the next an adjective, and the next a noun. Make them all start with the same part of speech.
- Bad font choices: Avoid fonts that are incompatible with other systems, whose bullet symbols change into question marks or letters touch too closely for scannability, or are hard to read because they are just too small. Keep it simple, and use a font installed with MS Word in a readable size such as Arial 10 or Times 11 for the body of the résumé.

Feeling overwhelmed? Start with a brain dump into a document on your computer to get everything out—your responsibilities, accomplishments, awards, challenges, and other recognition. Then begin sorting and shifting to create your dynamic new résumé. If you need formatting ideas and suggestions, look at annual TORI résumé award winners created by the professionals at www.careerdirectors.com/tori_all.htm.

Now, get started on your new dynamic résumé, which is going to help you stand out from the crowd and land your next interview!

Bio

Laura DeCarlo is known, as the "Career Hero" for her pioneering efforts in the career services industry for both job seekers and career professionals. She is the founder of the global professional association Career Directors International. She has earned two degrees and 11 industry certifications and has received the industry's most prestigious awards in résumé writing, career coaching, and job placement. Laura has authored three books and numerous industry courses in résumé writing, job search, interviewing, and Web portfolio development. She has been featured in numerous résumé compendiums, has acted as résumé expert for 54 national professional associations, and has received national publicity. Log on to http://www.careerdirectors.com.

36

EMOTIONAL INTELLIGENCE

Emotional Intelligence in the Job Search

❧

Brock Hansen, LICSW

The Emotional Brain

Each of us is born with an emotional brain in addition to the problem-solving capacity measured on IQ tests. The emotional brain rouses us for emergency situations and impacts social situations. It works well enough for basic survival. But none of us is born with a user's manual for today's complex social interactions, including the network of working relationships. Because the emotional brain is designed for emergencies, we are prone to overreact in social situations. Emotional intelligence involves monitoring and quieting the emotional brain when it's overreacting. This opens the door to the other skills described below.

How is emotional intelligence developed? We learn by imitating those we grow up with or by trial and error. If you were lucky enough to be born into an emotionally intelligent family, you have an advantage. Some children develop emotional intelligence as a survival skill in dysfunctional families. The trial-and-error approach is a long shot. It is not taught in many schools, so individuals who understand the value of emotional intelligence must seek coaching or training programs to understand the principles and learn how to practice them.

Application

So, assuming that you have now done your homework by learning and practicing emotional intelligence skills until they become relatively familiar to you, how do you put them to work in the job search?

- First off, don't panic. Panicking is natural as you see your funds dwindling and your contemporaries getting ahead. It's natural but not helpful. And one of the most basic emotional intelligence skills is recognizing and quieting unhelpful panic or frustration that may lead you to leap to wrong conclusions.
- Secondly, make a plan and stick to it, emphasizing what works and tweaking or eliminating the time-wasting things that don't produce results after a while. If you don't have a plan, talk to those who do or those who know until you find a plan you want to use. Then make it your own.
- If possible, in an interview, reference your familiarity with emotional intelligence concepts or any EI coaching or training you have had and how you think it has been helpful to you.
- Finally, cultivate relationships. By using the listening skills and assertiveness skills described below, build and maintain a network of people at varying levels of influence who know that you respect them and they respect you in return. If your emotional brain wants to be impatient or greedy, take a breath and quiet down. Those emotions are for an emergency, not the successful cultivation of good relationships.

Emotional intelligence skills will benefit you in love and family relationships as well as in work-related communications. Successful communication at work and home is the best key to overall happiness.

Following are five ways emotional intelligence skills give you an advantage in today's competitive job market.

1. Managing the Emotions

The best employers value applicants who know how to manage their own emotions so that they get along well with others, even others who can be difficult to get along with. They appreciate employees who are less likely to be distracted by anxieties or jealousies, or less likely to be intimidated into sitting on a creative idea. Simply knowing this protects you from the misleading assumption that your résumé alone will get you the job or prepare you to do well in it.

2. Listening Well

We all value someone who listens well, and the potential boss or mentor is no exception. In an informational interview, the prime ingredient you have to offer is your attention and respect. If you can quiet your own excitement or frustration well enough to pay true attention, ask good questions, and fully understand the other person's needs, you'll learn a lot more and gain that person's respect in the process.

Cultivating relationships with those who can help you requires more than a display of technical ability. Though most of us are born with a basic empathic ability, we need to practice to become skilled listeners. Cultivating mutually helpful relationships is an important key to success, and mentors enjoy their side of the relationship as well. Respectful attention is the contribution you can make to the relationship. In return, you gain access to the connections and experience that the mentor has to offer. In the workplace, listening well is at least as important as the brilliant idea you may have to contribute. By listening, you can determine whether someone else has had the idea already, how receptive the boss may be, and how to time your suggestion. By listening to others in a group, you can determine how others' suggestions are received, what works, and what doesn't.

3. Displaying Integrity

Integrity has been defined as the ability to keep a promise. From the simple courtesy of showing up on time, to the ability to meet a commitment on deadline, to the emotional courage to say no to a demand you know you cannot meet—demonstrating integrity builds your reputation as someone on whom the boss can rely. Integrity can begin with the promises you make and keep with yourself. As you choose wisely the commitments you make to yourself and follow through in keeping them, you will be rewarded with growing self-confidence that is well earned.

150

4. Asserting Yourself

Assertiveness is the art of asking for what you need in a way that makes it easy for the other person to give it to you. Knowing what you need is the first step—but it's not as obvious as it seems. You can be distracted by grandiose dreams into missing the next realistic step and falling on your face. Or you can assume that your humble service will be rewarded in time and forget to ask for what you need and want. Then your anticipation turns to disappointment and resentment without giving the boss a chance to say yes or explain why not. An appropriately expressed assertive request usually gets an answer, which gives you information even if you don't get everything you ask for.

To be effective, your expectation of what you need and what you want the other person to do needs to be realistic, specific, and timely. If it's something he can actually do for you now—such as giving you the name of someone else you can talk to—your chances of getting it are good. If it's something vague, unavailable, or off in the future—such as telling you when he might have a job opening that suits your needs—your chances of getting it are not as good. Why? Because unless he wants to offer you a job right now, you are creating a problem for him. He has to come up with something he doesn't have or disappoint you. His natural motivation is to forget this dilemma rather than spending a lot of time thinking about it. If you give him an easy way to meet your needs, and send him a thank-you letter later, he is more likely to remember you.

5. Understanding Criticism

Understanding how to use criticism as a guide to improvement rather than reacting to it as an insult or an attack is an important emotional intelligence skill. Criticism often triggers shame and anger, and these emotions interfere with a helpful analysis of constructive feedback and an understanding of how best to respond to it. For more on this topic, see "Dealing Effectively with Criticism in the Workplace" in *101 Great Ways to Enhance Your Career.*

Bio

Brock Hansen, LICSW, author of *Shame and Anger: The Criticism Connection*, is a therapist and personal effectiveness coach/trainer in emotional intelligence skills with over 30 years of counseling experience. Based in Washington, D.C., he is available for telephone or Skype video coaching as well as speaking engagements. Visit his Web site, http://www.change-for-good.org.

37

"Take This Job and Shove It"

Kieron Sweeney

Though I was not aware of the subconscious programming going on when I first heard Johnny Paycheck sing the lyrics to his song, they laid the foundation for the entrepreneurial mind-set I teach and embrace today. It took many years and some circuitous detours to eventually work out the paradigms I now embrace and share globally. But the central question I came to ask myself, and now ask my clients, is: "Do you have an employee mind-set or an entrepreneurial mind-set?"

Like many of us, I was raised to get a job. By age 11, I had bought a paper route, was cleaning my parent's house every Saturday (for cash), and working at a dog kennel. It was simple: I worked because I liked to make money. With money, I could buy the things I wanted. But every job I found, I found because I *pursued* the opportunity.

I continued my employee path, interspersed with volunteerism in developing countries through Canada World Youth and Up With People. Within these organizations, I performed in the 1986 Super Bowl halftime show and initiated many programs that resulted in new opportunities and projects within the communities I served. At university, I went on to enjoy stints as student government president and a multiple-award-winning independent filmmaker.

But as a young university graduate, my deeply embedded programming was still to get a job. I sent out 200+ résumés, and I didn't get a job. I was 27, broke, and living at home. I wrote articles; did contract work; and, eventually at age 28, landed a government job. I was quickly promoted to a senior position where I identified an opportunity. I presented a proposal to a senior bureaucrat that was accepted, and the next thing I knew, I was leading presidents of colleges and universities on educational trade missions in Europe.

Do you see the pattern of behavior here? Did I have an employee mind-set or an entrepreneur mind-set?

At the time, I had never been exposed to the possibility of succeeding as an entrepreneur. Everything I had been taught had suggested that success was achieved through exemplary employee behavior. My parents and the school system had conditioned me to get a job. Deep inside of me, however, there was always an insuppressible character trait of independence.

The truth is, I was never destined to be an employee. I found work by seeking it out and networking. In the employment world, I created opportunities (employers call it self-starter skills or initiative). The entrepreneur mind-set was natural in me, driven by what I later discovered were three fundamental desires: freedom, choice, be a millionaire.

I was educated and trained to work in a job. But something deep inside me was guiding me down a different road. It was, as M. Scott Peck wrote, *The Road Less Traveled.*

My shift toward entrepreneurship occurred while I was working for the government and started a part-time business. Eventually, I resigned as an employee and became a full-time entrepreneur. At 28 years old, I was a half-time entrepreneur. By 31, I was a full-time entrepreneur. I point this out because many of my clients don't realize it's fine to start a business while employed. In fact, I highly recommend it for the tax benefits.

I knew by 28 that the nine-to-five structured workday, driving in rush hour traffic one hour each way, and answering to someone else just did not match who I had become as a person. I wanted more. I wanted to be free, to have choice, and to be rich.

My initial entrepreneurial experiences—as an owner, shareholder, and salesman—exposed me to an industry that eventually became my love and my home: the personal development and business-success training industry. This is where my passions lie and, therefore, where I've really excelled. I've gathered all that I have learned as a student of the industry into the mind-set strategies I now teach all over the world.

This arena is also where I learned how my mind-set governs all outcomes in my life, inside and outside of my business dealings. I learned that how I think and manage my thoughts manifests the reality I experience in all areas of my life experience.

I chose to contribute to this book because I am a firm believer that our education system needs to evolve to adopt the psychology-based teachings of my industry so that it can meet the needs of all the various kinds of minds that are now being streamed into a curriculum centered exclusively on the employee mind-set.

My second son is a classic example. He has an entrepreneurial mind. He is curious and brilliant, but the educational system cannot serve him fully. He has a beautiful heart and wants to serve people. And, thankfully, he has two parents who are entrepreneurs and able to support his natural tendencies to seek freedom, choice, and wealth.

Many people are dissatisfied with life. They work in a job because they believe they have to work in a job. You may be one of them. If you're longing for more freedom, choice, and wealth, you may want to investigate your latent entrepreneurial spirit. Though you were most likely led to embrace an employee mind-set, that may not be your destiny. You may have an entrepreneurial mind-set or a combination of both.

Our politicians are constantly campaigning about job creation. Governments pour billions into job-creation programs and job-creation projects. Government departments provide literature and workshops on how to start a small business and become an entrepreneur. *Really*? I actually attended one of these government-led workshops and listened to a bureaucrat speak for two hours on why 95 percent of businesses fail. *Are you kidding me*? I estimated they spent $10,000 on a nice hotel room, nice looking brochures that provided little information, coffee, muffins, AV equipment, and three bankers who spoke about the unlikely possibility of your getting a start-up loan unless it was government guaranteed. Now, there are great government programs to help small business. However, my plea is this:

"Dear Government: Millions of people cannot find jobs, and many of them have an entrepreneur mind-set. They can participate in part-time businesses while employed or not employed. You need to provide funding to citizens to help them start a part-time business and promote independent thinking. Many companies that offer home-based businesses provide entrepreneurial training and personal development coaching."

To help entrepreneurs globally, I have created a Web show called "KieronTV. com" to provide entrepreneurs and wantrepreneurs™ with the mind-set teachings required to be an entrepreneur, as well as teachings on money management to create financial freedom, life purpose, relationships, social media marketing, and many more useful trainings to support entrepreneurs.

If you are looking for a job, consider this. You can work 40 hours a week for $40,000 per year for the next 40 years. Or you can gain the tools to invest in yourself and become an entrepreneur. What is your true mind-set?

Bio

Kieron Sweeney is an authority on the psychology of success, mind power, leadership, and public speaking. He has trained more than 200,000 entrepreneurs globally through live seminars. Kieron also privately coaches public speakers and trainers, increasing their sales by up to 500 percent. His global Web show, at http://kierontv.com, was created based on his belief that every success-destined person must create the habit of participating in daily coaching, or as he refers to it, Nutrition for the Mind™. Members pay $9.97/month and have access to 20 minutes of daily coaching. Start here: http://www.kieronsweeney.com and receive a gift.

38

How an Iowa Woman Landed a New Job and a $10,000 Pay Increase by Asking One Question

Glenn Shepard

September 14, 2013, is a special milestone in my career; it represents 25 years in business. The small business I started with in 1988 allowed me to make it to the top echelon of income earners by doing what I love—public speaking—while still in my 30s.

My speaking fee today is $15,000 for a 30-minute keynote, and it's not uncommon to make $20,000+ for a half-day seminar. I stay booked 12 to 18 months in advance and normally take at least three vacations a year with my beautiful bride. We live in a nice Nashville neighborhood made up of doctors, lawyers, and business owners. The house three doors down from ours is owned by Engelbert Humperdinck (though I've never met him). I have a life today that I could have never dreamed of when I was a kid back in the 1960s, growing up in a 700-square-foot house on a dirt road.

That's the happy part of my story. Here's the really, really sad part.

I try to give back some of what God has blessed me with by coaching other speakers who want to achieve what I've been fortunate enough to achieve in my career. They all ask what my secret of success is. I explain that any of them can be making a six-figure income within three years if they'll follow this simple two-step formula:

Step 1: Find out what makes people mad and make that the subject of their speeches, books, DVDs.

Step 2: Spend 75 percent of their time on marketing and 25 percent on everything else.

This is such a foolproof formula that people can screw it up and still make a killing at it.

Every speaker *says* he or she will follow it. Sadly, out of the 300+ speakers I've coached, I can count on one hand the number that has followed through (which helps explain why most motivational speakers are secretly broke). Most don't follow Step 1 because they speak on what they think people *need* to hear, instead of what people *want* to hear. To see what a bad idea this is from a financial perspective, drive through any town in America and notice how many more fast food restaurants there are than health clubs.

What people *need* is to exercise more and eat less. But what people *want* is to pig out on king-sized orders of french fries, milk shakes, and hamburgers, and that's what they'll pay for.

Most speakers don't follow Step 2 because marketing is boring and sometimes humiliating. Getting on the phone and selling yourself ("smiling and dialing") is not that different than being a telemarketer selling toner, insurance, or aluminum siding.

Here's how this applies to you.

The cruel reality is that the person who gets the job is not necessarily the one who's best qualified; it's the one who's best at interviewing. No matter what field you're in, the key to winning in today's job market is knowing what employers really want and how to sell yourself as the answer to all their problems. Interviewing is about making yourself stand out above other applicants who are just as qualified as you are, maybe even better.

The key to my success as a speaker is that I followed Step 1 so well that Step 2 was a breeze.

I knew my audience was management and HR, so I found out what frustrates them so much that they'll gladly open their wallets and pay any reasonable price for someone to scratch their itch. That one thing that drives management and HR up the wall more than anything is that the great American work ethic is going straight down the tubes while the entitlement mentality of today's workforce is going through the roof. It drives them *insane* that job applicants will walk into their office with a list of demands of what they want the company to give them.

For employers, hearing applicants say things like, "I need a job" or "If someone would just give me a job" is like hearing someone drag their fingernails down a chalkboard.

It goes back to John F. Kennedy's 1961 inaugural speech, when he said, "Ask not what your country can do for you; ask what you can do for your country."

Change the word *country* to *company* and you'll understand why employers are so fed up with applicants who are interested only in what the company can do for them and don't understand that the interview is about what they can do for the company.

Job applicants sometimes ask, "But shouldn't this be a two-way street?" The answer is no.

Some relationships are a two-way street. One example is marriage, where two people share in major decisions such as having kids and buying a house. No one would adopt a child or buy a house without involving her or his spouse in the decision. Both parties are equal partners (or at least somewhat equal in a healthy marriage).

The employer-employee relationship is not a two-way street because the employer pays the employee to serve the company. This sounds harsh the first time people hear it, but it's actually the only way things can work. Whoever is *paying* gets served, and whoever is *getting paid* does the serving.

When you walk into McDonald's, the workers there don't expect *you* to serve *them*. They expect to serve you because you're paying them to do so. McDonald's understands that businesses have one primary purpose: to serve the customer.

Walmart founder Sam Walton became the wealthiest man in the world because he understood this principle so well. His famous saying was, "There is only one boss: the customer. And he can fire everybody in the company from the chairman on down, simply by spending his money somewhere else."

This is not to imply that companies shouldn't be good to their employees. But it's crucial to understand that the company pays employees to serve them, not the other way around. If you'll let employers know that you understand this principle and detest the entitlement mentality as much as they do, you'll be amazed at how quickly you'll shoot up to the top of their list.

I explained this to Heather in Cedar Rapids, Iowa. The following is the email she sent after the interview:

"Glenn, I got the restaurant manager position!!! Thank you for your help and coaching in the hiring process. I said what you told me to say in the interview. Once I said that, the interviewer said 'I don't need to ask you any more questions. You've got the job.' Excellent! Also the pay increase is awesome—$10,000! Can you believe it? Thank you again for everything!"

The question she asked was, "What do I need to do to *earn* this job?" The employer, which happened to be the third largest hotel chain in the world, said no one had ever asked that before. Everyone else expected the job to be handed to them on a silver platter.

Bio

Glenn Shepard is a professional speaker and bestselling author of six books. For more free tools, visit his Web site at http://www.glennshepard.com.

39

Better, Faster, Cheaper, More Profitable:
An Employer-Focused Résumé

Andrew Pearl, CPRW, CEIP
Jennifer Alonzo Reule, CPRW

Why should a company or organization hire you? What makes you the best candidate for the position you want? What are the most important qualifications you have to offer a prospective employer?

Does your résumé clearly and confidently answer these three questions? If not, then it lacks one of the most integral components of an effective résumé: *employer-focused value.*

More often than not, job candidates completely miss the mark when developing their résumés; they fail to highlight the key qualifications and qualities that appeal to employers. Instead, they typically provide a bland accounting of their general responsibilities and perhaps one or two of what they consider decent accomplishments. They think like an *employee* rather than an *employer* when building their résumés. They don't fully consider a prospective employer's needs. Although it's important to paint a full picture of your career, which might include day-to-day duties, it's even more critical to emphasize results, or what is known as employer-focused value.

Understanding Employer-Focused Value

What is employer-focused value? Simply put: all companies and organizations—large and small—want the same results: better, faster, cheaper, and more profitable. A résumé must speak to those desires. It must provide concrete evidence that you have delivered tangible benefits to your previous employers because many prospective employers view the past as an indication of the future. Prospective employers want to know what you specifically can bring to the table.

Depending on the job you are targeting, the type of employer-focused value will change. For instance, a sales manager may be expected to surpass sales quotas and increase market share. A network administrator may be expected to establish a reliable and secure technical infrastructure for hundreds of employees. A financial controller may be expected to improve margins and strengthen fiscal discipline. But more than simply stating that you boosted bottom-line value or improved customer satisfaction, it's crucial to provide evidence to back your claims. Monetary values, numbers, time frames, statistics, percentages, and the like all serve as support for your assertions. They also differentiate you from the competition; no two job candidates possess the same career history.

Incorporating Employer-Focused Value

Throughout your résumé are several key areas where you must integrate employer-focused value. Two of those main components are your professional summary and career accomplishments.

Professional summary: The top one-third of your résumé is considered "prime real estate." It's where hiring managers and recruiters will likely focus the majority of their attention when conducting an initial review of your document. As such, you must include tangible details that will hook the reader. Your professional summary sets the tone for the body of your résumé. This is where you establish a core message and where you provide a brief overview of your value. If you can pique an employer's interest here, you are more likely to maintain that interest in the body of your résumé.

Career achievements: Many job candidates suffer from task-based résumés. That is, they tell a prospective employer or recruiter what they *do* but not

162

the *results* or *outcomes* of their efforts. A social media campaign developer may state that he created content for a company's Twitter feed but not that he increased the number of followers by 150 percent. A construction manager may state that she developed project plans and budgets but not that she led the construction of a 50,000-square-foot building at $50,000 under budget and a month ahead of schedule. You can see how integrating numbers and amounts bolsters the potency of career information; they establish context, accountability, and specificity, all of which appeal to employers. An effective résumé is driven by action-oriented accomplishments with employer-focused value.

Gathering Employer-Focused Content

Following is a brief list of leading questions to help you compile employer-focused content for your résumé:

- Did you increase sales, productivity, efficiency? What was the dollar or percentage contribution? How did you accomplish this?
- Did you save money? How much did you save? What were the circumstances? How do your results compare to your peers' results?
- Did you implement new systems, procedures, policies, or changes? Why? What situation led to the change? What were the results? Have your changes been adopted anywhere else in the company or organization?
- Did you earn promotions? Being promoted several times within a company or organization demonstrates your potential for growth and advancement as well as your ability to work well with others in management.
- Did you suggest new programs? What kind of programs? What were the results?
- Did you establish new goals, ideas, or concepts? Why were they adopted? What were results?
- Did you streamline or standardize processes or ease workloads? How? What were the results?
- Did you lead turnaround or transformational efforts? What problems did you address? What were the results?
- Did you earn company or organizational awards? When and why? Were you nominated by your peers? Out of how many other employees did you win awards?
- Did you lead key projects or initiatives? What was the scope of the projects and the situation, your actions, and the results?

- Did you contribute to substantial or ongoing business growth? How and by how much?

The bottom line: you are not paid to simply show up at work; you are paid to create value for your employer. Hiring decision makers select candidates who can deliver the most tangible results. As a job seeker, you will more quickly realize your professional goals if you spend the time and energy necessary to analyze and effectively convey the value you have to offer within your résumé.

BIOS

Andrew Pearl and Jennifer Alonzo Reule are two of the three cofounders of Precision Resumes, Inc., a professional résumé-writing firm. Andrew is a certified résumé writer and interview coach with seven years of career-services industry experience. Jennifer is an accomplished editor and certified résumé writer. As a team, they have developed thousands of high-impact résumés, LinkedIn profiles, and interviewing strategies tailored to job seekers' backgrounds and goals. Both are certified by the Professional Association of Resume Writers and Career Coaches. Visit their company Web site at http://www.precision-resumes.com; or contact them at info@precision-resumes.com.

40

Are You an Essence-Based Entrepreneur?

Jennifer Howard, PhD

People often think of entrepreneurs as bold, successful, even glamorous. It seems ideal, an easy lifestyle where your time is your own and you can be your own boss. The promise of autonomy and big bucks sounds enticing, but truthfully, the lives of most entrepreneurs require a deep commitment and large amounts of time. And even though many achieve some success, a much greater satisfaction and fulfillment comes from being what, I call, an "essence-based" entrepreneur.

Our *essence* is the deepest part of us and in relationship with what many might refer to as God, Spirit, or the Universe. Our essence is far more than our quirky personality; it's the source of our purpose and passion. I know these words have been bandied around a lot lately, usually describing a fun pastime or an intense interest. We might say we're passionate about cooking or football, but that's "passion light." When I say *passion* and *purpose*, I'm talking about something that comes from our very deepest source, our highest level of existence.

When we come from our life purpose and create a career rooted in our passion, it makes the work required much easier to do. When we're aligned with our essence, we have access to a knowledge and wisdom that allows us to consciously experience our connection with truth or being-ness itself. We're actually being who we were always meant to be. It just feels right and allows us to live an authentic life.

Our "essence connection" sustains our interest in our work. It generates the inspiration and commitment we need as we pursue our personal and professional goals. Rooted in this central part of ourselves, we are tapped into our passion, and we realize a genuine desire to make a positive difference in the world. In fact, this urge to help others with our work is an indication that we are connected to our essence. Our deepest purpose is to contribute our special gifts to others, and I believe this brings the ultimate fulfillment.

Communication flows so much more easily when we're aligned with our essence. We naturally connect with other people and can experience real intimacy more easily. When we conduct business from this place, we create meaningful and lasting relationships with our clients, customers, and colleagues. We're more present in our conversations, and we can hear a deeper level of communication. This benefits us not only in our work but also in every relationship we have. From here, we become a conscious entrepreneur.

You also hear the inner conversation that's taking place between your essence and you—your personal sense of self. This conversation often happens without your noticing because your essence, through your inner voice, is continually broadcasting its reaction to what you're doing. It's responding to what's going on around you all the time. It's a hunch about the next best move for you. And it's the wisdom that tells you who you really are and why you're here. What makes it a conversation is your willingness to slow down and listen; to become more sensitive to the subtle movements of thought, energy, and feeling within you; to act upon what you hear; and to see where it will lead and what response it will call forth.

In our culture, we tend to measure success by income, fame, and reputation. Some might say that to compete in today's marketplace, you need to compare yourself to others. Of course, you need to have the appropriate training, education, skill set, and experience needed for your profession, but being conscious and knowing yourself leads to being more relaxed, self-confident, and aligned with the very best you have to offer. We all have our own song to sing, and only we can sing it, so there's no value in comparing our expression to another's.

As we step into being an essence-based entrepreneur, we become less interested in the old definition of success, and we begin to broaden our view of success. We observe how clearly we receive our inner wisdom, the alignment

166

of our business with our spiritual values, and how often our actions are guided by the deeper inspiration within us. All these aspects flow from our fundamental connection to essence. Nothing we do and nothing we choose to be is separate from this. Our alignment with our essence determines our quality of life and guides us to take inspired action.

If we do the inner work to identify our mission, and we feel a strong sense of purpose in what we do, we may find it looks startlingly different from someone else's business plan. Imagine three accomplished painters side by side at easels, gazing at the landscape before them. Each will see the view differently. People don't perceive in identical ways. One artist may focus on the foreground, whereas the next is fascinated by the waves splashing against the rocks. The third is intrigued by the clouds over the horizon. All of these paintings are beautiful in their own right. No two works of art are alike, and so your essence-based business will have that specific stamp of you, your own unique perspective.

When we make an effort to consciously connect with and live from our essence, we're aligning not only with our highest energy but also with the highest and deepest energy that exists, existence itself. When we make this connection, we experience a clarity, confidence, and empowerment that isn't ordinarily available to us.

There are several ways to get started. To develop, deepen, and clarify our connection to essence, we need to turn inward, be contemplative. This can be greatly served by meditation. When we turn down the mental chatter that distracts us, and we begin to quiet our mind, we become open to the deep communication. There are many types of meditation: one-pointed focus with a mantra, centering prayer, cultivating silence, chanting, guided meditations. Whatever you choose, I encourage you to practice every day if you can. Meditation can also help us release emotional blocks holding us back, and it does wonders for the stress we carry with us.

Along with a contemplative practice, the essence-based entrepreneur engages in personal work. Whether its psychotherapy, coaching, energy psychology, energy healing, a specific spiritual discipline, or an entirely different modality, we continually seek to know ourselves and let go of the thoughts and beliefs that no longer serve us. We may have anxiety and fear that lower our energy, make us unsure of what to do next, and stop us from seeing the possibilities available to us. With our ongoing personal work, we can release our stuck energy and connect with our essence more easily.

As essence-based entrepreneurs, we love what we do because we've identified our passion, have clarified our mission, and finally have come to awaken and live our life's purpose. Our essence informs who we are and all of our choices and ultimately all that we bring to this world. As a conscious entrepreneur, your business will grow and thrive as you do. Your life and relationships will be energized and enlivened. Imagine the possibilities of living from your essence! What song will you sing?

Bio

Jennifer Howard, PhD, is the author of *Your Ultimate Life Plan: How to Deeply Transform Your Everyday Experience and Create Changes That Last,* which won a Gold Nautilus Award and Silver Benjamin Franklin Award. Dr. Howard is an internationally acclaimed author, life coach, licensed psychotherapist, professional speaker, energy healer, and spiritual teacher. She's a *Huffington Post* blogger, has appeared as an expert on numerous national network television and radio shows, and is the creator and host of the popular radio show *A Conscious Life.* She's @DrJennifer on twitter and DrJenniferFanPage on Facebook. Go to http://www.DrJenniferHoward.com to download the free recording "Reach Your Goals," and visit her virtual meditation room.

41

Everyone Can Work

❧

Lori Bell

I grew up in a nontraditional home, way before nontraditional was *even* remotely OK. In fact, my oldest sister, Georgia, was told by her sociology professor that our family would never be accepted by society. At the time, my mom worked and my dad stayed home. He was home not because he wanted to be, but because he had been battling with physical disabilities and severe depression that limited his ability to work.

During the early 1960s, my dad spent a brief time confined to a state psychiatric hospital. While there, he received electric shock therapy. On a number of occasions, he shared with me that he lost two years of his life because of those treatments. He could not remember the first years of my sister Elizabeth's life. He also shared how after one visit from the hospital psychiatrist, he was miraculously "cured" and told to go home. At some point during my father's care, he was also told that he needed to "retire early and apply for disability benefits." He would "never be able to work again."

Those words—*never be able to work again*—were a death sentence to my father. He was a successful manager of a loan company before his hospitalization. His self-esteem plummeted. He led a life riddled with anxiety and a need to take psychiatric medications. After being "cured," he remained in outpatient care for more than 15 years. He did go on to hold some volunteer positions—arranging summer camp opportunities for Fresh Air Fund kids and other social service projects. He was an accomplished writer with many published poems and articles and had been contacted by a local university to be a guest lecturer in a literature class.

I am here to tell you that the message my father received—*never be able to work again*—was an incredibly damaging statement that resulted in a life of confinement. It served only to diminish who my father was as a person and his potential later in life.

Approximately 20 percent of people in the United States suffer from some type of mental illness: depression, bipolar disorder, or schizophrenia. Having a mental illness does not mean that you cannot work. In fact, the United States Health and Human Services Division of Substance Abuse and Mental Health Services has developed a national consensus statement that indicates that employment is a key factor related to recovery from mental illness. Employment provides a sense of purpose in one's life. It creates social connections. It provides structure and the opportunity to learn new skills. Having a job normalizes who we are. It allows the mentally ill to be like anyone else. Employment provides a sense of financial stability and serves to move the mentally ill worker out of a life of poverty and into a life of self-sufficiency when proper supports are provided.

So what do you do if you have a major mental illness and every attempt at finding a job has failed?

One of the most important things that you can do is enroll in a state-of-the-art, evidence-based individual supported employment program. Supported employment (SE) services are different from traditional vocational rehabilitation programs. Traditional services rely heavily on skills assessments and testing, which can take weeks to months to complete. Individual supported employment that follows a best-practice model does not involve extensive evaluation and testing because they are not good predictors of workplace success for people with mental illness.

A successful SE job specialist will instead help you figure out what skills you already have that will help you be successful on the job. Figuring out what your skills are could involve enlisting the help of your family, friends, and other mental health service providers. Success at work involves much more than just being able to perform the basic function of a job. Being able to relate to others, finding an environment that supports your needs (quiet and slow paced, noisy and full of energy—whatever best fits your personality and mental health needs), and being able to ask for help when you need it are keys to being successful at work.

If you have minimal work experience and aren't sure about what kind of work you would like to do, an employment specialist can arrange some opportunities with employers for you to visit worksites to see what is involved in different jobs through a process called situational assessment. If you want to work in retail, for example, your employment specialist might arrange for you to talk to an employer of a retail store and have you shadow an employee who already works there. This would allow you to see what is involved in the job and give you opportunity to ask questions about the job before actually applying for it.

In SE, the focus is on rapid job placement in a job that you choose, and on providing support to help you keep the job. A good job coach will help you walk through every step of the job-searching process, from the type of jobs you are looking for, to filling out applications and writing résumés, to practicing for an interview. In some cases, a job coach may also go on a job interview with you, if you choose, to let potential employers know that you have an illness or disability.

A job coach will also offer you support after you get a job. A coach can visit you at work, if you choose, or provide support to you after hours. Support may be around how to deal with coworkers, how to ask for time off for medical appointments, and how to ask for an accommodation such as modifying your work hours if taking medications makes you groggy in the morning. If you have legal issues related to your illness or disability, a job coach can help you work around those issues too.

If you have a documented disability, you can find an individual supported employment program through vocational rehabilitation services in your state. If you do not have a documented disability, but need assistance in getting and keeping a job, do an Internet search for individual supported employment programs in your state. Make sure that the program you choose to work with uses an evidence-based model that follows best practices for employment.

A job is out there for anyone who truly wants one. I worked closely with a young man who experienced his first episode of mental illness at the age of 17. He wanted to be an astronaut more than anything else in the world. Clearly, with his disability, this was not an option. His family and his caseworker pushed him to sign up for disability benefits. He had other plans. He went to community college and graduated. He tweaked his dreams a bit and wound up working in a museum that focused on air and space travel. He would not have been able to accomplish these things without the assistance of an employment specialist navigating him through the system.

"Employment is nature's physician and is essential to human happiness." — Claudius Galen

Bio

Lori Bell is founder of Creating Powerful Change, LLC, found at http://www.help-me-change.com. She offers tips, tools, and techniques for implementing successful change in your life. Lori has an MA in counseling enhanced by graduate-level course work in business administration and organizational development. She has over 20 years of experience working in mental health as a therapist, career and employment specialist, contract manager, and mental health manager. Lori is also experienced in small business development and is well versed as a contract negotiator.

42

Does Your Executive Career Need a Rebrand?

Deb Dib

Follow these 12 ditch-dare-do personal brand-
ing rules to win in volatile markets.

The market has changed fast, thoroughly, like an earthquake. This seismic shift has left even the most accomplished top talent feeling a bit lost in the present and thoroughly uneasy about the future. In this volatile climate, it's tempting to try to alter who you are—to become who you think the market needs you to be—so you can protect your current job, rise faster, or secure a new position.

But changing your *personal* brand is a "no can do" because your personal brand is the core of who you are. Like the color of your eyes or your blood type, your personal brand is indelibly you.

However, you *can* change your *executive* brand—what you are known for in the marketplace, what your personal brand looks like when you take it to work, and what the perceived value of your brand is today. When you intentionally and authentically evolve and retool your personal brand, you shape a message that resonates with decision makers (I call it your Why-Buy-ROI™).

First, to retool your executive brand you need to embrace the ditch, dare, and do plan.

DITCH: Understand your brand and the market—what the market needs now and what in your executive tool kit of ROI contribution intersects with that need. Then shatter (DITCH) old mind-sets that aren't working!

DARE: Dare to have passion! Dare to take risks. When you take risks based upon passion and what the market needs, your executive rebranding puts you in your zone—in your sweet spot.

DO: Build and maintain focus. Focus is about staying on your new course every day and *doing* what needs to be done to build your new executive brand presence.

Then, to win in volatile markets (or any market), follow Deb Dib's 12 ditch-dare-do rules for executive rebranding:

1. Do your homework. Learn what the market needs, strategize how you can help, put an action plan in place, and start to build the executive brand you now want to project (DO).
2. Stop thinking branding is spin (DITCH). Make sure your new executive brand remains grounded in your personal brand and is authentic and comfortable to you (DO).
3. Make sure your brand is *valuable* to an employer or market. Make sure you can *prove* the ROI of your executive brand through stories of previous accomplishments that relate to your new brand (DO).
4. Try to be as niched (specialized) as possible to increase your value. Scarcity value sells (DARE).
5. Stop being safe (DITCH). Get passionate about evangelizing your new message (DARE). If you can't be passionate about it, you may not yet have reached the clarity of a deeply visceral and valuable brand—keep working for that "eureka" feeling that tells you you're there (DO).
6. Create a strategic plan and timeline for maximizing your new brand's exposure (DO). If you are employed, don't forget that you need to do this within your company as well as in the marketplace (DARE).
7. Remember—a résumé won't build your career (DITCH)—but rebuilding or establishing your new branded online presence via LinkedIn, Twitter, Facebook, Namz, Google+ will help do so (DO).
8. Make all decisions brand decisions (DARE). Ask yourself, "Is the answer on brand or not? Will this decision strengthen my brand presence or weaken it?" (DO).

9. You can't be branded and be all things to all people (DITCH). If you decide to do something off-brand, understand the consequences. A muddy brand dilutes your impact, confuses your stakeholders, and erodes confidence—your own and that of the marketplace. Honestly, it's not worth it. Turn it down (DARE).

10. Educate your "personal board of directors" as to your new direction—get some passionate advocates working with you (DO).

11. Stop going it alone (DITCH). Give to get. Be open and generous with on-brand knowledge and help. The "career karma" William Arruda and Kirsten Dixson talk about in *Career Distinction* doesn't happen in a vacuum. And it feels really good to help others while building a nest egg of career capital (DO).

12. Embrace the knowledge that building, strengthening, and refining an authentic and valuable executive brand never ends. It's an evolving and exciting continuum that helps you rise faster, earn more, have fun, and change the world (DITCH, DARE, DO).

Bio

Known as the "CEO Coach" for innovators and change agents who "do capitalism right," Deb Dib has a penchant for bucking the status quo and a passion for propelling visionary, gutsy leaders to rise faster, earn more, have fun, and change the world—without becoming sharks or suits. A Reach master brand strategist and longtime career industry leader, Deb is the first recipient of the Dick Bolles Parachute Award for innovation. Her latest book, *Ditch. Dare. Do! 3D Personal Branding for Executives*, reached No. 1 in the "Hot New Books" careers category on Amazon. Reach Deb at http://www.ExecutivePowerBrand.com; http://www.LinkedIn.com/in/DebDib; or https://twitter.com/CEOCoach.

43

Overcoming the Fear of No

Harvey Mackay

Rejection is a part of life. You can't avoid it, whether you're a salesperson with a tough quota or a shy nerd hoping for a date with a supermodel. You can't let the fear of rejection paralyze you from the start, or you'll never get any sales—or any dates.

Like many of us, Jonathan Robinson, now a professional speaker and author, was shy as a young man—painfully so, especially when it came to women. One day in college he decided to do something drastic about it. He handed a friend $50 and told him, "Don't give this back to me unless I get rejected by 10 different women by the end of today."

The idea was to push through his fear of rejection, with money as a motivator. Robinson headed through the campus, looking for women to ask out. The first time, he barely stammered through his question. The woman he approached thought he was babbling and blew him off. After a while, he grew calmer and the prospects warmer.

Then something unexpected happened: his seventh target agreed to go out with him. Robinson was so shocked he was tongue-tied, but he managed to get the woman's phone number. Number eight also said yes to him.

In all, he collected six more phone numbers and had to resort to consciously chilling his charm to reach his quota of 10 rejections to get his $50 back. He not only got his money and plenty of dates but also vanquished his fear of

176

rejection. I'm not recommending the Robinson gambit to beat rejection, but it pays to know your worst fears are usually trumped-up traumas.

Early in my career, when I was struggling to start my company, I made a list of all the accounts I wanted to sell. Some were immediately attainable; others were far out of my reach. That list was the impetus for my eventual success. It made me really listen to my potential customers and find out what I needed to do to change "No, thanks" to "Where do I sign?"

You can't escape rejection, I learned. But you can let it go. That requires programming your mind-set. Here are some exercises that paid big dividends for me:

- *Dissect thoughts under the microscope.* When faced with a challenge, what do you tell yourself? "I'm no good." "This is too hard." "I'll never make it." Don't let negative self-talk sabotage your attitude. Size up the evidence objectively. Chances are you'll realize your worries aren't accurate or realistic. Drain the power out of irrational fears.
- *Identify realistic fears.* Whom do you fear? What might go wrong? Knowledge is power, so clarify the facts: Who has the power to reject you? Why would that person say no? The answers will help you prepare your best offer, and facing them will help you keep your composure.
- *Focus on the moment.* Keep your perspective. Rejection lasts only a moment, and once it's over, you'll be able to move on to the next opportunity. Overcoming your fears can be an exhilarating experience, so savor your triumph. Great athletes and ace competitors of all sorts are masters of deftly moving through both ups and downs and not wallowing in either.
- *Be more assertive.* Most fears of rejection rest on the desire for approval from other people. Don't base your self-esteem on others' opinions. Learn to express your own needs—appropriately—and say no to requests when you genuinely can't help. People respect peers who stand up for themselves.

Reprinted with permission from nationally syndicated columnist Harvey Mackay, author of the *New York Times* No. 1 bestseller *Swim with the Sharks Without Being Eaten Alive.*

BIO

Harvey Mackay has authored some of the best-selling business books in publishing history, with more than 10 million copies sold worldwide. They have been translated into 37 languages and have sold in 80 countries. All of Harvey's books are available at bookstores everywhere. *Swim with the Sharks Without Being Eaten Alive* was a groundbreaking *New York Time*s No. 1 best seller for 54 weeks. You can visit his Web site at, http://www.harveymackay.com.

44

Finding Work: 4 Ways to Get a Job

Brian Tracy

To earn what you are really worth, you have to be in the right job in the first place. Sometimes you could earn more just by walking across the street and getting a new job if your special talents and skills could be used to get more valuable results for a different employer.

This is a challenging time in human history to be out in the job market and working to survive and thrive. However, in spite of problems in the economy, there are countless opportunities and possibilities for talented people to find or create great jobs and earn more than they ever have before.

Do Your Homework

When you are looking for the job you want, you engage in the same activities that a sales professional would. The three activities essential to sales success are prospecting, presenting, and following up.

Your job is to *prospect* thoroughly and develop the greatest number of leads that you possibly can. Then you meet with and make *presentations* to as many prospective employers as possible. Third, you *follow up* with the very best opportunities until you get the job you want.

One of the most important keys to success in selling today is what is called *pre-call research*. Do your homework. Find out everything that you possibly can

179

about the individual, the organization, and the industry before you call on anyone the first time.

Fortunately, with the Internet you can do more and better research in a few minutes than has ever before been possible in human history. And you cannot imagine how impressive it is when a job candidate calls on a person with a file full of information on that individual and his or her organization and industry. It gives you a critical edge in the final decision. This critical edge can open a door for you that can change the entire direction of your life.

Internet Job Search

Getting a job on the Internet is not easy. It is a skill that you must learn through practice. You start by visiting the main Internet job sites that you see advertised all around you. If you don't know where to start, go to a search engine such as Craigslist, Aol, or Bing and go to the employment section. Examine the various job categories and then read the job description for positions that are being offered.

Get as much information as you possibly can about the various job sites. Some Internet job sites specialize in one kind of employee, and some specialize in another. Some are local, and some are national. When you list on an Internet job site, your résumé and your information become instantly available to potential employers nationwide.

There are many opportunities for you to post a brief description of your abilities and the job you are looking for at no charge. Some sites will charge you a placement fee, but these are usually worth it because they are much more aggressive in tracking potential employers to the site. Remember, you always get what you pay for in life.

There are also job career fairs held in every community every year. These are advertised in the newspaper and on the radio. You should visit these job fairs and talk to the various employers exhibiting there. Find out what they are looking for today and what they will be looking for in the future. Even if you are currently employed, keep sowing seeds everywhere you go so that you can create a rich harvest of employment in the future.

The more seeds you sow, the more likely you are to get the job you really want.

Look for the Names of Decision Makers

Look for the names of key people in various companies and departments of companies. Especially look for the names of those who have been recently promoted. People who have been recently promoted often make immediate staff changes and create job opportunities for people who call.

Look for active, growing organizations that are announcing a new expansion or increased profitability. These companies are always looking for more good people. They offer lots of opportunities, and they pay well.

Look for new product releases and the introductions of new services. Wherever a company is expanding its products or services, there are job opportunities to sell the product, distribute the product, service the product, install the product, and handle the administration and details associated with the product.

Whenever you see a company that is expanding and an executive who has been promoted, phone the company immediately, and tell the person you talk to that you are looking for a job in that industry and that this company is of interest to you. Ask the receptionist for the name of the person you should speak to. Arrange to go in and see the person and interview for a job. It is absolutely amazing how many great job opportunities you can uncover by simply taking action on the news and information all around you about the business and industry that you want to work in.

Sell Yourself Professionally

The job interview is really a sales call. You are in *sales* when you are looking for a job. You are going out to sell yourself to someone else. The type of job you get and the type of salary you command will be a measure of how well you have sold yourself at this critical point in your career.

Many people don't like the idea of selling. They don't like to see themselves as salespeople. Unfortunately, this is the type of attitude that leads to under-achievement in life. The fact is that everyone who wants to sell his or her ideas or services to others is a salesperson. The only question is whether or not you are any good at it.

B<small>IO</small>

Brian Tracy is a top business and motivational speaker, consultant, and best-selling author. In the last 30 years, he's consulted for more than 1,000 companies—including IBM, Ford, Federal Express, and Hewlett Packard—and has spoken to more than five million people worldwide on sales, business, leadership, self-esteem, goals, strategy, and success psychology. He's the top-selling author of more than 55 books, including *Eat That Frog!*, and has produced more than 300 audio-video learning programs, including the world-wide best-selling Psychology of Achievement. He's one of the most sought-after success coaches and has transformed the lives of millions of people. For more information on Brian Tracy, go to http://www.briantracy.com.

45

The Future You

❧

Andrew Christison, MBA

Fulfill your career and lifelong aspirations. Become the you who is capable of accomplishing your dreams and desires. Become your future self that attains all that your present self requests out of life. Grow into your future self thoughtfully, methodically, and strategically.

Your present self is nothing but the composite of who you have become every day of your life through this moment. Your present self has strengths and weaknesses, personality quirks and saboteurs, intelligence and skills, hobbies and interests, dreams and desires. Your present self has likely obtained much from life, but your future self will bring you what you still want.

Your future self is the you who will build your own empire or be recruited by the top firm in your industry or climb to the top of the corporate ladder. Your future self is the you who will make your dreams come true, if you dedicate yourself today to influence and serve others more effectively, by developing the mastery that only your future self can embody.

Employ these seven steps to become the future you.

Step 1: Feel That You Deserve Achievement

Feeling entitled to be educated, successful, and worthy of your goals and aspirations is vital for you to become the future you you are seeking. You *can* fulfill your goals; you *must* believe that you are worthy of them. No matter where you are right now or what your past may look like, you deserve to forgive yourself for past failures and disappointments and to feel that you deserve future success. Don't just know that you deserve achievement—feel it!

Step 2: Create a Personal Strategic Plan

Creating a personal strategic plan means to take a full inventory of the resources and capabilities that you have right now. Then add the capabilities and resources your future self has. Once you identify your gaps in knowledge and expertise, you will be able to shift your focus toward your personally identified high-value areas to catalyze the acquisition of these skill sets. Your future self will still have all of the talents, knowledge, and skills of your present self. But to fulfill your future goals will require new growth and acquisition of further talents, knowledge, and skills. Have a personal strategic plan to give yourself a guideline for the realization of your goals.

Step 3: Become Prominent in Your Industry

Whether you are on your first day considering your field of interest or you are already a seasoned expert, staying on the cutting edge of your industry and becoming competitively knowledgeable in corollary fields will give you the depth and breadth of knowledge that will attract people to you for advice. By gaining the knowledge or having the resources to access the knowledge, you will gain the influence that your future self needs to accomplish your goals. Reflect how others have established their prominence in your industry. Consider what you can learn from them, and do likewise.

Step 4: Get Expert Advice

No matter what industry you are in, others are already recognized as experts in it—likely scores of people. Seek their advice. The easiest way to find expert advice is to stop by the library or bookstore. By simply reading books and listening to audiobooks, I've had the privilege to receive advice from Warren Buffet, Oprah Winfrey, Jack Welch, Tim Ferriss, and nearly countless others, without ever meeting them in person. Dedicating time to reading nonfiction books from your industry and corollary fields will make you attuned, flexible, and adept in your marketplace. If you know experts in your organization or industry, reach out to them. Let them know why you are interested in their advice and what your goal is. Then ask for advice on what to read or do, depending on the circumstance. The very act of asking and following through on advice from experts you know will honor them and make you memorable to them in the future. After you have taken their advice and followed through, report back to them and, gratefully, let them know what you learned, and ask to discuss it with them.

Step 5: Take Daily Disciplined Action

A small action toward your goals, completed every day, will build for you the life that you envision. Not one singular action, but a series of daily disciplined actions will get you to where you want to be. You act every day to get into the habit of progress. In life, you are either progressing or regressing. You are either becoming more or becoming less. You are either moving toward your goals or away from them. You are either moving forward or backward. By taking daily disciplined action toward becoming your future self, you are honoring yourself and ingraining within yourself a habit for progress.

Step 6: Prioritize Your Activities

More than a dozen times a day, ask yourself, "Am I serving my future self, right now?" Keep the vision of your future self at the forefront of your mind. See the world and modify your actions in the context of how it serves your future self. When you prioritize your activities in service to your future self, you establish clear judgment focused on your personal purpose. This judgment will make you fully aware of your actions, giving you the opportunity to carefully amend them.

Step 7: Take Full Responsibility for Your Decisions

Being accountable for serving your future self and becoming your future self is solely up to you. Who you are today is the combination of the choices that you made yesterday and every yesterday before that of your life. If you have chosen or not chosen to serve your future self today, recognize that that was *your* choice. You have the freedom and liberty to choose who you become. When you take full responsibility for your decisions and actions, you empower yourself to grow and to change. You empower yourself to personify self-control. You empower yourself to become the future you.

Follow these seven steps to get on your personal road to fruition. Set goals and achieve them. Maneuver through and around obstacles that deject others. Find strength, hope, clarity, and expertise. Have certainty of vision and tenacity to follow through on your engagements. Employ these seven steps and you will become the future you.

Bio

Andrew Christison, MBA, founder of CollegeStudentAdvice.com, is an author, advisor, communicator, and true student of lifelong learning. He believes that sales, business, interpersonal relations, and a positive frame of mind are intertwined threads woven together to transcend a good life and that the pursuit of worthy goals is essential for healthy well-being. Learn more about Andrew at http://www.collegestudentadvice.com.

46

Uncovering Hidden Jobs Fast

☙❧

Jamar Cobb-Dennard

Business Week, *FOX News*, Harvard, Yale, and Cornell have all reported or conducted studies that suggest that 60 percent to 80 percent of jobs are found through networking. The days of turning to the classifieds to find a new job are long gone.

The wave of wholly effective online job boards has also passed. Employers who advertise on job sites get inundated with résumés; don't have time to go through them; and find disconnected, unqualified candidates. As a result, many of the best hiring managers have forsaken job boards altogether.

The best jobs are not advertised, and the best candidates are not responding to mass advertisement. Job connections are now made through networking. There are three types of networking:

1. Direct
2. Six degrees of separation
3. Strategic

Direct networking involves building relationships directly with your target employer. An example of this is going to your industry's trade association and networking with members who could be potential employers.

Six-degrees-of-separation networking is based on the premise that everyone knows someone who knows someone, and if you ask enough people whom you need to meet, you'll find them within six asks. If you're networking

187

through general community events, service clubs, or church, you are using the six degrees method.

Strategic networking places the focus on building relationships with people who are engaged with your target employer over and over again. An example of this for job seekers is partnering with recruiters. They work with dozens of employers who are looking for candidates just like you.

Direct and six-degrees networking yields results—but only in small unpredictable quantities. Engaging multiple strategic partners can bring your search dozens of leads. The key to finding a job through networking is partnering with professionals who see your target employer and are willing to open up their contact database to you.

To find the right strategic partners, you first have to know your target market. Your target market is your ideal role. Be clear about what your perfect job looks like. If you settle for anything, you'll get nothing. They key to finding a job quickly is knowing exactly what you want and going after it with every bit of vigor that you have.

As you brainstorm, consider these questions:

- Which industry would you like to work in?
- Which position is best for you?
- What are your minimum income requirements?
- What would you like your position and earnings to be within three years?
- How soon would you like to get started if offered a job?

What are the top five must-haves for your perfect next job?

1. _____
2. _____
3. _____
4. _____
5. _____

Because you now know what you want, you can effectively share it with potential partners.

The second part of knowing whom to partner with is identifying who regularly sees the hiring managers at your ideal job.

Here's an example to get you started. This concept starts with your target market and who else sells to it. McDonald's has toys, play places, and clowns, and markets to kids, right? Who else sells to kids? Day cares, Disney, pre-schools, toy stores, amusement parks, Gymboree, Nickelodeon. McDonald's is smart. Every time a new Disney movie comes out, McDonald's features the toy in its Happy Meals. Disney cross-pollinates its client base with McDonald's, and both of their ships rise in the tide.

Now, take the hiring manager for your ideal job. Who else is selling to her or him? Write down a few of your ideas.

Typically, recruiters, HR consultants, payroll salespeople, group health sales-people, personality test salespeople, temporary staffing companies, and other applicants are also calling on hiring managers. Your job is to go to network-ing events, scour your database, and search LinkedIn to find people in your desired industry who fit the categories just mentioned.

If you know who your job-hunt partners are, you're good to go. The next steps are to actively pursue them, build a relationship with someone you can mu-tually benefit, and begin trading notes on who to contact at the right places.

Here are some simple ways to use strategic networking to find a job.

- *Join HR associations.* Most association meetings can be attended a few times as a guest for a nominal event fee. Don't worry about selling your-self too hard; just figure out how you can help the HR managers achieve their goals.
- *Partner with HR consultants.* HR consultants are in and out of multiple companies that are hiring. Focus on connecting them with more hiring managers who could use their services. The consultants will return the favor by introducing you to jobs that could be a good fit.
- *Partner with recruiters.* You can partner with recruiters who can help you get a job. You can also use them as a resource to break in to seeing hiring managers who have been unresponsive. Send a recruiter the con-tact information of your target company, and see what he or she can do to get you an interview.
- *Partner with other job seekers.* What? Partner with my competition? Refer your friends to great positions that may have been a poor fit, and have them do the same thing for you!

- *Join employment groups.* Find other job seekers to partner with, and lead the charge of keeping the energy light and enthusiastic within the group.
- *Email your professional and personal database.* Don't just send an email to your friends that says, "Hey guys, just got fired. Let me know if you hear of any good jobs!" Lame. Send the description of your ideal job to your contacts so they know exactly how to spot the right role for you.
- *Attend job fairs.* Use job fairs to speak with hiring managers, and remember to also connect with other job seekers and potential strategic partners.
- *Serve on not-for-profit boards and committees.* Join a cause that you care about, whose volunteer members are closely aligned with your industry. You never know what opportunities will come of it.
- *Join LinkedIn discussion boards.* If you share high-quality content in the discussion boards, readers will view your profile (that states you're seeking a new position), notice that you are open to job opportunities, and reach out to you because you appear to be an expert.
- *Attend trade associations.* Consider partnering with a vendor member who knows all of the members who are decision makers. The vendor member can make neutral introductions to all of the right people for you.

Finding a new position through networking is fun and easy. Using the strategy I've just outlined will add focus to your relationship building and will help you land your next perfect job quickly!

Bio

Jamar Cobb-Dennard is a principal at Outsourced Sales Force, a sales recruiting firm that helps companies without a sales force have a sales force. Jamar is a sales, networking, and recruiting expert. In 2002, he built a team of 70 salespeople in four months and later recruited 8 to 30 new salespeople a week as a hiring manager. Jamar has built small businesses from $800 to $30,000 in monthly sales entirely through networking He was recognized as the Rainmakers Rookie of the Year and a Top 50 Business Connector. Find more on sales, networking, and recruiting at http://jamarspeaks.com.

47

Stop Chasing Job Postings, Ignite Your Job Search, and Turn Job Hunting into Opportunity Finding

Laura M. Labovich

When I was thinking about writing this article, I thought, "Maybe I'll call it job-search strategy because that is really what I'll be sharing." But then I thought, "I better get a catchier title because, to be honest, job-search strategy sounds like a class from college that I wish I had slept through."

But it is so important that I truly believe that every job seeker, every successful job seeker needs a strategy; it's the foundation of your job search. You go to driver's education before you earn a license; you draft a blueprint before you build a house; you go to a bridal show (or hire a wedding planner) before you get married. But so often in our job search, we have one method and no instruction: we apply online. We hit "Send" and wait for the job to come to us.

But, surprisingly enough, even with job search, there is an instruction manual, and it's not just about posting your résumé to job boards and applying online. So let me share with you how you go about creating a strategy and a foundation for yourself. Trust me: this will shorten your job search substantially.

When you wake up in the morning, do you ever find yourself unsure of what to do with your day? In the absence of a formal plan, you log onto your computer, check your email, search the job boards, submit résumés, and wait. And that next step simply eludes you, so you wash, rinse, repeat. You spend crazy hours refining your résumé for this job and that job, customizing cover letter after cover letter, all along believing you'll get that call.

I'm sure you won't be surprised to hear that this is a very stressful, reactive, ineffective way to conduct a job search. But what are your other options? You're about to find out.

First, let me provide you with a bit of background. These statistics are consistently consistent: 85 percent of the jobs are never posted online in the first place. When you go online and apply for them, you are applying for only 15 percent of the jobs available to the job-seeking public. The other 85 percent (that are never posted) are found within what is affectionately referred to as the hidden job market. Sadly enough, only 2 percent to 4 percent, of job seekers who apply for a job online actually land one this way, yet they often spend upwards of 90 percent of their job search time on these unproductive activities!

So chasing job openings is futile. These jobs are going to candidates who are known, candidates who got there before you did, in advance of an opening. They have networked their way in. They are insiders. They have researched the company before it had an opening and did so with a blueprint. They did so with a strategy.

Instead of becoming a job finder, become a company finder and a people finder. Targeting is the key.

What is a target and how do you do it? How do you get focused in your campaign? There is a formula, in fact. What I hear from most people is: "What if I don't know exactly what job I want?" Or, "What if I don't know where I want to live? What if I don't know what industry, organization, or type of company I want to get into?" If this is you, you have some prework to do.

Here's how targeting works. Instead of logging online every day and applying for jobs and trying to make your cover letter and your résumé fit the job posting, I recommend that you craft a strategy around a target. And a job target is very specific. A job target includes three things:

1. *Title or function*: This is the first part of your target. What job do you want? Marketing manager? Research analyst? Cake decorator? Getting clear on this is priority No. 1.

2. *Geography*: Let's say you live in Bethesda, Maryland, and want to travel for work only a short distance to Kensington, Rockville, Chevy Chase, and perhaps a few other cities in the neighboring area. Or you may want to stay in the D.C. Metro area. Either way, this is your specific geographic region.

3. *Industry or organization size*: You may say that you don't care what industry you want to work for, but I will tell you something for sure: the employer cares a great deal. The employer cares that you know the lingo, that you understand what is going on in the company, and that you understand what is going on in the industry. Ask yourself, "Do I want to work in a nonprofit? Corporate America? University, hospital, publishing, manufacturing? It does make a difference. These industries are all very different, and their jargon is different.

If you don't want an industry or you are undecided, decide on company size. Perhaps you prefer the feel of a small company: that's OK. Are we talking 10 to 20 employees or 400 to 1,000? If you don't decide on an industry, you can at least decide on a company size.

What this looks like in action is this:

Neighbor: "So John/Jane, I hear that you're in a job search. What do you want to do?"

You: "I'd like to be a social media consultant for a consumer products or energy company in the D.C. Metro area."

You: "I'd like to be a marketing manager in the manufacturing industry in the Atlanta area."

Next, target some companies in manufacturing or consumer products, and put them on a sheet of paper with "Target" written at the top. This is called a personal marketing plan. A question I often get is, "How many companies should go on my PMP"? A good number is approximately 40 for most folks, but if you're at a very senior level, you'll need more because there are fewer SVPs in any given organization than there are people at the manager level.

Now, instead of going after job openings, you want to try to get meetings within your target companies. Remember, you need to be an insider, the person who gets there before the job is posted. So don't worry anymore about whether they are hiring. It doesn't matter!

Your goal is to network with people at least one or two levels above you. If you are a marketing manager, you look for directors or VPs of marketing. They are in a position to hire you when a position becomes available.

What do you do when you meet these people? You want them to meet with you. (Heck, offer to bring them breakfast!) Right, there is no job, so don't ask for one! But, statistically, if you target enough companies, there will be a job at some point in the near future. When you meet these folks, establish a connection. Cultivate the relationship. Make meaningful relationships. Say, "I know there is no job right now, and that's OK. But I have been researching your company, and I really believe I would like to work there in the future. I hope that you have just a couple of minutes to speak to me. It would really mean a lot." And, because there is no job on the table, they are (in most cases) more than happy to meet with you.

To recap: Create your target. Make a target company list. Do the research to target those ideal decision makers before they open up a job. And get meetings with them. Now, wash, rinse, repeat. And watch how your job search transforms!

Bio

Laura M. Labovich is the CEO of The Career Strategy Group, a career management and outplacement firm in Bethesda, Maryland, that offers job seekers a solution to shave months off a challenging job search. She is the coauthor of *100 Conversations for Career Success: Learn to Network, Cold-Call and Tweet Your Way to Your Dream Job*—affectionately referred to as the communication bible for job seekers and a Forbes Top 5 pick for Best Career Books of 2013. Laura is an in-demand speaker at conferences nationwide and has been seen in and heard on NPR, Sirius, XM, NBC, *FOX News* and more. Laura can be reached at http://www.thecareerstrategygroup.com.

48

Handling Inappropriate Questions in a Job Interview

Liz Cassidy

When I was a young, naïve engineer learning interview skills for a student recruitment campaign, our HR manager grilled into us: "Never ask an interview question of anyone that you would not ask of a white, Anglo-Saxon, Protestant male."

That advice has stood me in good stead. And to that list I would now add *heterosexual, able-bodied, and in his prime.* When you put any candidate in this context, there are a number of questions that don't need to be asked.

Unfortunately, very few managers have gotten that same advice or exposure to the early training that I have received. As a result, some well-meaning *but unaware* interviewers ask the silliest questions, often without realizing that the question itself may be illegal.

Before we go any further, it's useful to acknowledge the difference between a question that is *illegal* and a question that could give rise to *criminal liability.* Most questions taken at face value as illegal do not create a crime. There is a vast difference between criminal liability and civil liability. For criminal liability to exist, there must be a motive or intent to commit a crime.

Most of the illegal questions I have heard and been asked are a result of either ignorance or good intentions; that is, ignorance of what is legal, ignorance of what questions are valid, and ignorance of how the answers might be misused in a discriminatory way. They are not asked from malice. There may still be civil liability even when there was no criminal intent.

So how do you respond when you have been asked an inappropriate question? Given that most illegal questions are asked in innocence and ignorance, if you try to be politically correct, then you will probably put the interviewer on guard and create an early end to the interview.

Examples of inappropriate questions:

- Are you planning a family?
- Are you planning to retire in the next few years?
- Do you need time off during the day to pray?
- Are you pregnant?
- Do you think you could cope as the only male in an all-female workforce (or vice versa)?
- How will you handle getting up and down the stairs with one leg?
- Does your religion prevent you from working weekends or holidays?
- Do you have any use of your right arm at all?
- Do you have any preexisting health conditions?

So how can you be diplomatic and rescue the interview from falling off the cliff? The choices are yours.

- You may choose to be politically correct and assertive, correcting an obvious error and ending the interview and this career opportunity.
- You can be brief and succinct in your answer and then change the subject.
- You can ignore the question and change the subject.
- You can ask if there has been a previous issue in the organization that has caused the question to be asked to find out the real and underlying concern. Then you can alleviate it and show yourself to be caring, flexible, and tactful. For example, you could say honestly, "There is nothing about my personal health or status that would get in the way of my performing well and doing a great job for you." This shows you to be courteous and professional in the face of unprofessionalism.

Caveat 1: If you feel that you cannot perform the role for some reason, thank the interviewer for his or her time and move on to a role that you can do and is a better fit for you.

Caveat 2: Beware of your need to be a hero. I have a very dear client who is a delightful person, a high achiever, and outstanding employee. Six years ago he accepted a role in an organization that had a totally different values set from his own. He didn't fit, and the end of the employment was messy. My client knew he was "in the right," and in his heightened emotional state, sued the organization for unfair dismissal. He won and it was a legal test case.

Now, when you put his name into a search engine, the first three items are about his dismissal and the court case. He is job hunting again and lives in stress that potential employers and recruiters will put his name into a search engine and find out his history. He has done nothing wrong. But he is worried how his need to win legally six years ago could reflect on him today.

The reason for telling you this story is to give you pause to reflect if you are unfortunate enough to be asked inappropriate questions in an interview.

Do you want to be right? Or do you want have a stress-free and successful career? If you choose to take a legal remedy to a real or perceived slight in an interview, then, as a minimum, you will be buying into months of stress. Your name will also go into court documents and will be available to anyone who searches the Internet looking for your history.

Bio

Liz Cassidy, No. 1 Amazon Best Selling Author and founder Third Sigma International and LiveOutLoudPublishing.com, is a speaker, facilitator, and publisher. With 28 years of industry and business experience in multinationals, nationals, and small businesses, in the U.K. and in Australia, within production, operations, distribution management, sales, and professional services in traditional and online businesses, there are not many aspects of building, leading, and managing a business that Liz has not experienced and coached her clients in. Now based in Brisbane, she travels to the United States extensively with her business and is recognized and acknowledged for her skill and ability in assisting her executive coaching clients to overcome business and leadership blocks. Liz has been a guest on local and national radio and has articles in a number of business magazines. She is also a qualified practitioner in a range of tools including Myers-Briggs Type Indicator and

Apollo Profiling and is the author of Job Interview Questions and Answers. She has a BS in Chemical Engineering. Contact Liz via her Web site, http://www.LiveOutLoudPublishing.com.

49

Increase Your Odds in the Job Market

~~~

John J. La Valle, MBA

Having been in various corporate positions before deciding to go out on my own, I have interviewed many people. As a consultant, I have also been in the position to interview executives as a second pair of eyes and ears for the hiring manager. People want definite qualities when they are hiring someone. And these qualities are valid for companies that outsource for consultants, although most of those jobs are initially found through very good networking. Competition in the marketplace is fierce only because of the vast number of people out there searching for work, but they don't all fit that high-quality of criteria that jumps out at the person hiring.

First, there is the résumé, that dull-looking piece of paper that, if stuffed with the right information, can make it onto the pile that gets looked at next. That piece of paper, loaded with results you have achieved.

No one really cares that you were the president of your fraternity or sorority. How much money did you generate for the charities you were raising money for? No one really cares that you were a project manager overseeing 20 people. What did you achieve? How much money did your project make for the company, or how much did it save the company? No one really cares that you were a manager of some department with 25 people reporting to you. What was the turnover rate? What was the safety record? What was the attendance rate? Was it a line position or staff position? How much did your wonderful department save the company or contribute to the bottom line?

Whatever you do, don't fudge numbers or dates. If you were out of work for a short while, that's OK. Don't even try to hide that fact. We would look for missing dates and ask about the times missing. Did we care that the person was out of work for a time? Not as much as we were about the person's honesty. What were you doing while out of work, anyway?

Now, assuming this gets you noticed and onto the next pile that gets you an interview, the hiring person will be looking for certain things. Here are some tips to help you.

- *Be well dressed.* Not fashionable, but solid business attire. I once lost out on a good job with a major pharmaceutical company because, as the recruiting agency told me afterward, my shoes reflected other than a conservative attitude, and the three people interviewing me loved my responses and experience and everything else but that. Believe it.
- *Be well groomed and clean.* Have only minimal carrying cases with you, no iPods, iPads, cell phones, or other devices. Leave them kept away and turned off.
- *Have the best attitude for getting hired.* Many managers want people who are proactive, not reactive. This can and will come across in your language and the way you carry yourself. You may not believe it, but people make most decisions quickly and unconsciously. They may think of this as intuitive, but rest assured it is going on all the time. Use active verbs and complete sentences. These convey strength and character.
- *Have great questions ready for the interviewer.* Although it's important to get the cursory info—benefits, salary, hours—be interested in the company, where it's headed, what markets it's in. Is this a company you really want to work for?
- *Have great questions about the manager's style of managing.* Ask him or her questions such as, "What kind of manager are you?" And, "Would you allow me to interview some of your employees to find out how they like working you?"

Strange questions? They sure are. Do you want to be part of the status quo or portray the person who is different enough to be remembered?

Remember one more important attitude check: aren't you also interviewing the company and the manager?

<u>B</u><small>IO</small>

John J. La Valle, MBA, is the coauthor, with Richard Bandler, of *Persuasion Engineering®*. John has a strong background in sales, manufacturing, and human change technologies. He is well known for his ability to take seemingly complex issues and breaking them down into easily solvable opportunities for organizations. John holds an MBA from Mount Saint Mary's College in Emmitsburg, Maryland, and is a member of the ASTD. He consults both organizations and individuals to assist them in achieving their outcomes. His consulting style is open, supportive, highly participative, energetic, and results oriented. He also publishes a monthly newsletter available at http://www.nlp-newsletter.com. You can contact him at the through the Web site http://www.PureNLP.com or through Facebook at https://www.facebook.com/john.j.lavalle.

50

6 Ws of Informational Interviewing (aka Networking)

⁓

Kristin Johnson

Networking can strike fear into the heart of any job seeker. If you prefer solitude, haven't done much networking before, or you're having a crisis of confidence, it can be extremely intimidating. Can you relate?

If you have reservations about networking, try conducting informational interviews instead. A slightly different take on networking, this strategy can help you get started talking to your contacts. These one-on-one conversations will help you to build your confidence. After techniques used in an informational interview are mastered, they can then be used in any networking conversation.

The greatest number, 24.5 percent, of all external hires (job seekers who were not already employees of the company) come from referrals, according to the 2012 CareerXroads Sources of Hire study. Conducting informational interviews can keep you top-of-mind as openings arise and improve your chances of getting hired this way.

This strategy makes so much sense and is so natural that soon you'll be a networking pro. To get started, use the 6 Ws—Who, What, When, Where, Why, and hoW—to answer common questions about this technique (not necessarily in that order, though).

Who Might Consider Doing an Informational Interview?

Anyone from a student to a C-Suite executive can benefit from doing this type of networking. Active job seekers, career transitioners, and careerists desiring a promotion are people I commonly teach this strategy to, but anyone with a question about his or her career will get results from informational interviewing.

Whom Should I Ask to Do an Interview With?

You have several options for whom to contact.

- *Career coaches or counselors*: These professionals can provide help if you are unsure of your career goals. They may have ideas about whom you could talk with and can even facilitate an introduction.
- *People in your network*: Identify people you know whom you can talk to about their jobs. Ask them to introduce you to their connections or tell you about organizations they belong to.
- *Professionals in your target company*: Even if you don't know them yet, others are often open to answering a few questions about their job.

Remember that you are looking to your contacts for their expertise and advice. When you show this respect, people are often eager to share their knowledge and lend a helping hand.

Why an Informational Interview?

Because the interviewee is the one doing the talking (you're just asking the questions and giving her or him the floor), this is an excellent learning opportunity. You can glean a myriad of information such as:

- Insider information about the culture at a target company
- Typical duties for someone in a new career
- Salary or benefits information for a position
- Personality traits or professional needs of company leadership
- Additional contacts to broaden your network

What Kinds of Questions Can You Ask
in an Informational Interview?

Some excellent articles on ask.com and quintcareers.com outline questions to ask in an informational interview. You may ask general questions about the person's occupation, for example:

- What education is required for the position?
- How does one gain work experience as a _____?
- What opportunities for advancement are there?

Or functional questions such as:

- What is a typical workday like for this position?
- What are the most rewarding aspects of the job?
- What is the toughest thing about this work?

Because these meetings are less formal than a hiring interview, you can also ask questions about topics that would be considered taboo in a formal interview. You can ask about not only salary and benefits but also length of the workday, challenges with competitors, marketing strategy, internal processes and procedures, or other sensitive topics.

This is an opportunity to get an honest, firsthand perspective from someone at your target company. Your interviewee might be more forthcoming if you ask, "What's the best thing about working for Mr. Smith? The most challenging thing? What is his management philosophy?"

Be prepared with your questions written out ahead of time. Depending on how the conversation goes, you may not get to ask all of them because you want to respect your interviewee's time, but that may give you a reason to reconnect for an additional meeting.

When and Where Should You Schedule
an Informational Interview?

The interview should be scheduled at a time and place that's convenient for the interviewee because that person is doing you a favor. Your contact may prefer to have you come to the office, or she or he might be more comfortable meeting you for coffee after work. A brief phone conversation and a series of emails are other options.

How Do You Request an Informational Interview and What Do You Say?

People often have different ways they prefer to be contacted. Some people are phone people; others are more likely to respond via email. Judge which mode of communication your contact might prefer, but try another if your request goes unanswered. You might try going through a contact's assistant if he or she is hard to reach.

However you make contact, your message should:

- Include a polite salutation.
- Tell your contact how you know him or her or if you have a mutual connection.
- Inform your contact of your objective: to meet, talk via phone, or simply exchange emails.
- Be clear that you want a brief meeting to discuss a specific set of questions, and that you are not inquiring about a job or seeking feedback on your résumé.
- Provide two or three options for your meeting so that it is easy for your contact to check his or her calendar and schedule the appointment in return email.

Don't focus solely on one or two connections. You want a list to work through so that you aren't being too persistent with one person. If you feel as though it's time to move on, trust your gut.

What Else Should I Know?

Other helpful guidelines to follow:

- Dress at the professional level you would anticipate to see on a typical workday for the company your interviewees work for.
- Demonstrate how pleasant and helpful you would be to work with.

- Don't ask for a job or be demanding in any way. Being polite and understanding is essential, especially if you are visiting interviewees at their workplace. They are doing you a favor.
- Respect their schedule; be brief.
- Informational interviews may lead to an employment opportunity, either with the interviewee's company, or with a connection of his or hers. Word your questions carefully and professionally.
- Ask for referrals to other contacts of interviewees who would be good for you to speak with.
- Thank them immediately following your meeting via email.

In our digital age, there can be a plethora of information about your desired target online on company Web sites, blogs, or social media sites. However, certain topics are less likely to be so openly discussed, such as corporate culture, salary, or ease of promotion. Instead of leaving questions about these things to your imagination, set up a meeting with someone in the know. And use the 6 Ws for a successful informational interview.

Bio

Kristin is a TORI award-winning, six-times certified résumé writer, job search coach, and social media consultant. Her approach is cutting edge, creative, and kind. As owner of Profession Direction, LLC, she works with professionals and aspiring executives across the country. Her clients enjoy the reassurance of having professionally written, SEO-optimized documents. They find clarity and direction in their job search, feel at ease with social media and in-person networking, and earn more income faster. To provide the most current resources to her clients, Kristin attends careers industry training from Career Directors International and The National Résumé Writers Association. Her credentials include certified advanced résumé writer, certified career management coach, certified job search strategist, and certified online professional networking strategist, among others. She would love to help you "target your success today."

51

How to Answer the Top 10 Interview Questions

❧ ～ ☙

David Couper, MA

1. Tell me about yourself.

This is often how a job interview starts, but it doesn't mean it's a good opener. "Tell me about yourself" is often more accurately translated to mean that the interviewer is thinking: *"I don't know to what to ask. But I heard someone ask this question and it seemed to go OK. So I'm going to use it too."* The main problem with this question is that you don't know what the interviewer wants and needs. You are just guessing.

Best advice is to answer that open-ended first question briefly. Outline your education, professional experience, and key skills in a few minutes flat. Be bold, be brief, and be to the point.

Then begin your questions to find out what the employer actually wants from this hire. The interviewer doesn't want to know everything about you. He or she doesn't care about half the things you have done. And if you take time to answer this question fully, you will give out a lot of information the interviewer doesn't want or, worse, will hold against you.

All the employer wants to know is:

- Can you do the job? Do you have the skills?
- Will you fit in? Are you going to be productive in this team?

207

- Will you cause any problems? Are you going to leave after two weeks, sue us, get us sued, or be a pain to work with?

Focus on what you do and then highlight what makes you different. Differentiating between yourself and the competition is a smart thing to do.

2. What do you consider your most significant accomplishment?

Don't ramble on about everything and anything you've ever done, from winning first prize in a science fair to having children. Instead, discuss your hard work and accomplishments that relate to the job—and only to this job. Make a list before the interview of your most significant achievements, narrow it down, and then discuss that in two to three minutes. Remember to use stories to get your point over.

3. Why are you leaving your current position?

Whatever you do, don't bad-mouth your previous employer or old coworkers. Instead, focus on the benefits of the experience gained in your last position.

4. What do you consider your biggest weakness?

An interview is a sales exercise. Soda manufacturers don't advertise their products as sugar water. No, they talk about the positives—how it makes you feel good and quenches your thirst. You should do the same. Instead of talking about weaknesses, talk about something that you have worked on and is no longer an issue. Preferably, this is something that was earlier in your career. Or talk about an issue that everyone knows is an issue, for example, dealing with international business and juggling time zones.

5. How have you handled stressful/frustrating/ difficult situations in the past?

The interviewer is looking to see if you can deal with petty problems on a daily basis. Make sure you address your common sense, perseverance, and patience in these situations. Have a relevant example you can cite. Use one that highlights how you used your unique persona to solve the issue.

6. Our company has to deal with X. How would you handle this?

Don't come up with a complete solution. Instead, talk about the process you would go through to get to the solution. Hypothetical questions are often trick questions. The employer often knows the answer because rather than being fictional, it's real and something the company has been through. You are at a disadvantage in this situation because you don't know the details of the problem, how the culture works, and what options have failed. If you launch into a solution the employer already rejected, you don't look smart; you look naïve and unprepared.

7. So what makes you think you are qualified for this position? You don't seem to be.

This question is designed to provoke a response. The response the interviewer is looking for is not the answer but how you react to confrontation and conflict. You need to pick two or three main ideas about the job and about yourself and connect them. It's a good idea to target the skills directly related to the position and then provide a brief story to show your success in the past. Don't get combative with the employer, but prove your worth.

8. Where do you see yourself in 5 or 10 years' time?

On a beach in Mexico. … No, just kidding. Make your goals realistic. Too much ambition does not look good in an interview. Promotions usually come in one to three years, so work with that. Don't talk about your dreams that don't relate to work and then give the interviewer the impression you are not committed or not going to stay.

9. Why should we hire you for this position?

You need to summarize your skills in a way that is directly relevant to what you have learned about the position in the interview. Be thoughtful, be organized, and be genuine.

10. Is there anything you would like to know about the company?

This is often the last question asked. It's a good idea to have a few questions prepared regarding the position and the potential for growth. Leave questions about vacation time and pay raises at home. You want to be offered the job before you get into specifics. You should do your research on vacation time, pay, and other benefits with HR, with the recruiter, and with other people in the industry.

Bio

David Couper is a career coach who gives real-world advice that works. His clients find the perfect jobs, earn more money, and create new careers. Because he has been a hiring manager and a senior executive in major companies, he knows what works in the job market. He has successfully coached managers in major companies wanting a new challenge, frustrated souls wanting to make their dream come true, and frontline employees laid off and desperate to get a job. David has published eight books. His latest, *Outsiders on the Inside: How to Create a Winning Career...Even When You Don't Fit In!*, was published by Career Press. He has appeared on television and radio and has been quoted in *Forbes*, *Fortune*, CareerBuilder, Yahoo, Monster, and *CNN Money*. David has a degree in communication, a postgraduate qualification in education, and a master's in psychology.

52

How to Interview an Organization

❦

Steven J. Burks, PhD

Competing successfully in today's job market requires your evaluating your career options with the same level of due diligence that you would take when making a major purchase such as buying a house. Yet many job candidates forget that an interview is a two-way street when it comes to an evaluation. This chapter focuses on how to interview the organization you are thinking of joining to determine if joining the organization is a great career move for you.

You can greatly accelerate your career by investing time gathering information in advance of an interview. Profitable traders know that they make their money at the beginning, when they purchase the item they are going to sell. If they buy the item at a low enough price, the profit margins are excellent when they sell. Planning for the interview process will give you a foundation of information that will enable you to further your career.

Parts of the Interview

A successful interview has three basic parts: preparation, presentation, and closing. The sequence varies, but during the interview process you still need to execute the three basic steps of the cycle.

Preparation involves studying the position profile and researching the company. Use your contacts to learn about the position and company. And develop a list of strategic questions.

The actual presentation part of the interview should be focused on learning about the enterprise and individual goals within the organization. Obviously, you need to know the goals of the enterprise, but how does each member of the interview team want to be supported by this position? Try to get an insight into whether expectations are in alignment. If they aren't, then address the misalignment. If the interview team is not aligned, it could mean a red flag for you. Practice your strategic questions before interviewing. Hold an imaginary conversation between you and an interviewer. Nothing is more important than active listening. If you don't understand something, ask for clarification.

In an interview, the closing must be done subtly. Begin by addressing an important point that many candidates find uncomfortable. As the interview nears its end, ask if the interviewers have any concerns about your ability to meet, or exceed, their expectations for the position. This is your indication if you can be successful in this new role. Don't be afraid of the question or their response; address concerns forthrightly. Make sure you have a clear understanding, and address your own concerns during this final discussion.

Strategic Questions for the Candidate

Following are some excellent questions to ask during an interview. The answers you get early on during the interview will help you answer later questions. Don't hesitate to ask the same question of different people to check for consistency. You should have more questions than anyone has the time to discuss. Of course, not all questions apply to all situations. Focus on four major areas to properly evaluate the position: culture/company, boss, position, and success factors.

Culture/Company

Each company has its own unique culture—for example: intense, laid back, rigid, process focused, formal, entrepreneurial, flexible, has no rules.

- What is the corporate culture and the chief binding force among employees?
- What are the characteristics that the company finds attractive about itself?

- What are the principal strengths of the company?
- What is your company's management style?
- Is the growth strategy through internal development or through acquisitions?
- What key things drive results for the company?

Boss

The boss can have many management styles: micromanager, hands off, strategic view, detail oriented, share lots of information, or share little information. A boss can be great at getting people promoted or do nothing to develop people.

- If I should have questions of you after the interview, may I call you directly?
- What is the company's attitude toward attendance at professional meetings or community involvement?
- Why did you come to work for this company? Have your own expectations been realized?
- What career path can I expect, given good performance?
- Tell me about how you manage a project within your group.
- Tell me how the organization views this division, group, or business unit.
- For others who were in your group at some point, can you tell me what they went on to accomplish within the organization?

Position

It is important to understand the new role from many perspectives. Learning what the position responsibilities are, the expected outcomes, what resources are available, who the key people you will work with are, and how the position contributes to the company's success will help you decide whether there is alignment of enterprise goals and individual expectations within the company. It will help you decide if it is a position that you will want to accept.

- What are some of the major short- and long-range objectives of the company?
- What challenges do you see for yourself and the company over the next five years?

213

- From the kinds of things that we have talked about, where do you see a good fit between my qualifications and the position? Are there any areas where you need some information to strengthen fit?
- How does this position contribute to the organization's success?
- When you look forward 60 to 90 days from my starting with the organization, what will I have accomplished that would make me successful in this role?
- What is the most important thing I have to accomplish in the first year?
- In what period would you expect a very solid contribution from me?

Success Factors

To be successful in a new role, understand the position, the company, the mission, and how to bring value to your boss and the company. Being successful at a new company is determined by many factors. Being able to integrate quickly and smoothly into a new organization is one key factor that is often missed by candidates during the interview process.

- What outside influences affect your company's growth?
- What strategies do you think have contributed most to the company's growth over the last five years?
- What are some of the common attributes of your successful employees?
- Do your employees understand that you are going outside to fill this position? Do they agree with the need to go outside?
- Why do you believe that the existing team will play ball with a person hired from the outside? What preparation has been done to bring in someone from the outside?
- How important are new products to the achievement of the company's goals over the next five years?
- How is individual performance evaluated throughout the company? How often?
- How does the company plan to deal with the challenges it faces?

By asking good questions and probing in the four areas of focus, you can achieve the desired outcome. You will have a comprehensive picture of the potential next step in your career. You will know you are stepping into a new role that will result in career success.

BIO

Steven J. Burks, PhD, is CEO of Sanford Rose Associates—Crystal Lake Executive Search Consultants. He earned his BA, with highest honors, from Earlham College, and his doctorate in chemistry from Miami University. Steve entered executive search from a chemicals industry career, where he served in executive positions in technical and sales/marketing. He helped launch three start-up chemical businesses during his career. He was global manager at Momentive and held executive positions with Eastman, Air Products, PPG, and Solvay. He has authored dozens of scientific papers and patents. He is adjunct professor at McHenry County College. Email: steve@careerfasttrack.com; Web site: http://www.careerfasttrack.com.

53

10 Steps to Prepare for a Job Interview

Shanna Landolt

It's been my experience that most people do very little preparation for an interview. The thinking is, "After all, I'm talking about me and my experience. I'll just be myself."

This is lazy thinking, and often great candidates lose the opportunity for a fabulous job because of a lack of preparation, not a lack of skill set or fit. Here are some tips that can help you ace your interview:

1. *Research the company.* Be prepared to answer the question, "What do you know about our company?" Have an answer that goes beyond the obviousness of what is on the Website. Try to find something to say about the organization that would indicate that you went above and beyond to learn about it. Print a couple of pages of your research and have them with you and visible in the interview. Your interviewer will understand immediately that you have done your homework. It will demonstrate your interest.

2. *Research the people who will be interviewing you.* Go on LinkedIn. See if you are connected to anyone who knows someone who will be interviewing you. Call those connections to see if you can garner any insight into their style or personality. You can also Google your interviewer to see what else comes up. You may find that he or she is an avid runner or a board member of a charity. This will allow you to bring it up in conversation, and you can build a sense of relatedness.

3. *Contact current employees.* If you know someone who is a current employee of the company you are interviewing with *and* you have a great relationship with that person, call her or him and say that you will be coming in for an interview. Your contact might just put in a good word for you. It's critical here that the person you are calling will think or say only great things about you. This can backfire if the current employee has had a negative experience with you in the past.

4. *Get recommended on LinkedIn.* Try to get a sense of what the most important experience or skill set is for this role. Turn to your own network to see if someone who has worked with you will write an authentic recommendation on LinkedIn addressing that particular area as a strength of yours.

5. *Rework your résumé.* Update your résumé to address examples that are relevant to the job description. Before the interview, send the interviewer an updated version of your résumé.

6. *Anticipate questions.* Think about what some of the standard interview questions could be, and write out and rehearse your answers until you like what you are saying. Standard interview questions include:

   • Tell me about yourself.
   • What are your strengths/weaknesses?
   • Why did you leave your job? (Have any answer for each job in the last six years.)
   • What were your responsibilities?
   • Tell me about an accomplishment that you are proud of.
   • Tell me about a time that you worked as a member of a team. What was your role?
   • Why are you interested in this opportunity?
   • What questions do you have for me?

7. *Read and reread the job description.* Go through every bullet point of the duties and responsibilities and answer the questions: "Tell me about a time when …" or "Tell me about your experience with …" for each bullet point of the job description. Typically, almost all of the interviewer's questions are based on the job description. Write out your answers and ask yourself, "Is that my *best* example?"

8. *Be prepared to provide specific answers.* Often senior executives assume that the interviewer thinks they are qualified and will provide generalized answers instead of specific answers. If you can't provide specific examples using an actual scenario, the interviewer may think you don't know your stuff. Sometimes people generalize because they are concerned about giving away confidential information. If you can't say the exact name of a client or project, then be specific without using the name. Rather than say, "I was working on the Telus account," say, "I was working on an account for a major telecommunications company."

9. *Be brief.* Make sure that your examples and answers can be communicated within two to three minutes. If you ramble on, the interviewer is more likely to tune out. I like this format best for interview answers:

   - *R—result*: This is the outcome. Now tell what happened. Give the ending away first. This way the interviewer isn't trying to figure out where you are going with your answer.
   - *S—situation*: Describe the situation you were in or what you needed to accomplish.
   - *T—task*: What goal were you working toward? What did you have to achieve from that situation?
   - *A—action*: Describe the actions you took. Focus on what *you* did instead of *we*. What did you do and why did you take those actions?
   - *R—result*: Summarize again with the result, the outcome, what happened. Did you meet your objective? What did you learn from this? Don't be shy about taking credit for your contribution.

10. Videotape yourself answering interview questions, and watch the video. How you think you communicate and how you *actually* communicate may be very different. Watch your tone, posture, body language, and eye contact. Look at the way you are dressed and your hair. Ask, "What impression am I leaving?"

If you complete all 10 steps of this interview preparation, you will be ready to put the best *you* forward in the interview.

"Success always comes when preparation meets opportunity." — Henry Hartman

Bio

Shanna is president of the Toronto-based executive search firm The Landolt Group. She has been in executive search since 1997. Her search experience covers the business-to-business, not-for-profit, pharmaceutical, biotechnology, advertising, public health care, and consumer packaged goods sectors. Shanna is a frequently requested speaker at outplacement centers and networking groups. She has been featured as an industry expert in human capital on the Life Network and on Rogers TV. She has a passion for people and is committed to making a difference with everyone she meets. You can contact Shanna by email at shanna@landoltgroup.com; by phone at (416) 849-3855; or at her company Website, http://www.landoltgroup.com.

54

Reneging on a Job Offer: Is
It Ever Acceptable?

Gayle Laakmann McDowell

A candidate recently came to me seeking the advice for the following situation: A few weeks after accepting a software development position with Dell, he received an offer from Microsoft as a program manager. This was his dream job, and his dream company, but he would have to turn it down. Or would he?

I wanted to tell him to do "the right thing" and turn down the dream offer, but I couldn't. Why? Because, about seven years earlier, I was in a nearly identical situation. And I did the so-called "wrong" thing.

In 2004, I was interviewing for an internship. I didn't want to go back to Microsoft—three internships there was plenty. Google and Apple had both rejected me, though Apple told me that I was their "No. 2" candidate for this position. So though I was pretty lukewarm on the position and would never join there full time, I accepted the IBM position. I had stopped all other interviews and had every intention of completing the internship.

Then, six weeks before the internship was supposed to start, I got an email from the Apple team. Their No. 1 candidate just reneged. Was I still available? This was my dream job. I loved the company. I loved the product. I loved the team. So I said yes.

The Aftermath

Here's where I'm supposed to say that it caused some horrific impact on my career. Recruiters no longer trusted me. I got blacklisted. And ever since then, I've regretted my decision, or something like that. But the truth is that none of that happened.

IBM was annoyed, but they replaced me. Word didn't get out about that awful thing I did. Even the other IBM recruiters had *no idea* what had happened. And why would they? It's a huge company and one candidate reneging is just not *that* big of a deal.

But it was a big, big deal to me.

Should You Renege?

I can't—and won't—advise anyone to renege. It can certainly hurt your reputation. You may be seen by others as unreliable. People who know about the situation may hesitate to recommend you to a company in the future. And, of course, there is definitely an unethical component to it. You're breaking a promise, and a promise you made in a professional context. That's never good.

At the same time, I do feel that much like an awesome salesperson will recommend a competitor's product if it's clearly a better fit for you, an awesome recruiter should understand the position you're in. This is your dream job; you don't just walk away from it. (And, in fact, the Apple recruiter was supportive when their original candidate reneged and would have eagerly interviewed him in the future.)

Additionally, unless the original offer was from a very small company or for a very high-level position, the impact on the company probably pales in comparison to the impact on you. Is it really so wrong to renege? Rather than the knee-jerk "ZOMG-it's-wrong" response, think seriously here. What is so special about committing to a job offer?

What's So Special About This Promise?

You shouldn't promise to see a movie with friends but then shop around for better plans. You shouldn't get engaged if you're not sure you want to get married. And you shouldn't offer a friend a ride to the airport if you don't have a car. But sometimes your parents unexpectedly come to town, sometimes relationships fail, and sometimes cars break down. Life happens.

So let's all move away from this absolutist "it's always wrong" mind-set and be honest: we break promises all the time *and we're OK with that.* Life happens, and things come up. And sometimes that thing is your dream job. Why do we accept broken promises in other cases, but think that it's always wrong for a job offer?

Bio

Gayle Laakmann McDowell is the founder and CEO of CareerCup.com, the leading Web site for technical interview prep, and the author of *Cracking the Coding Interview* and *The Google Resume.* Gayle has worked as a software engineer for Google, Microsoft, and Apple, and has extensive interviewing experience on both sides of the table. She holds a BSE and MSE from the University of Pennsylvania in computer science and an MBA from the Wharton School. She can be reached at gayle@technologywoman and found online at http://www.technologywoman.com or http://twitter.com/gayle.

55

Are You Tracking the Most Important Activity of Your Job Search?

Lisa Rangel

With all the job-search activities a job seeker has to do in this employment marketplace to conduct a successful job search, it can easily become overwhelming. Submitting résumés to job postings, going to networking events, reaching out to your contacts, and introducing yourself to new people at target companies—and we have not even included social media interactions, interview preparation, and many other actions. It's enough to make your head spin, if you let it.

Through my years of recruiting and job-search consulting, I have boiled all of the activity down to one real job-search activity metric that needs to be tracked. Tracking this metric each week provides a litmus test for you to determine if all of your social media interactions, in-person venues, online research time, and phone activity is purposefully focused or just plain busy work.

The metric to track is this: *How many conversations are you having each week with people who can help you with your job search?*

(To be clear, I define a *conversation* as a back-and-forth dialogue about your job search among two or more people that can happen over the phone, in person, or in email.)

Yes, that's it. That is what all of this activity comes down to.

223

The number of conversations per week in an active job search can vary based on the person's situation—but I would say any active search with fewer than five conversations will experience slow progress. Ask yourself if all of this social media posting, résumé submission, networking event attending, coffee meeting, lead generation, online research, and blog writing is getting you qualitative conversations with the right people who will lead you to getting hired.

I pose this question to job seekers often. This is often the pivotal point missing from the job search when people are experiencing lackluster results and bordering on job-search burnout. Diagnostic conversations I have with frustrated job seekers who are not seeing results often go like this:

Job seeker: I am spending 10 to 30 hours a week on my job search, and I am not receiving many (or any) calls for job interviews. I am getting really frustrated.

Me: What activities are you doing for your job search?

Job seeker: I do all this research online for jobs, and I have submitted to more than 150 job postings over the last three months. I have received two phone calls for interviews, and I am frustrated.

Me: How many conversations have you had with people at the companies or people who can introduce you to hiring managers at these companies during the course of those 150 plus submissions?

Job seeker: Well, I do not really talk to anyone at the companies directly at this point. I hope they call me when I submit my résumé. I mainly submit through job postings and attend job-seeker support groups.

Me: Are you speaking to contacts who are employed, as well? Are you asking your network at these events you attend who they know at those companies to help you gain an introduction?

Job seeker: Not really. In hindsight, I am asking if they know of open jobs that I can apply to.

You see, it all comes back to the conversations you are having to gauge if the activities you are doing are moving your job search forward. Here are other ideas to help you audit your effectiveness:

- Are you posting on LinkedIn, Facebook, and Twitter but not getting much from it? What do your profiles look like when people find you? When was the last time you reached out to a person from these mediums to speak on the phone or meet for coffee in a public place? Use social medium as a gateway to conversations.
- Not see much activity after a networking event? Are you following up properly after a networking event with people who can provide you introductions or be a conduit to other influencers? The job you find probably won't come directly from the networking event—you need to follow up with people after the event to find those gold nuggets.
- Are you researching for hours? Feeling like you are not getting anywhere? Ask yourself how many outbound calls or emails to *people* did you make/send as a result of that research. Sending emails to job postings does not count as communication activity. People hire people. So reach out to people and track it accordingly.
- Submitting to job postings? I wouldn't say stop, but for each submission you make, spend time finding a possible hiring manager to introduce yourself to and find contacts that can help you with an introduction to the firm.

The goal of all your job-search activity is to generate conversations that advance your job search. To help you stay focused on the right activities to pursue, ask yourself before your next job-search action, "How is this going to help me chat with a person about my search?"

Bio

Lisa Rangel, managing director of Chameleon Resumes, is a moderator for LinkedIn's Job Seeker Premium Group; a former search firm recruiter; certified professional résumé writer; and holder of six additional job-search certifications. As a former recruitment professional for over 13 years, Lisa knows firsthand which résumés receive a response and land interviews from reviewing thousands of résumés to identify talent for premier organizations. She has been featured on LinkedIn, Yahoo!, Monster.com, *US News & World Report*, Fox Business News, and *Good Morning America*. Lisa is the career services partner for eCornell, the online division for Cornell University. She has authored three books, including *99 Free Job Search Tips from an Executive Recruiter* (http://chameleonresumes.com/99-free-job-search-tips/). You can follow Lisa on Facebook at http://www.facebook.com/chameleonresumes; on Twitter at @lisarangel; or on LinkedIn at http://www.linkedin.com/in/lisarangel.

56

Should You Announce You're Looking for a Job on Your LinkedIn Profile?

&ec ~ ℘℘

Mary Elizabeth Bradford, CARW, MCD

Executives often present me with the following question: "Should I join LI Jobs or post in my profile that I am looking for another opportunity?"

Let's talk about overexposure for a minute and dispel a few myths. Back in my recruiting days, companies paid me handsomely to bring those three "perfect" candidates that matched exactly what it was they were having such a hard time finding (often no easy task). Unfortunately, if he or she was currently in a job search or between companies, that candidate lost some cache—even if the candidate was a perfect fit. Because search fees are substantial, there was a lot of pressure on me to bring my client companies candidates they perceived they could not find on their own. And I think that is the key—client companies didn't want to pay me a fee to find someone who was already available. They frowned on that.

That is why recruiters are not looking for people who are looking for jobs.

Now, this is just a hunch, but I believe my theory should be given serious merit by job seekers who are thinking of posting their availability on their LinkedIn profile.

It is unlikely, but possible, that you might lose out on a position because you did not post that you were available. In the end, you must choose based on your own unique circumstances. I think, as a whole, executives need to look at the problem of branding and overexposure. What, after all, are you trying to create with your branding message?

One of your goals should be to communicate a story line that demonstrates your unique value. You do this by communicating your specialty strengths and attributes, your leadership skills, and your quantifiable results, or what happens when you do what you do. Tie it all up in a short message that says, "This is the promise of the experience you are going to have by knowing/ working with/hiring me." In this message, you want to create cache, allure, and intrigue.

In my 17 years' experience as both a recruiter and résumé writer/job-search coach, I haven't seen anyone accomplish this by screaming from the rooftops that she or he was in the job market. I know some might disagree with me, but please consider that my perspective is based on real-world experience working closely with more than 1,000 executives, to date.

What do you want to convey in your job search? Leadership. Confidence. Control. A professional attitude. You are not desperate. You are not "eagerly seeking your next opportunity." The more people think they may not be able to have you, the more they will want you—it's just human nature. This special place is not reserved for the select few—all professionals who care about optimizing their career should strive to market themselves in a compelling way. This is Marketing 101. And in a job search, one of the best investments you can make in your career is learning how to create a marketing plan for yourself and how to market yourself. No ad says, "BUY ME! BUY MY PRODUCT!" No, the ads are geared to make us *want* the product. Of course, we're not products; I'm just making a marketing observation.

Even if you find marketing distasteful (or, worse, disingenuous), if you can't communicate why someone should hire you, then how are you ever going to have a chance to help that person or company? Your dream job at your dream salary isn't distasteful, is it? Exactly. Learn how to market yourself or pay someone to show you how. Your ROI will be tremendous.

Bio

Mary Elizabeth Bradford is a top award-winning career-services industry expert and is known as "The Career Artisan." She has 16 years' experience providing job-search coaching and marketing and branding documents for mid-to-senior-level job seekers. Known as a hidden job market expert, Mary Elizabeth has shown hundreds of professionals at all levels how to get off the job board treadmill and land interviews. Her Job-Search Success System is a revolutionary system that teaches job seekers, step by step, how to set up an easy, turnkey job search that gets results in the hidden job market. Mary Elizabeth lives in the beautiful Hill country of Texas with her husband and daughter. Log on to her Web site, http://www.maryelizabethbradford.com.

57

JOB SEARCH NETWORKING

Keys to Successful Job-Search Networking

❧

Tim Tyrell-Smith

A lot of people still struggle to grasp networking. It is in some ways really simple and other ways painfully difficult. I hope this short case study knocks a hole in the wall for you and lets some light in. I'll try to keep it painless.

Recently I met with someone I knew from earlier in my career. We had briefly worked at the same company in the early 1990s. But we hadn't spoken since then. Staci and I reconnected via LinkedIn. Although we were not connected there yet, she found me and sent a *personal and friendly note* asking if I would meet with her. Because she sent a *personal and friendly note*, I was open to hear what Staci has to say. She took the time to make me feel important by spending a few extra minutes on that note.

We met at a coffee shop *near my house*. Staci could have suggested that we meet in the middle (she lives in Los Angeles; I am in Orange County). Her decision to drive to me shows a respect for my time. Let's face it—she made it easy for me to say yes.

She offered to buy my cup of coffee. Not everybody does this; in fact, most don't. Those who do, again, send a clear message of appreciation. It doesn't matter if that message has a value of $2.50; it still matters. A few months ago I met with a recruiter and got some advice on my blog. Although that recruiter wouldn't let me buy breakfast that day, you better believe she got a gift card from me a few days after our meeting!

Providing some early value is critical. Staci did this by *bringing a CD* filled with recruiter names and company lists that she thought I could use. I appreciated the effort on her part and thanked her. During our meeting, I gave her everything I could, including résumé feedback and an introduction to the free downloads on my Web site. I told her everything I knew about the market for jobs and finished our meeting absolutely spent but happy that I could help and glad that we had connected.

Now, it could have ended there, as most networking relationships do. But Staci extended our relationship and made me want to stay involved in her search. At the end of our chat, she said *those magic words: "How can I help you?"* I've learned to always have an answer for this one. I told her that if she knew of anyone who might be helped by my blog or Web site, to please send a note or let me know.

Over the next week, Staci reinforced her interest in building a relationship. She *introduced me* (and my work on my blog) to two people who run an outplacement company in Los Angeles. These are great targets for my content because they are always looking for new ideas to help their job-seeker clients. And I love new ideas!

In the meantime, I sent her leads on two great career coaches, something she mentioned during our meeting as an interest area. She *sent me contact information* for the head of her graduate university's alumni career center. Again, a place where potentially I can gain additional exposure for my blog. She *attended a networking group presentation* of mine and made sure to grab me before and after to reconnect. She also *sent me a note afterward* to tell me how much she enjoyed it.

 She *commented on a blog post* and offered some very relevant thoughts on the topic. As a blogger, I appreciate comments; they provide an important part of interacting with readers. They also help support better search engine results by showing the value of your blog to the community. She helped me.

Now, every networking relationship is different. Clearly, the stars aligned a bit to allow Staci and me to meet and work well together. But you can implement a version of every one of these ideas. A couple of key things to notice here:

Staci *made a big and broad effort to say thanks to me—before, during, and after our meeting.* Most important, I think, was her postmeeting effort. She went out of her way to help me. Based specifically on my answer to her question. Remember those magic words? I will remember her gracious offer to *meet me near my home* and *buy the coffee,* and I will appreciate her *referrals.* They added long-term value and addressed something important to me: the opportunity to increase awareness of Tim's Strategy, the concept I've worked so hard to create.

She *maintained contact for a few weeks,* cementing her search objectives in my mind. Instead of a quick thanks and monthly email follow-ups, Staci *delivered value in multiple steps.* As a marketer, she clearly understands reach and frequency!

Staci has left me *feeling that I got the better end of the deal.* This matters because her need is still in my head. I feel as though I owe her a referral or a lead to balance out our networking relationship. Not literally, but I do want to help and she has given me several reasons to be looking out for her.

Networking is hard work because you have to prepare and execute a plan with each person. You have to know what to ask for and what to provide in return. And you have to know when and where to put in the bigger efforts. Had I been a junior IT professional, perhaps Staci would have focused her energies elsewhere. But I am a good contact for Staci (as she is for me) because we are in the same industry and in the same function. It's not always as simple as a coffee and a thank you. But it's a start.

Bio

Tim Tyrell-Smith is founder of Tim's Strategy, a site that helps professionals succeed in job search, career, and life. Follow Tim on Twitter, @TimsStrategy, and stop by his site (http://timsstrategy.com) to learn more about how his strategy can help you find the right job faster.

58

Great Ways to Compete in Today's Job Market

～◆～

Arleen Bradley

The title of Hillary Rodham Clinton's book, *It Takes a Village,* reminds me of the successful job search. The electronic technology available to us has created a global village. We no longer live in a vacuum, nor can we afford to if you want to be productive. The speed in which technology advances can boggle the mind and cost a fortune to keep up. We become interdependent with many others to help us make our way through this difficult job market.

Today's job search is different from when you got your first job. You can be sure the change is permanent; it won't be going back to what it was. If fact, it's a rapidly changing process. To be successful, you want to be able to respond to and implement the changes quickly. However, as quickly as the process changes, more steps are added, and the time it takes to get hired has increased since you were first hired.

To compete in today's job market, you need a job-search networking support group.

The job searcher rides an emotional roller coaster during the lengthy job search. Couple that with rapidly changing techniques, and you have a job searcher who will be frustrated and stressed. To cope with all these feelings, the job searcher needs a support system. This system is called a job-search networking support group. Each member brings something to offer the group. Members give and take as the need arises. No one has all the answers, but together they have—or they know where to find the answers.

233

Your Support Team

The following list illustrates the roles members need to play to have an effective job-search networking support group. Although this list is not an exhaustive list, it's meant to underscore the need to incorporate the skills and contacts of others to be successful in your job search. Here are some of the "villagers" you need.

- Just as your *mother* kept after you to brush your teeth and to do your homework, your mother will keep you at your task. A prolonged job search drains your energy and confidence. Some job-search activities you don't enjoy, but, to succeed, you must do them. Your mother will keep you at your task with gentle reminders and explanations of why you must do the things you don't want to do.

- A *teacher* teaches you today's fundamentals and how to use them in your life. A teacher also helps you develop critical thinking skills so that you can adapt and respond to the rapidly changing job search process. The skills you learn from your teacher will help you think outside the box.

- A *miner* digs up the treasure trove of jobs and brings them to your attention. Today, many jobs are either buried deep inside the Internet or completely hidden from view because they aren't posted anywhere.

- A *cheerleader* builds up your confidence and encourages you to keep going, no matter how the search is going. Your cheerleader is there from beginning to end to support you during the ups and downs during your job search. To boost your confidence before an interview, make a phone call to your cheerleader.

- A *confidant* listens to you when you need to vent when you are discouraged and feeling down. You get your problems off your chest. This person helps you do it by allowing you to talk through your problems to arrive at your solutions without interfering and keeping the information confidential. Your confidant is someone who won't judge you or try to fix you—you aren't broken. Your confidant won't be able to fix the situation, but she will provide the emotional support that you need.

- A *small army* aka *network* is a must. More than 80 percent of all jobs are obtained through networking. The more people you have in your network, the better your chances of success. Your network needs to continue to grow in numbers. Remember to build relationships with these people instead of asking for help. People help others they know, like, and trust.

They may not be able to help you, but when they know, like, and trust you, they will introduce you to the person who can.

- A *proofreader* is the second pair of eyes that makes sure your résumé, cover letter, thank-you notes, and any other written materials you send out are perfect in spelling, grammar, and format. Because each résumé and cover letter will be tailored for each job you apply for, you will be cutting and pasting from one to create a new one. This person will be an objective set of eyes to make sure everything you send out is impeccable. (Tip: Many cover letters are addressed to "Dear Hiring Manger." Those letters and résumés are tossed out of the running.)

- A *coach* prepares you for the big single elimination event you face—your interview. Your coach will have you practice and fine-tune your interview skills. Your coach will video a practice interview session to help you remove what interviewers find annoying and show you what you are doing right and what you can improve upon.

- An *image consultant* helps you manage your brand so that your message matches your intent. Your image consultant can advise you on your appearance. As a job searcher, you should always look current and at your best because you never know if you are going to meet your prospective employer.

- An *activity director* looks at your work–life balance. Finding work is work. Balancing your job search with enjoyment keeps you on an even keel. The many ups and downs of the job search are tempered by taking your mind off the search, even if only temporarily. Take time off from a long-term task when your become exhausted and hit a roadblock. When you come back refreshed and recharged, your work begins to flow.

- A *village manager* coordinates all the events so that the appropriate person is ready to step in when needed. The village manager knows that different people are needed at different times and when each one is needed.

Everyone Wins

The workings of this group of villagers bring to mind a story of another village where hungry soldiers arrived to a frightened and cautious village. The villagers claimed they had nothing to offer, but as they began to know, like, and trust the soldiers, one by one they brought something to share. The result was that everyone shared in the feast when each gave her or his one gift.

A job searcher can succeed alone. But it will take longer and be more difficult. When many job searchers and people with jobs join their resources, everyone wins. The job searchers find jobs, and people with jobs have made an ally for when they need help.

Bio

Arleen Bradley puts the care in career. She is the owner of Arleen Bradley Career Coaching. A certified career management coach, certified job search strategist, and certified job loss recovery coach, she provides state-of-the-art job-search strategies and needed assistance from job-loss grief. She is the founder and facilitator of two job-search networking support groups. Having walked the path of many of her clients, she understands the needs of unemployed job searchers. She mixes compassion, motivation, and accountability when working with her clients to obtain job-search success using the latest best practices. You can contact her by email at arleen@arleenbradley.com; visit her Web site at http://www.arleenbradley.com; follow her on Twitter at http://www.twitter.com/arleenbradley; or connect with her on Facebook at http://www.facebook.com/arleenbradleycareercoaching to learn how she can help you succeed in your job search.

Twelve Steps for a Highly Successful Job Search

❧

Gary Erickson

Executive Search Partners has created a job-hunting guide called *Twelve Steps for a Highly Successful Job Search* based on our experience both as executive recruiters and as executives who have hired hundreds of people.

Our search process has four stages:

1. Creating your marketing material
2. Marketing yourself
3. Networking and interviewing
4. Closing the deal

For this article, we concentrate on the first two stages, which include Steps 1 to 7 of our 12-step process. You can download our entire complete *Twelve Steps for a Highly Successful Job Search* as well as a sample résumé at www. execsearchpartners.com.

Stage 1: Creating Your Marketing Material

Think of yourself as a product that you are trying to sell. You must know your attributes and benefits and be able to articulate them. You also need to have some sales literature (résumé) that presents your attributes in a compelling fashion. Here is how to create your marketing materials:

Step 1: Write down your accomplishments. A good rule of thumb is to write down 10 accomplishments for each of your last 10 years. Use the problem/actions/results (PAR) format, and write each accomplishment in two or three sentences (at most).

- Problem—describe the problem you tackled.
- Actions—describe the actions you took.
- Results—list the measurable results achieved.

As an example: To improve the timeliness and accuracy of order processing, designed and implemented a new computer-based order-to-ship process that reduced order-to-ship time from two months to two days while increasing order accuracy from 72 percent to 99.5 percent.

Step 2: Develop a professional summary. In four or five, sentences describe your background and capabilities.

As an example: Senior information technology executive (CIO, vice president) with 22 years of increasing responsibility experience in several industries, including automotive and manufacturing. Have been responsible for a global organization of 425 professionals and an annual budget of $65 million. Recognized by Deloitte and Touche as one of the top CIOs in the country in 2011.

Step 3: Create your résumé. Now you have all of the material you need to create your résumé. We strongly prefer the reverse chronology résumé in the following format:

PROFESSIONAL SUMMARY (from above)

PROFESSIONAL EXPERIENCE (reverse chronology format with each position)

Company name and description of the company

Your title, dates

Responsibilities described in narrative form

Three or four selected accomplishments from the PARs

Use the third person. Do not use the words like *I* or *my* or *me*.

EDUCATION (dates, degrees, activities, and honors)

OTHER (recognitions, awards, other distinguishing activities and accomplishments)

We recommend that when you email your résumé to a hiring manager or a recruiter, you include a short message in your email that summarizes why you are a fit for *that* position. Usually your modified professional summary will suffice.

Step 4: Update your LinkedIn profile. Make sure that your LinkedIn profile is up-to-date and that it includes the revisions you made to your résumé. Get some people to write recommendations for you and post them to your LinkedIn account.

Stage 2: Marketing Yourself

Now that you have completed your marketing material, start letting people know that a superior product (you) is now available in the marketplace. Most jobs are found through networking, not by sending letters and résumés to companies or in response to a job posting. If you see a job posting that you are interested in, try to find a way to network yourself to the hiring manager. This is done by developing and executing your marketing plan.

Step 5: Create your marketing plan. The marketing plan is the list of people with whom you will network, recruiters you will contact, and companies you want to target. Here is how to create it:

- Identify your geographic focus. First, ask yourself if you will move. If no, confine your marketing plan to the area within acceptable driving distance. If yes, identify your target cities and focus your efforts on those cities also.
- Create a contacts spreadsheet/database. Create a list of the people, companies, and recruiters that you want to contact. This list should be kept in a spreadsheet or database with notes. Add to this list as you network, and use it to follow-up with key contacts.
- Identify target companies. From your own knowledge and a variety of publications, review job openings on Monster.com, HotJobs.com, ExcuNet.com, Dice.com, TheLadders.com, and others job Web sites.

Look in the local papers and the *Wall Street Journal* for opportunities that look interesting, and add those to your list.

• Use LinkedIn. LinkedIn is ideal for linking companies and contacts. When you have identified some target companies, see who you know who works there or who you know who knows someone who works there. Then try and network into those people.

Step 6: Create your "30-second commercial": Using your professional summary as your guide, write and then practice saying a 30-second commercial about you. You should know this so well that it comes off naturally. You will use this for both networking and interviewing. The 30-second commercial is your best answer to the frequently asked question, "Tell me about yourself."

As an example: I am a senior information technology executive (CIO, vice president) with 22 years of increasing responsibility experience in several industries, including automotive and manufacturing. I have been responsible for a global organization of 425 professionals and an annual budget of $65 million. In 1994, I was recognized by Deloitte and Touche as one of the top CIOs in the country.

Step 7: Execute your marketing plan by networking. Networking is *the key* to any job search. You should identify as many people as possible with whom you can meet. Your purpose is to ask for their help in your job search. You want to walk out of each network meeting with at least three names that they recommend you contact.

Here is a typical networking approach:

Hello, Mr. Jones. My name is Gary Erickson. Fred Smith suggested I give you a call. I am … then launch into your 30-second-commercial.

Fred thought you would be a good person for me to talk with about my job search. Would you have 30 minutes sometime in the next two weeks to discuss my background and offer suggestions about possible companies or individuals with whom I could meet?

When you meet with Mr. Jones, treat the meeting as if it were a job interview. There may be some opportunities within Mr. Jones' company, and if you do well in the meeting, he may ask if you would be interested in talking to someone in the company.

At the end of the meeting, ask for names of at least three people with whom they would recommend you meet. Here is where your marketing plan is important. If you have any specific target companies you would like to get into, ask the people if they know of anyone at the target companies. Ask their permission to use their name when contacting their referral.

Your networking should lead to job interviews. For how to handle job interviews and more, see the rest of this document at www.execsearchpartners.com.

Bio

Gary Erickson is the managing partner of Executive Search Partners. Founded in 2002, Executive Search Partners conducts searches on behalf of its clients for senior-level information technology positions nationwide. Gary has over 30 years of management and executive experience, including the positions of CIO for three companies, COO, director of sales, and global director of quality and manufacturing. The article "Twelve Steps for a highly Successful Job Search" comes from Gary's experience in both looking for positions for himself during his career and in helping others find new opportunities. Gary holds a bachelor's and a master's in computer science from Dartmouth College and an MBA from the University of Michigan. You can contact him by phone at (248) 470-9976; by email at gerickson@execsearchpartners.com; or through the Web site http://www.execsearchpartners.com.

60

Dear Job Seeker, Are You Ready for Some Relief?

❧～❧

Irene Myers MA, PCC

In my coaching, I ask clients a lot of questions that stimulate them to think differently about the challenges and changes in front of them. As a "translator," I help them make sense of their work and life history and put it into future terms, leading to unexpected rewards. Typically, the way we work inspires them to go for something bigger than they had originally thought possible.

Information on the job market tends to become outdated quickly. Recommended strategies for the hunt change with technology. Job-seeker anxiety ratchets up. Let's shift the focus to you, the job seeker, with a set of enduring concepts that will help give you an edge in your search and, at the same time, take the edge off your anxiety.

Don't Panic

Realize you probably need only one job right now. A job description is a company's wish list. What an employer is looking for is the ideal job candidate. There may not be any real-life job seekers who fit that description, so don't let the list of requirements scare you. If your experience is not a perfect match, but the job has a big draw for you, what compensating qualifications do you have? Are you good at getting people to work together as a team? Do you have public speaking experience? Have you organized major events?

Get with Your Strengths

Get with what you're good at and love to do. Know who you are and what you can contribute. How do you know which jobs you could fit? Turn it around. Determine your profile of top skills and traits and then set your radar for a job that matches who *you* are. All seven of the seven employees in one of my strengths workshops found better fitting, more satisfying jobs without leaving their organization.

Show You Know Who You Are

Demonstrate self-knowledge. It enhances your credibility around what you claim you can do. Be able to talk about how you operate at your best and what contributes to your success.

An interviewer or someone you are networking with will likely ask some version of, "Tell me about yourself." You can steer the conversation in your favor by giving an answer to a better question. Example: if you've been in real estate, someone might say, "Describe the kind of home buyer you have worked with most successfully." You can say, "People who are looking for an agent who is willing to go at their pace for the time it takes to find the home that fits their dream."

Distinguish Yourself from Others

Among the ranks of job seekers with your qualifications, only you have your combination of those qualifications plus any number of the following:

- *Successes you can describe*: Be able to talk about problems you encountered in your work, what actions you took to address them, and positive results that occurred because of your actions.
- *Misses that have taught you what success otherwise could not have*: It adds to your credibility when you can explain the value of times when you did not score a win.

- *Transferable skills*, especially those suited to the job you would be doing: Transferable skills come with you wherever you go. They stem from natural aptitudes.
- *Personal style*: How are you most motivated to direct your energy and attention? Are you wired as the *Arranger* or the *Visionary* or the *Decoder* or the *Originator* or the *Strategist* or the *Elder* or the *Synthesizer*, etc.? (www.irenemyers.com has a sample of my Archetypes of Calling model plus client success stories.)
- *Deficits that have a flip-side advantage*: Maybe you've changed jobs several times within the same field. That gives you inside knowledge about the competition.
- *Attitude*: Can-do, customer-oriented, win-win—these attitudes make life easier for your boss. This is big!
- *Job-related interests*: What you naturally do outside of work for pleasure can add dimension to the expertise you bring to your work.
- *Life history facts*: From a big family? You know about cooperation and adapting to changing situations involving several people with differing priorities. Only child? You may have extra confidence or an expectation of attention.
- *Values,* your most motivating values: If, for example, sustainability is a high value for you, you have an extra degree of compatibility with organizations that promote sustainable practices.

Know What You Want and Get Comfortable Communicating It

That doesn't mean you have to state a specific job title when people ask, "What kind of job are you looking for?" You can respond by naming the three, four, or five most satisfying and most proven strengths you most want to use in your work. "I'm good at collaborating with diverse groups, synthesizing large amounts of data, and making good decisions under changing conditions, and I want to be able to do these things in my work."

Get Assistance

A career coach or counselor can help you recognize what your history and unrealized passion have set you up to succeed at next.

When You Network, Tell Your Truth

Telling is compelling. And don't assume you know where an indirect path might lead.

Fresh out of graduate school with a master's degree in German, I went to work at a bank in its international department working in letters of credit. Years later I bemoaned my not ending up teaching German. I called one of the German professors at my alma mater who had become a friend and colleague, but I didn't ask her for help finding a job. What I did do was tell her this truth for the first time. I said, "I have to say, I am rather disappointed that I didn't get into teaching German as my career." Short silence. "Would you like a job teaching here?" It was not a rhetorical question. One of the other professors was going on sabbatical. The instructor who was to fill in couldn't accept. The faculty remembered my success as a teaching intern there. Would they have extended the offer had I not been up front with my truth? In jaw-dropping astonishment I said, "Why, yes, I'd love that!"

Watch Out for the "Yes, Buts"

In co-active coaching, we speak of "the gremlin." This is the wired-in source of doubt that speaks up when any change is being considered. It prefers even a painful status quo to anything unfamiliar. When you evaluate a course of action, it's necessary to distinguish between a) old gremlin-driven doubts (e.g., your father/mother/brother would never approve) and b) reservations that are more legitimate. Even those don't have to be obstacles.

Listen to Your Gut: Tune In to Home Base

That means you. Check in with yourself to know which of the possible next choices along your career path grabs you the most, apart from recognizing the "logical" choice. A steeplechase rider, asked how he and his horse managed to jump the fence time after time, replied, "You have to throw your heart over first." And so it is with success in our work and anywhere else in life.

As an example to my coaching clients, I need to walk my talk. I found a way to spend a year in Sweden refining my playing of traditional Swedish music while continuing my coaching. There were challenges to meet. Could I get into the music program I wanted? Could I afford it financially? The phone connection with my clients? My mortgage payments? I knew that I had to do this music sabbatical as part of what is mine to do in this life—this was my version of throwing my heart over first. Within a few short weeks I re-arranged everything. My clients were inspired by my striking out on this big adventure and wanted to stay on. I switched to an Internet-based phone system. Two visiting professors rented my townhouse. Once I was in Sweden, wonderful friends filled in gaps and helped with logistical details back home. And now my clientele extends to Sweden.

When you want something badly enough, you will find a way to get it. When the goal is big enough for you and you go ahead and throw your heart over first because you know at a deep level that this goal is part of the life you are called to lead, the plan to achieve it can come together more quickly than you could ever imagine, with bigger results.

There is work to do that has your name on it. How many lives do you have to live? When will you start living this one?

Bio

Career and life coach Irene Myers MA, PCC, principal of Career & Life Design based in Seattle, Washington, is celebrating 20+ years of client successes. She and her clients thrive on the synergy of working together co-creatively. They are attracted to her work because she offers a one-of-a-kind combination of three proven approaches: Dependable Strengths Process (created by career development expert Bernard Haldane), wholistic co-active coaching, and her own Archetypes of Calling model. (http://www.irenemyers.com).

61

Journaling: Your Ultimate Career-Counseling Tool

Mari L. McCarthy

Whether you have lost your job, you are a new graduate trying to figure out your next steps, or you have just decided that it's time for a career change, journaling will empower you to create the future you want!

The important thing to understand about journaling to improve your career is that it is a very focused kind of journaling. Whereas everyday journaling can be about whatever comes to your mind, your goal with your career-related journaling is to focus on the most important aspects of your job: your current performance and activity, your short-term projects, your long-term goals, your wants and needs.

So as you set out to journal about your career, consider these two different scenarios and how your journaling can help you achieve success in either case: the job search and climbing the ladder.

Job-Search Journaling

When journaling about your job search, open up each journaling session by reflecting on your day's job hunt. What did you do well today during your job search? For example, if you made a specific business contact, it might be good to reflect on how that meeting went. Likewise, if you failed to achieve some benchmark today, reflect on what caused you the trouble. And your journal is the perfect place to unload your job-search frustrations, angers, and anxieties when you need to.

Then you could use the journal to think about your weekly job-search goals. You can use it to set weekly goals such as how many applications you need to send out each week, and you can use it to adjust those goals. Likewise, you can use it to write out answers to potential interview questions if you get an interview.

Finally, you can write in the journal about what sorts of jobs you would really love to get. This reflection can examine what skills you have, what sorts of tasks you like doing, and how you interact with others. You should reflect upon how those skills can translate into your dream jobs and how they can translate into jobs you'd be willing to do.

Journaling About Your Current Career

Just as journaling can help you during your job search, it can help you rise through your current career.

Each evening come home and spend 30 minutes reflecting on your work-day. Think about the work you accomplished that day. Were you productive? When were you at your best? When did you feel yourself fading? If you can be aware of the productive ups and downs of your day, you can begin to work to improve your weaknesses. Also consider interactions with your supervisors and coworkers. How did these interactions go? What was communicated well? What was confusing or frustrating? Your self-reflection can help you improve how you interact with others in the office.

You can also use the journal to work out how you will accomplish your various short-term projects in the office. What do you need to do to get the report done by your supervisor's deadline? Will you need to get it done a day early to go over it again? How are you going to motivate your team on this complex proposal? Use the journal to figure out these tough questions; you'll find yourself getting the harder thinking done before work so you can get right to accomplishing what you need to do.

Finally, you can reflect on how you plan to grow your career. What are the 5- or 10-year goals in your career? What do you need to do to achieve these goals? What sorts of attitudes make you a great businessman or business-woman? What personal characteristics do you need to work on to improve yourself so that you can realistically meet those goals? By constantly reviewing and journaling about your long-term plan, you can make sure you keep your eyes on the prize, so to speak.

Discoveries and New Interests

Another great benefit of journaling is self-discovery. Just as a productive brainstorming session at work or in school have helped you and your peers come up with ideas none of you had ever thought of before, journaling can cause you to produce and develop ideas you've never considered.

For instance, say you blindly apply for a position not really knowing much about the company but somehow land an interview. After meeting with a hiring manager, you feel you can really see yourself there and start exploring other ways to just get your foot in the door. You might find yourself jotting down these ideas and possibilities and start thinking of how you can make them happen. The more you think and write about it, the more likely new ideas will come to you, making it a form of personal, effective brainstorming.

Who knows what you'll discover or learn about yourself and your interests once you start journaling? It may unearth new passions and guide you to a completely new career path!

Bio

Mari L. McCarthy is the founder of CreateWriteNow.com, home of Journaling for the Self of It™. She is the author of 15 e-books, including *Do What You Love! 7 Days Career Journaling Challenge*. It guides you through the process of uncovering your passions and talents to find a career that will make you happy, fulfilled, and engaged.

62

Your Perfect Career and the Law of Attraction

❦

Dena DeLuco

"Don't ask what the world needs. Ask what makes you come alive, and go do it. Because what the world needs is people who have come alive." —Howard Thurman

In the late 1980s, I was a single mom. With no fancy degree or discernible career path, my jobs barely kept food on the table for my son (Isaac, two at that time) and me. Truth be told, I even reached out for welfare. It went against the very core of my nature. It was a hard pill to swallow.

At one time, I was a typesetter for a printer, worked in a greenhouse, and delivered balloons for birthday parties. Oh yeah, I also sold skin care and cosmetics. At the end of many months, I found myself having a pay-the-rent sale just to make ends meet.

Day after day I filled my future life with hope. I'd think, "Everything will change when Isaac starts school. I will find a good job and finally get ahead."

Amazingly, soon after Isaac began kindergarten a door opened: a full time job with benefits! Not only that, but it completely shifted the trajectory of my career path. In the first year, my income went from $6,000 (*not per month, per year!*) to $12,000. The next year, it doubled again to $24,000. In a few short years, I went from living on food stamps and government cheese to a six-figure income (in Youngstown, Ohio)! One month I actually cried when

I realized that my deductions (for one month) were more than I used to make in an entire year.

Now, you may be wondering how this story will help you get a job. I had done something that I had never even realized until decades later. The Law of Attraction was working on my behalf. Looking back, it is all so clear. Yet, at the time, I was unaware of what I was creating. During all of those years of affirming a better life, a well-paying career, and getting ahead of the bills, my future life was being created. Behind the scenes, I was accumulating dividend-paying declarations that one day would become my reality. And I didn't even recognize that I was doing it! If the "scenic route" is no longer serving you, maybe my past meandering will shine a light on a more direct route.

The Law of Attraction has been under the microscope lately. Some people have experimented with it and not seen the results they were looking for. Others dabble in it, using it to find a better parking space at the mall or to catch the green lights on the way to work. But what if by following the deepest desires of your heart, you could find your dream job? How would that work for you?

If an undereducated, small town single mom can create a six-figure income in one of the most depressed areas of the United States, *without having a clue* how she did it, can you imagine what *you* can create for *yourself*?

For years, my reasons (excuses) for not having a better life were surrounding a victim mentality. It was because of my ex-husband—yes, he was to blame! Then I began blaming God. "Yep, if God would just tell me what He wanted me to do, if He would just tell me my purpose." And then one fate-filled day it hit me! There was a reason I loved to help people. I was really good at seeing people's higher potential better than they could see it for themselves. And once they caught a glimpse of that higher vision, something magical happened! Their lives began to shift. The aha moment that transformed me? *My passion is my purpose!*

You are extraordinary at many things. But what makes your heart sing? These are your clues, your indicators that you are heading in the right direction.

Now you may be thinking, "I just need a job. I just need to pay my bills, put food on the table." And, of course, this is the desired outcome. But what if you could create your dream job (and income) simply by following the urgings of your heart?

Practically Working It Out

I believe that we come from a source of unlimited supply. Further, this same source pours out from the abundance as we ask. That being said, maybe we've just been taught to ask for the wrong things, or in a way that takes us further from our desired outcome.

Of course, we think we are asking for what we truly want. But if the Law of Attraction is valid, then what you are experiencing *is* what you are asking for (on a deep, unconscious level). We send out our prayers, petitions, affirmations in quotes. We set aside time to ask. But what about the remainder of our life? This type of prayer/affirmation is like tossing a bucket of sugar into the ocean and expecting it to be sweet. What if this source (or law) listens to every word, action, thought, intention, and emotion? With this in mind, what are your daily emotions and fears sending out that will be echoed back to you?

If you are unemployed or underemployed, I invite you to notice all the blessings that you already have. Appreciate that as your belief expands, so do the prospects of greater opportunities. Competition, lack, and scarcity are merely conditions of the mind, misinformation. As we open ourselves to upgrading these old limiting beliefs to more honoring truths, we liberate ourselves from the shackles of restriction.

What limiting beliefs do you hold about finding a job or earning a substantial income? No matter your beliefs or how they originated, once you become conscious of them, you have the power to create new beliefs about your options that are more empowering.

In a nutshell, *a belief is merely a thought in your mind that you hold as truth*. The law of life is the law of belief. You are being guided through life by your unconscious beliefs. Your thoughts and the emotions and actions that accompany them are creative and will, over time, reshape your unconscious beliefs. Therefore, by *choosing* more empowering beliefs, it stands to reason that you will experience more empowering results. If you are unsure of your current (unconscious) beliefs, simply look at your results. That's a great place to start.

I invite you to shift to more powerful beliefs as a practice with no blame and no guilt. Some days we are on top of the world; the next, we plummet down the rabbit hole of doom, fear, and self-loathing. It is human nature to beat ourselves up when we stray from the path. As soon as you notice you've veered off your path, simply pick yourself up, and remember who you are. Practice gratitude. Follow the things that make your heart sing. You come from an infinite source. You are unlimited potential just waiting to be awakened!

Sending you love and abundant blessings for your magical, amazing journey!

<u>Bio</u>

Dena DeLuco is a passionate and inspiring teacher who has an exceptional gift for helping people get unstuck. Her compelling workshops merge ancient wisdom, modern science, and universal laws and principles, translating into paradigm-blasting tools that help you uncover your hidden gifts and talents, adding new dimension and purpose. Dena currently has her private practice in Boardman, Ohio, where she is a certified NLP success coach, hypnotherapist, Reiki master teacher, and hypnotist trainer. She is the coauthor of the book *Step into Your Best Life*. Dena is a member of the International Hypnosis Federation and Toastmasters International.

63

Leadership Development: You Are a Great Leader!

~~❦~~

Clarissa Leary

Ever wondered if great leaders are born, or do they have to learn the skills? Does everyone need a certain level of leadership skills? And what does it take to be a leader? There are two elements: leading yourself and leading others. Here you will learn the key elements to becoming a great leader. Whether you are in business or employed, you will be a leader to yourself, your team, and your business.

To become a leader, you first must be open to learning, being passionate and motivated, and willing to take responsibility for your actions and personal development. Whether you're in a job or in business, it's better to be motivated and love what you're doing than to be doing something you really hate and don't want to get up every morning for. This is your choice to make if you take the time to work out what you want, what personal development you need to be undertaking, and what education you require for your chosen field of work. This will put you in good stead for being a great leader.

Being a leader doesn't always mean that you are leading someone; it can mean that you are taking control, taking responsibility, and delivering results for yourself. It also means you are able to follow others when required.

The Key Elements of Becoming a Leader

Treat people as real people. You are here to serve (giving) and be served (receiving). If you understand that when you are serving, your focus is on your customers; they deserve your full attention. At times, you serve, for example, when you deal with customers. Other times, you are served, for example, when you are out to dinner or buying from the supermarket. If you don't deal directly with customers, still have the attitude that you are in service. What you do will eventually come out to customers, so have pride in what you do, even if you are not face to face with them.

Continue your personal development. Learn and learn some more. This should be a priority for your whole life. There is so much to learn about you. What personalities do you show with certain people at work, at home, with your partner? What makes you passionate? What do you hate? What is your result? What are your values and beliefs and why? Do these values and beliefs serve you? Are you balanced in your four lives: relationships, financial, physical, and spiritual? In today's world of social media, computers, job pressures, relationships, and lots more, we tend to lose our identity, what our purpose is. We become disconnected from ourselves because of all the outside influences. Take time to find out who you are. You are beautiful; you are talented; you have the right to be happy.

Learn from your mistakes. If you're going to get upset about your failures, then do so and move on quickly. The next step is working out why the mistake happened. What could you have done differently? How can you change things next time? What did you learn?

Educate yourself. Being employed or in business, you need to keep learning about your chosen field. What are your competitors doing? What can you be doing? What can you do better? What makes you unique to your customers? If you're an employee, learn how you can do things better, safer, and easier to achieve greater results.

Hone your people and team skills. Communication is the key to ultimate success in business because you deal with your team, experts, media, suppliers, and clients. You need to communicate with a variety of different personalities so that you can achieve your ultimate outcome. Most of us don't realize that when we are dealing with people, the way we communicate with them will be the outcome. If you are in a meeting with your team with an ego personality, you won't get that team giving you 100 percent. We all have different personalities that we use when dealing with people. We need to understand how we use these personalities and with whom. This is about being aware of how you are acting, being, and speaking and whether you are achieving the results that you ultimately want. Or is it always a win/lose situation?

Take responsibility for your actions. I can't stress this enough—take responsibility for your own actions. If you make a mistake, admit it, find a solution, fix it, learn from it, and move on. That takes courage and commitment and is the basis for being a great leader. You show your team you are human and can take responsibility.

Act. Nothing happens unless you act. Be aware of your sabotaging, resistance, and when you are procrastinating. Whether you are working now or not, write down how you spend your time. What tasks are you doing? How much of this time is wasted? Checking emails, talking on the phone, taking unnecessary breaks, daydreaming—you'll be surprised at how quickly time goes on nonproductive tasks.

Be engaged, committed, and motivated. Being engaged, committed, and motivated in your employment or business comes back to your personal development and purpose. Being engaged works in with your being focused on your results. Being committed is your "why." Why are you doing what you are doing? Motivation comes in line with being passionate. Love what you are doing. Enjoy the journey and the experience.

Focus on results. If you want results, you have to focus on the results. What are your outcomes? What is your business vision and mission? What are your next steps to making the business vision come true? The only people who can make it work are the people in the business. That takes vision and passion. Give 100 percent commitment to your workplace.

Key Points for Team Leadership Skills

* Give praise and honest appreciation.
* Call attention to people's mistakes indirectly. Give solutions rather than criticize.
* Talk about your own mistakes before criticizing the other person.

- Ask questions instead of giving direct orders.
- Let the other person save face.
- Praise the slightest improvement and praise every improvement. Be "hearty in your approbation and lavish in your praise."
- Give the other person a fine reputation to live up to.
- Use encouragement. Make the fault seem easy to correct.
- Make the other person happy about doing what you suggest.
- Be sincere. Don't promise what you can't deliver. Concentrate on the benefits to others.
- Know exactly what is it you want the other person to do.
- Be empathetic. Ask yourself what it is the other person really wants.
- Consider the benefits that person will receive from doing what you suggest.
- Match those benefits to the other person's wants.
- When you make your request, put it in a form that conveys to the other person the idea that he or she will personally benefit.

Your next step? Practice and act!

Bio

Clarissa Leary is a passionate business owner and entrepreneur in Australia who focusses on helping business owners with personal development and business-growth strategies. She is well known for her passionate drive and awareness of how personal learning and awareness can rapidly bring increased business success. If you teach yourself, you will be rewarded in business and life. Her expertise extends to property-investing strategies, online lead generation, Web site development, business consulting or mentoring, and personal development for teenagers. To learn more and get the free *Business Mindset Strategies*, go to http://www.clarissaleary.com.

64

The Art of Leading Others
Through Inspiration

Janet Kinkle, MNLP, MTD, MHT

What would it look like to have such a *strong* connection with others that they would follow your lead without saying a word? The answer is quite simple: live the best version of *you* every single day! You will quickly find out that once you adopt this simple rule, it affects not only your life but also the lives of those who look to you for guidance.

While sitting in a quiet space, imagine what that feels like. Be specific. Be aware of who you truly are. This is a critical step because we humans can sell ourselves on the idea of who we *consciously* think we are. We can even trick ourselves into thinking that we believe it.

Let's try something. Go back to that moment not long ago when you were consciously thinking about who you are as a leader. As you are in that moment, shift your focus to the moment just before that, the moment before the moment. That is the moment that you hadn't noticed before now. That is the unconscious moment that you need to be aware of. Having the courage to discover who we are at an *unconscious* level or, what I call, our "truth space" is where the magic happens!

How different is your dialogue in that unconscious moment? Listen closely to all the thoughts and words that are brought to your attention. Put no judgment or meaning to these thoughts and words; be an observer. Pay close attention to your inner dialogue because when there is conflict in the *moment before the moment*, even if you are consciously unaware of it, the *energy* attached to that internal moment will also be in conflict. Understanding that we are all made of energy, imagine the mixed signals you send out before you even venture to speak a word!

We've all experienced this. You randomly meet a person and instantly feel very connected, as though you've known that person your whole life. You are buzzing with excitement! In a different scenario, you meet a person and—you can't explain it—you just feel uncomfortable and look to get away from that person.

3 Key Questions to Ask Yourself

1. *What is my intention*? As a leader, you are ultimately responsible for those who follow you. You must be clear in your intentions. You will know your intentions are ecological (good for you, good for others, good for the world) because when you sit in your truth space, there is an internal congruency. It's OK if you feel incongruent in this space. It's the *perfect* time to find out what the conflict is and adjust either the action or the value so that it is no longer in conflict.
2. *Who am I being*? This is a big one. This is where the inspiration comes in! Again, in your truth space, take a genuine look at your values and beliefs. Are your values and beliefs aligned with your actions as a leader? Is your inner dialogue aligned with the words you are saying out loud? Focus on this as if you were holding a giant magnifying glass. Again, it's OK if you feel incongruent in this space. Your goal is to discover conflict within and to shift your actions to align with your values and beliefs, or to shift your values and beliefs to align with your actions.
3. *In what do I trust*? Trust in yourself and your ability to *create* an environment in which others feel safe and secure.

In following that third simple rule, you will find that you create *that* thing, that sense of community that includes not only your employees but also your friends and associates. Trust yourself in all of your conscious and unconscious ways. Be a witness to your own security. And include yourself in everything that you think, feel, and do.

"If your actions inspire others to dream more, learn more, do more and become more, you are a leader." —John Quincy Adams

Bio

Janet Kinkle is a successful entrepreneur and business owner. Through her humble experiences of building several companies from the ground up since the age of 25, she has learned profound life-changing lessons, both financially and spiritually. At the end of 2011, Direct Sales Resources, LLC was formed. With a focus on leadership development, DSR grossed $850,000 in its first year and is on track to triple that number in its second year. DSR's secret to success is: "Take care of our people and the business will take care of itself." Janet is master certified in business strategy, NLP, timeline dynamics, and hypnotherapy. She resides in Southern California with her husband/business partner, Chad, their three children, and two dogs. Contact Janet directly at janetk@dsrcompanies.com or at her company's Web site, http://www.dsrcompanies.com.

65

Ostriches, Eagles, and African Grey Parrots: Lessons from the Aviary for Entrepreneurs and Job Seekers

k d Marlee

One option open to the job seeker is to work for himself or herself instead of working for someone else. In the American marketplace, the entrepreneur has been the source of most available jobs. Looking at economic history, the entrepreneur has also been responsible for the expansion of developing a stable and growing economic base. Being an entrepreneur comes with risk and uncertainty, but it can also bring personal and economic rewards. Birds offer many good examples for the fledgling entrepreneur.

But first, to be a successful entrepreneur or job seeker requires specific traits:

- Having a vision and the passion needed to bring that vision into reality
- Having the self-discipline necessary to build a solid foundation, a critical aspect to making a vision come true
- Having the ability to define the steps needed to achieve goals
- Being open to exploring a variety of options in the process of creating what you want
- Having the ability to find a way around the obstacles to keep the business going
- Having the willingness to keep on learning

- Having the ability to communicate ideas effectively and to inspire others to join you in your vision

Our first example of a good set of skills comes from the ostrich. Aspiring entrepreneurs can learn good skills from ostriches. Contrary to popular myth, ostriches do not bury their heads in sand when danger threatens. They hunker down and lie low along the sand while they assess the situation. They know that sometimes it is better to wait for more information before acting. Likewise, entrepreneurs and job seekers with this skill know when it is time to act and when it is better to wait.

Ostriches may not fly, but they can sprint up to 40 miles per hour, and they have the endurance to run long distances up to 30 miles per hour. Entrepreneurs and job seekers need to be able to move swiftly to seize opportunities when they arise and have enough persistence to keep going. The marketplace changes rapidly, and the successful person must adapt accordingly, altering strategies to match the marketplace.

Eagles soar high above the ground; from 1,000 feet they can see a range of almost three square miles. In spite of their bird's-eye view that gives them the overall picture of what is going on, they still see details as small as an individual rabbit. The successful entrepreneur is able to emulate the eagle, being aware of overall trends that can affect the business as well as keeping an eye on the smallest details of the business operation.

A small detail that is absolutely vital to a successful business is having a stable foundation. Most new business owners do not realize the amount of back office work that is required to have a thriving business. Their goal is to make money. But without the foundation of back office functions, they will never know if they are making money or not, nor will they have the information required to make good decisions to keep the business prosperous.

The most crucial of the back office functions is handling money. Like the eagle, the owner of a thriving business can read the financial statements for the big picture of the company's finances while still being able to focus on the details. Cash flow has been cited many times as the No. 1 reason why a business fails. Successful entrepreneurs understand where the money comes from and how to increase the amount of money coming into the business through marketing. They also know where the money is going and how to minimize the expenses of the business. It is important to focus on the small details that can derail the business in order to make changes quickly.

Entrepreneurs wear many different feathers in the course of doing business:

- The CEO, who makes the executive decisions about the company
- The CFO, who determines the budget and handles the finances
- The operations manager, who runs the day-to-day operations of the business
- The marketing director, who researches the marketplace to know what products or services are in demand and decides how to fulfill those demands better than the competition does
- The sales manager, who devises strategies to get the products or services in front of the target market and tracks the results
- The head of research and development

Ultimately, entrepreneurs must determine what is a good return on the investment of time and money. From all of this analysis, they will be able to determine what works to bring in the income or what strategies waste their resources.

Finally, wise entrepreneurs can learn from African Grey Parrots. These birds work together to accomplish a desired goal, using individual skills and strengths to benefit both the individual and the group. Owners of thriving businesses know that their business could not be as successful without the help of other people. Good entrepreneurs know their personal strengths and weaknesses. They know when to enlist assistance from other people in performing all of the necessary functions. They understand the value of their time and hire others to handle the aspects of the business that they do not have the skills or the time to handle themselves.

Entrepreneurs can choose to hire employees to take care of certain aspects of the business, or they can engage the services of other professionals. Some of the other birds in the business forest are:

- An insurance agent who knows what kind of liabilities the entrepreneur has and provides policies to cover those liabilities
- A bookkeeper or accountant who can track the details of the business' money and keep the owner informed
- A business attorney who can advise on legal matters for the business

- A CPA (certified public accountant) to handle the taxes
- Others such as Web designers, graphic artists, a payroll service provider, marketing specialists, or a business coach

Given the ultimate potential and benefits, the option of exploring entrepreneurial opportunities should be a consideration for every job market participant. Even if the job seeker realizes that being an entrepreneur is not the right path for her or him, each of the lessons from ostriches, eagles, and African Grey Parrots can also be applied to employees. Being able to move quickly and adapt successfully to current situations as an ostrich makes the job seeker more desirable to a potential employer. The eagle's ability to see the big picture without losing track of the details is extremely valuable to employers. Very few people have this skill. Working in cooperation with others as African Grey Parrots do is vital to the corporate culture of teamwork. Staying passionate, focused, and disciplined is critical for anyone in today's job market. Whether you are working for yourself, owning and running a business, or working for others, applying lessons from the aviary will make you more successful in whatever endeavor you choose.

Bio

k d Marlee is the pen name of two writers who live in the Pacific Northwest. They met in 2003 and began collaborating in 2006. Their interests are nature, writing, music, poetry, spirituality, and reading. They enjoy the playful connections with their animal companions and have a commitment to lifelong learning. See more of their writing at http://www.catalystforcreativeliving.com.

264

66

13 Essential Tips for Landing a Job on LinkedIn

Lewis Howes

I hear countless stories every week from people who land amazing full-time positions at great companies thanks to engagement on LinkedIn. Although there are a number of approaches you can take when hunting for the right job, start with these 13 important tips for using LinkedIn effectively.

1. Complete Your Profile 100 percent

If someone is thinking about hiring you for a position, he or she is going run a Google Search for your first and last name. For many, a LinkedIn profile will rank in the top five results. This gives you a certain level of control in showcasing your best talents with your profile. Make sure your profile is 100 percent complete, and position yourself as an expert in your niche. A profile that is only 55 percent complete, without recommendations and an updated work history, may not make a solid first impression when people find you through a search.

2. Add a Compelling Headline

Your headline is the first thing potential employers and hiring managers will see after your name. First impressions are an important aspect of the interview process, and this holds true for your LinkedIn profile as well. Be clear and to the point with your headline. Try to tell people who you are, what you do, and how you can help them in as few words as possible. This simple step will help you stand out from many other LinkedIn profiles.

3. Add All Past and Current Work Positions

It's important to include where you have worked in the past and where you are currently working. Obviously, the more work experience you can list, the better. You never know which position will earn you the respect of the hiring manager and give you the edge you need to land the job. There's always a chance the hiring manager has worked at one of your previous companies or has hired other professionals from that company. Situations like this may help you get the job security you are seeking.

4. Give and Receive Recommendations

On your traditional résumé, you are supposed to have a limited number of recommendations. However, on your LinkedIn profile, the more people who can vouch for you, the better. If you only have two recommendations on LinkedIn, most people won't take your profile seriously. It's unfortunate because there are a number of qualified and experienced professionals who aren't active on the network. This can hurt their reputation. Remember, in the online world, perception is reality. If people believe that no one will recommend you because there are no visible signs of approval displayed on your profile, why would they want to hire you?

The best way to receive recommendations is to give them first. The more you give on LinkedIn, the more you will receive. Take some time to write a few recommendations for those you know, like, and trust, and a majority of them will write you one in return.

5. Connect with Everyone

There are some on LinkedIn who believe you should only connect with a small percentage of professionals you know and trust. Others say (including myself) you should connect with everyone, even if you vaguely know them. When looking for a job, you never know who will be able to recommend you or who is looking for someone to fill a position where you would be a perfect fit.

When connecting with others, make sure you *always* send a personalized message. This doesn't have to be an essay, but make sure you mention why you are connecting or how you know one another. Also ask if there is anything you can do to assist them. By offering your services to help, this breaks down any initial barriers and gives others another reason why they should hire you.

6. Be Concise in Your Message

When you communicate through your LinkedIn profile, structure it in a way that will help people clearly understand you and what you are after. There are three main components:

1. *Provide a preview so people know what comes next.* In your headline, give them the intro to who you are and what you are all about.
2. *Give them the facts.* Let people know who you are by injecting your personality into your work experiences, your summary, your specialties, and in how you help people.
3. *Summarize and reinforce your message.* Finish up strong by adding in your honors, awards, personal Web sites, and case studies. Provide a call to action on how to connect with you and ways to follow up if they want to learn more.

7. Stay Active

I believe half the battle of finding a job is simply letting others know you are alive. There are so many résumés being submitted to open positions that it can be tough to break through sometimes. Luckily, LinkedIn works in your favor if you are active and constantly engaged within the community.

Each time you take action on LinkedIn, it shows up on the home page of everyone you are connected to. The more people who see your picture, read your name, and check out the compelling content you are delivering, the more likely they are to think of you when a position opens up. Stay active, and the opportunities will be much more abundant than if you don't participate at all.

8. Join Niche Groups

Groups are a great way to find a position because they have built-in job boards with new jobs being added on a regular basis. Some groups have tens of thousands of decision makers within them. As a member, you are able to send a message to almost every person without having to upgrade to a premium account. LinkedIn also has a great advanced search function, and once you find who you want to connect with, you can often message them directly through mutual groups without actually needing to be connected.

9. Create a Group

Being a group owner has many advantages. It allows you to send messages once per week to all the members, and you are perceived more as a decision maker and thought leader. Start attracting potential employers as opposed to seeking them out all of the time.

10. Add Your Honors and Awards

Including honors and awards is just another way to increase your value to potential hiring managers. Employers want to hire winners and those who know how to excel. Be sure to show them what you are made of, and post everything relevant to your success in your past work history.

11. Answer Questions

This is a great way for job seekers to showcase their talents and expertise and stand out from the crowd. It's also valuable to entrepreneurs and business owners for gathering leads. Add the Answers widget on the right-hand side of your LinkedIn home page with the industry topic you know the most about. When you see a question pop up that you can answer, make sure you give your two cents and provide as much information and value in your answers as possible. The more you give to and serve others, the more job opportunities will come your way.

12. Import Your Blog and Twitter Feeds

There are a number of ways to beef up your LinkedIn profile and make its content more compelling. Adding your blog and Twitter account is a good first step. Simply connect with your Twitter profile and check the box to make sure your tweets are syndicated to LinkedIn. This will save time and make it look like you are more active on LinkedIn as well. Adding your blog to your LinkedIn profile is a no-brainer. This not only drives organic traffic back to your site but showcases your regular activities and expertise.

13. Connect Others

I'm a big fan of connecting people. Whenever I see someone with a certain career need, I try to think of the right people I can introduce them to. I want to create a mutually beneficial gain for each party. The more I do this, the more career opportunities come my way. When you help two people without asking for anything in return, you leave a lasting impression on all involved. This will help amplify your own job prospects, as people will be more likely to help you achieve your goals in the future.

Don't get discouraged if you don't immediately see results. Effectively building your LinkedIn presence and online network won't happen overnight. Remember these tips, and start to actively engage. Take action and be consistent, and you'll soon be exploring a wealth of new professional networking opportunities.

Bio

Lewis Howes is a former professional athlete, world record holder in football, and author of the LinkedIn book *LinkedWorking*. He is the founder of the Sports Executives Association and the popular sports and social media blog SportsNetworker at http://www.SportsNetworker.com.

67

Media Exposure

Create Celebrity For Your Career With
Local TV, News & Talkshow Interviews

Clint Arthur

You could and should be on ABC, NBC, CBS, or FOX news next week. Media exposure is a great way to establish yourself as an expert in your field.

Before I appeared on TV the first time, I remember thinking to myself, "Why would anybody want to put *me* on the news? I'm an unknown middle-aged guy. I'm not a celebrity, not a movie star, not a politician; I have no TV experience. My book is self-published. Why would any producer want *me*?"

But money is an amazing thing. I agreed to pay a publicist $1500 for every local TV interview she got me, and a week later I received this email: "Congratulations! Just booked you on ABC Phoenix TV Friday, January 29, 2010."

And after that one, three more followed in short order. I ended up paying that publicist $6000 for my first four interviews. She was thrilled. I turned out to be pretty horrible on all four shows. Didn't even budge the needle for my book on Amazon.

After posting the fourth video clip on YouTube, I was faced with a tough decision. As a businessman, I had a hard time rationalizing an ROI of zero, but I knew that becoming great at TV interviews was important to my career as a writer. So I decided to do the only thing that made sense: I learned how to book myself on local TV shows.

It took months of trial and error, but I finally broke the code. Since then, I've booked myself on 55 interviews in cities all across America, including New York, Las Vegas, New Orleans, San Diego, Albuquerque, Boston, Houston, Dallas, San Francisco, Chicago, and Los Angeles. I 've made it to national television seven times.

Once I knew what I was doing, it got so easy that I started teaching my friends and business associates my tricks and secrets. And now my students have booked themselves in Connecticut, Virginia, Memphis, Atlanta, Arkansans, St. Louis, Phoenix, Las Vegas, Los Angeles, and New York!

Turns out, it's *better* to book yourself on local TV shows than to hire a publicist on many levels:

- Booking yourself is free. All it takes is time and phone calls. We call this "smiling and dialing." You can do it yourself, or you can have an assistant or secretary do it for you.
- Booking yourself gives you the opportunity to "audition" for a producer right there on the phone, and using this form of instant audition often gets you booked on the spot.
- Booking yourself allows you to respond and modify your itch to meet a producer's needs. Two of my students are specialists at teaching people how to make toasts. When a Las Vegas producer didn't have time in her schedule before New Year's Eve, they switched gears on the fly, modified their pitch to work for early January, and got booked for *8 News NOW* in Las Vegas on January 2, 2011.
- It's better to book yourself because you actually care about *your* career, as opposed to publicists who only care about *their* careers. You don't have to be Wise King Solomon to know that nobody really cares about anyone besides himself or herself.
- When you book yourself, if producers say no, at least you really know that they are saying no. When my publicist told me, "*Good Morning America* isn't interested in you," I always wondered if *Good Morning America* had ever actually heard about me.
- When you book yourself, you get to maintain total control over your relationship with the producers. Great relationships with producers have resulted in my eight appearances on FOX5 San Diego, repeat appearances three times on stations in Las Vegas, four times in Houston, and twice in both Chicago and Boston.

- You may have more than one topic or area of expertise. So if a producer says no to one pitch, you can instantly switch to another pitch while you've got the producer on the phone. You can make a second pitch for yourself, but a publicist will probably pitch a different client.
- Local TV producers will actually book you off a voicemail message. I got booked on ABC 7 Chicago my first time like that.
- Local TV producers will actually book you off an email. Once you have the right media assets properly displayed on your Web site, you can get booked in major markets simply by sending out a segment proposal in an email. In the last two weeks, I've appeared in Dallas (No. 5 Neilsen Market) and Los Angeles (No. 2 Neilsen Market) off emails that I sent to producers who had never even spoken to me before meeting me in their studios.

When I originally started booking myself on TV interviews, I was intimidated and shy about pitching. After all, *who was I to be calling up these producers?* And wasn't it egotistical of me to pitch myself? I had a lot of insecurities, but as the number of interviews increased, I've come to realize this is perfectly acceptable.

Along the way, I've met other authors who also book themselves. Stephanie Ashcroft has done more than 1,000 local TV news interviews and credits this publicity with helping to make her book, *101 Things to Do with Cake Mix*, a *New York Times* bestseller.

Since releasing my New TV Power training program, I've taught hundreds of students how to start working their way up the ladder of local TV shows, and it has been extremely rewarding to watch them flourish on mass media.

Veronica Grey started New TV Power on October 26, 2011, and has done 10 interviews to promote all three of her books and her independent movie since taking the course! I'm so proud to share that she's made it all the way to the No. 1 market in America, appearing on ABC NYC with a pitch I created for her: "Will Your Cellphone Make You the Next Spielberg?"

If you're an entrepreneur, author, speaker, coach, seminar leader, filmmaker, or anyone with a message who needs to be shared with the world, local TV news is a wonderful forum to get the word out. It's also a great way to hone your craft of being a great television interviewee, so that when the big day comes and *Good Morning America* calls you, you won't suck!

You can promote any book or product on TV, and if you don't have a product, you can use TV news interviews to position yourself as an expert. My student Alan Ladd, of the Web site Interview the Best, doesn't have a book to back up his credentials. Nevertheless, he has appeared on FOX 11 Los Angeles three times as an expert on how to get a job. Now he's an expert because *FOX 11 News* says he is.

Booking yourself on local TV interviews is a wide-open playing field. The producers need you to fill time on their air. As long as you know how to give them what they need and how they want it, they'll be happy to let you use their shows to position yourself as an expert, build your platform, and promote your products/services.

Instead of asking yourself, "Who am I to want to be on TV?"; a much better question is really, "What am I waiting for?"

Bio

Clint Arthur produces the WORLDS GREATEST MEDIA TRAINING event *"Celebrity Launch Pad"*, and has used his New TV Power system to publicize his books *What They Teach You at the Wharton Business School*, *The Last Year of Your Life*, *The Income Doubler*, and *Daddy Loves You* on TV shows across America, and has been a featured speaker on the topic of local TV interviews at The National Publicity Summit, Author 101 University, and Steve Harrison's Quantum Leap program. For more information on how you can use local TV to become a celebrity in the eyes of your target market or clients, go to http://www.instantlocalcelebrity.com.

68

MOTIVATION

Staying Motivated in the Job Market

❦

Josephine Harewood

Staying motivated in the job market can be challenging and depressing if you do not stay focus on what must be done to achieve your ideal job. Let's look at some areas that you can focus on to stay motivated.

Your Attitude Toward Work

Take some time to evaluate your attitude toward work. Whether you are unemployed or looking to change careers, work is a service you provide in exchange for an agreed payment. In providing this service, you have to be able to use your skills and talents to solve a problem for some company or some client. This service you provide is not merely for financial rewards; rather, it is creating a life for yourself. In creating this life, be aware of what you are thinking. What kind of job are you looking for? Is this your true purpose? If you get this job, how will you feel? Will you be satisfied?

Start with a Plan

Having a plan will keep you motivated and focused. It keeps the adrenaline flowing to achieve your goal of that dream job. Develop a detailed plan with small call-to-action steps to get your desired job. Review and work on this plan daily. Call-to-action steps make your plan easier to handle.

Figuring Your Ideal Job

Sometimes you may want to change jobs but may be unsure of your career path. It can be helpful to take some time and be quiet. Just still your thoughts, and ask your creator to provide direction so that your ideal job can be revealed to you and that you are given the skills, talents, courage, and wisdom to do this job well. Some people use a life coach to help them discover their path. You can also create your ideal job by visualizing yourself in that job.

Start Fresh and Use Affirmations

Being on the job market is an opportunity to start fresh. You can start each day by being grateful and thanking the universe for the new opportunities that are being sent your way, the new doors that are being opened, and the people who are coming to help you. Affirm daily, "I now have a wonderful job with wonderful pay." This particular affirmation I have found to be very helpful. It has opened doors where previously I felt nothing was available. You can also affirm, "I am in the right job with the right people; I now have my ideal job." You have to believe that you have your ideal job.

Know That You Are Worthy

When you are looking for a job or changing your career, know that you are worthy of getting a job. You should not become depressed or let negativity step in because your last supervisor or boss said that you needed improvement in certain areas. Use all negative feedback opportunities for advancement. Always ask yourself what you do well and what your strong points are. Good sales representatives never focus on what went wrong. They focus on what went well and how to improve further. Do the same.

Look at your previous job. We all have been given skills and talents to utilize. If you believe you are lacking in some skill, now may be the time to acquire those skills. You can be as good as anyone else if you choose to be. The only difference between you and the expert in your field is your thoughts and actions. Are you focused on what job you want to be in? Are you taking action to realize that ideal job?

Reward Yourself

When you accomplish those call-to-action steps in your plan, be sure to reward yourself to avoid frustration. Reward yourself for enrolling in a course to acquire additional skills. Reward yourself for taking that first step by meeting with a life coach to discover your true purpose. Reward yourself for revamping your résumé. Your reward can range from a scoop of dark chocolate ice cream to a movie.

You Can Turn Things Around

You have the power to change things around by your thoughts and words, so engage in positive, constructive thoughts and words. Always use positive words when you say I am: "I am worthy." "I am full of life." "I am good at what I do." You are the only one who can turn things around for you.

Taking Care of You

Dress and walk with confidence and a winning attitude, and take care of your health. You are not going to be any good to any company if you are not healthy. Indulge in foods that keep your spirits up and your mind focused. Eat foods such as dark chocolate, coldwater fish (salmon, sardines), and organic whole grains. Learn to relax your mind and body. Take up yoga or practice meditation.

Stay Close to Friends Who Can Support You

Stay close to friends or connections who support your efforts and who are knowledgeable about your field. Negative people will encourage you to worry and start focusing on the "what-ifs" The "what-ifs" can be very depressing. Your attitude should be one of positivity and faith. Know that by having faith in yourself and your creator, you can accomplish anything.

Review

- Change your attitude about work.

- Develop a written plan.
- Break your plan down into small call-to-action steps.
- Work on your plan daily.
- Figure out your ideal job. Meditate or get help from a life coach.
- Visualize yourself doing your ideal job.
- Use affirmations. A good one is, "I now have a wonderful job with wonderful pay."
- Know that you are worthy of getting your ideal job, and use negative feedback as opportunities for advancement.
- Focus on your strong points or the things you do well.
- Reward yourself.
- You alone can turn things around. Engage in positive and uplifting thoughts.
- Eat foods to keep your mind and body healthy.
- Practice relaxation.
- Keep company with positive and supportive friends and associates.
- Have faith in yourself, and know that you can accomplish whatever job you set your mind on.

From now on, see yourself as the expert in your field, full of confidence and wisdom and solving problems for other people. See yourself excelling in your field. You alone can do whatever you are called to do.

Bio

Josephine Harewood is an experienced business operations consultant and life coach. Using her experiences and skills, she helps supervisors, managers, high-stressed professionals, and owners of small and medium-sized businesses find solutions to both their personal and business problems. Her background includes operations management; policy development; human resource management; life coaching; and social media marketing. She provides weekly motivational and health tips via her Web site, http://joseylifeline.com. She can be contacted at joseylifeline@gmail.com.

69

Using Music in Job Search? Of Course!

Herky Cutler

When it comes to job search, it seems that the emphasis is often placed upon things such as résumés, cover letters, interview skills, tapping the hidden job market, using social media, and so on. Maybe rightly so. After all, if an individual is looking for work, or deciding upon changing careers, these activities would be necessary and apropos.

Job search in itself implies that one is ready for work. So what does work readiness really mean? For me, it means two things. One relates to being able to work, physically and emotionally fit to handle a job. Not necessarily a full-time job or a high stress job, but some kind of job.

The other aspect of being ready for work has to do with self-awareness, or self-exploration. What do we truly know about ourselves? What do we value? What are our interests? What are our skills? What is our passion? Without knowing as much as we can about ourselves, how can we determine if the jobs we are searching for are good fits for us? I believe that career consultants, coaches, counselors make a critical mistake when they pay only little, or no, attention to this aspect of job search.

One may ask then, is it important to find a good fit from the get-go? Arguments suggest that if we just keep trying different things, different jobs, we will eventually find the right one. Maybe one of our goals in life should be to find meaningful work that fits our personality and, therefore, do whatever we can to get to know ourselves better.

If we don't pay more attention to the self-exploration aspect of job search, the trend of the majority of people feeling disengaged from their work will continue. According to a Gallup Poll conducted in 2011, 71 percent of American workers were feeling either "not engaged" or "actively disengaged" from their work.

There is much data and speculation about why people are unhappy with their work. I question if there is any connection between how we make decisions about the type of work we do and the degree to which we pay attention to the self-exploration aspect of job search.

This is not to say, however, that the self-exploration aspect around job search is being ignored entirely. I realize that there is a myriad of assessment tools to help individuals figure out who they are, and these tools are being used. The question is: How reliable are these tools when it comes to finding out what our values, interests, and passion are?

There are formal and informal career assessment tools that help people become more aware of their values, interests, and passions. Formal assessments include such tools as the Myers-Briggs Type Indicator (MBTI) and the Strong Interest Inventory. These tools are scientific in nature in that the results are geared to how a user responds on that particular day at that particular time. A computer program tabulates the user's responses and formulates them into personal attributes, preferred learning styles, and personal interests and even yields occupational choices that the computer believes the user would be good at based on his or her answers. The program then becomes the "expert" in terms of identifying things about the user's personality and occupational fit.

Many of these tools are available, and they come in many forms. In this chapter, I focus on how to use music as an informal assessment tool to "tune" into one's values, interests, and passion.

Why music to help articulate our interests, skills, and passion? We all use music for one reason or another—to relax, to change our mood, to motivate us, to feel something. Music is universal and found in every culture. It is known to have a soothing effect on the spirit and to stimulate intellectual development. Studies have shown that music can increase mathematical ability, reading comprehension, and reasoning skills. So why not extend its use to the job-search process by taking a much closer look at the music we listen to?

Another key way that we use music, especially when we're younger, is to help us create an identity. If you ask a group of people, for example hard core rock and roll music fans, what the attributes of people are who listen to rock music, you will get a comprehensive list of personal characteristics. In workshops where I have facilitated this exercise, words such as *rebel*, *thinking outside the box*, *independent*, *risk takers*, and *free thinkers* have emerged. These are identity descriptors, things that people value.

I have developed a methodology to help individuals discover their values, interests, and passion from the music that they listen to. Here's how the process works. An individual shares a song that moves her or him, a song that has an emotional impact on the individual and not one that she or he just appreciates for the beat or because the listener likes the band. We listen to the song and look at the lyrics. Then we have a discussion around why and how this song moves the listener. This reveals much about the person's personality, values, interests, and passion.

Here is a series of questions that will help the individual dig deeper to find out more about himself or herself:

* Why did you choose this particular song?
* What is it about the melody that appeals to you?
* What do you think the song is about?
* What themes do you think are in this song (e.g., love, good vs. evil, political protest, honesty)?
* Which of these themes is the most important to you?
* What does that theme mean to you?
* What about the next theme?
* What about the next theme (and so on)?
* What does this song tell you about *your* personal interests, values, and passion?
* Did you learn anything about yourself that you didn't already know? If so, what?

I recommend that individuals write out the answers to these questions. Once that has been completed, I suggest going through the answers and creating a list of the things that can be considered as a value, an interest, or a passion. Repeating this process with two or three songs will undoubtedly expand the list, in addition to showing patterns where certain themes will emerge. This list is the very essence of who that individual is.

Now, unlike a formal assessment that might match this list of interests, values, and passion to occupational choices, I cannot make that connection, nor do I wish to. Occupations-based career development or job search has some inherent flaws. First, there isn't any tool that I'm aware of that lists every known occupation in the world. Second, there isn't any tool that I'm aware of that can predict all the new occupations that are emerging at an alarming rate due to technological advances. So I can't say to an individual that based on his or her list, he or she would make a good _____.

What I can say is to take that list, and whenever that individual is thinking about doing a certain type of job, match what the job requires to the list. If there is not a good fit, the chances are great that the individual will end up as one of those unhappy-in-work statistics mentioned earlier.

Music is already a huge part of our lives, and whether we realize it on a conscious level or not, the types of music we listen to that move us emotionally also hold the key to who we really are.

Bio

Herky Cutler is an organizational consultant, speaker, trainer, and facilitator who has spent the last 15+ years developing innovative programs, curriculum, and resources to help individuals and organizations align with who they truly are. His book *Using Music as a Career Development Tool,* for example, has given career practitioners another way, besides formal career interest inventories, to "tune" into people's interests, values, and passion. In the workplace, Herky is a master at helping organizations identify and remove barriers that hinder maximum efficiency, as well as building cohesive, multigenerational teams. You can reach him at (403) 627-5044; at herkycutler@gmail.com; or through his Web site, http://herkycutler.com.

70

The Truth About Passion and the Truth About Work

❧〜❧

Genevieve de Lacaze

The following article is extracted from and strongly based on the book *Passion Pays: How to Make a Living from Your Passions... and Change the World Too.*

What Passion Is

Describing your passion and describing your career or your job are completely different things. Dictionaries commonly define *passion* as "a very intense feeling of love or anger." When it comes to our job, career, or what we do for a living, yes, our passion may be borne out of what we love or out of what makes us angry in the world. However, in the latter case, we would translate that negative energy into a positive, solution-oriented engagement. Our focus would shift from what we hate to see to the change we would love to create. Here is my own definition of passion, which forms the basis of the Passion Pays journey.

Passion is "the heart-rooted energy fuelling the desire to express your self with pure intent through the joyful creation of value in service to the world."

Imagine your passion is the energy making up a tree (see Figure 1). Just like a tree, your passion is deeply rooted and connected to universal energy, the

282

life force through everyone and everything. Just like a tree, your passion has an underground, unseen inner world and an aboveground, manifested outer world. Both worlds are intimately interconnected. In fact, the two make one. So, just as there is no tree without roots, there is no passion without deep desire. Figure 1 depicts how this universal energy flows from your (inner) self to the (outer) world (low to high) and how it can be translated (left to right).

What Passion Is Not

The term *passion*, whose original meaning—now obsolete—was "suffering," can still refer to negative emotions and behaviors. However:

Passion isn't superficial. Passion isn't to be confused with frivolous bursts of enthusiasm. Some people seem to change "passions" more often than they change pants, with every new ephemeral subject of attention always even hotter than the one before. Such people aren't talking about passion; they probably just need new pants.

Passion isn't overpowering. Although passion is a powerful energy, it has no agenda to crush, control, or cause any harm. Admittedly, there are still lessons to be learned, even in the worst passionate behaviors.

Passion isn't irrational. Although operating beyond reason, passion doesn't operate without reason. From your inner self, the energy that is passion translates in the outer world in a structured way that requires emotional intelligence and wise execution.

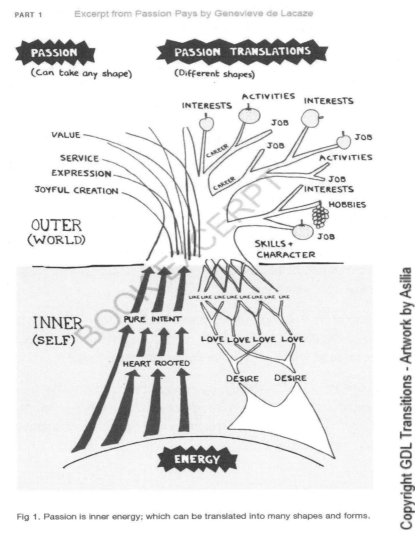

Fig 1. Passion is inner energy; which can be translated into many shapes and forms.

Work Expectations Gone Mad

You want to be happy at work? "Get real" is a comment you are likely to have spit back at you if you dare say this out loud. Or maybe, after you graduated in a subject you didn't particularly care for, your parents told you to now just "get a job." But not any job. A proper job. Of course, "proper" being defined by the rules of the masses of our current world. A proper job is one that is common, standard, low risk, ennui prone but most of all secure. I'm sure you can relate to this. So can I.

Work has been considered as merely a way to make money, "the necessary evil," not a way to be productive, creative—even less so—to be happy. As long as work is seen as the necessity to survive, work will be subject to mentalities and individualistic behaviors of survival, which breed on fear. That's why the road most traveled is to seek security at all costs. Security is the No. 1 priority, and to get it we just have to pay the price. I now have two grounds for objection:

1. The illusion of security: Following the recent recessions, it isn't a surprise to anyone that job security, as we fearfully seek it, is nothing but an illusion. There is no guarantee of eternity. As much as useless, precarious positions are often created, worthwhile and long-standing occupations are often terminated. Is it fun? No. Does it make any sense? Not even close. Has the world gone crazy? There's pertinent evidence, that's for sure. But it happens, nevertheless, with or without recession. We must come to terms with the fact that in this current system, everyone is expendable. This is not necessarily bad news.

2. The invaluable price to pay for security: The other problem, which we are now facing in our human evolution, is that of the countereffects of seeking security blindly and fearfully. Countless studies have been done about stress, anxiety, and depression at work. In Japan and China, the problem goes as far as death with their official words for "death by overwork"—*karoshi* and *guolaosi,* respectively.

This attitude of selling yourself for money is like being a prostitute to money. Like it or not, it's a fair point. When what we do to make a living prevents us from enjoying life fully and peacefully, isn't it time to wonder what the point actually is? Do you believe a change is possible for you? Do you actually care? As you ponder these questions, pay attention to your own feelings and to your own thinking. This will determine whether or not you give yourself a chance to have your passion pay.

Work Expectations: From Madness to Happiness

Whether you are living your passion or not, jobs and tasks have to be done for our society to function. Can you see the beauty of the bigger picture? Can you see how you fit into the whole?

Work is also a source of personal worth, creative expression, family stability, peace in the community, economic growth, and opportunities for enterprise development. So passion is an expression of who you are, not what you do, but passion is putting who you are in what you do.

Considering that work consumes so much of our time, it is important to realize that our working life now adds up to be life itself. We all deserve to be happy in life, so we all deserve to be happy at work. Many people are plagued with a sense of uselessness and waste of potential. The times that we are currently facing do make the case for happiness: global crises that don't spare anyone anywhere wake in us the desire for fulfillment and satisfaction as a life necessity, whereas in previous generations, they were luxury. Plus, in our information age, we do have the opportunities to use new avenues to translate our heart-rooted energy.

You may be feeling trapped under the illusion that you can't leave your unfulfilling job or that you can't afford to leave. It's all right to feel this way. Your immediate next step is small: nurture the sense that change is possible, with the help of experts as you can find throughout this book.

Bio

Genevieve de Lacaze is a writer, speaker, coach, and broadcaster who loves passionate conversations and ventures. She is the founder of GDL Transitions, an organization that supports people to make a living from their passion, and consults for organizations to reconcile mission with profits. She is the international head of CPD at the International Institute of Coaching (IIC), and she hosts the *Get Passionate* radio show. She writes articles and delivers talks, presentations, and workshops on many empowering subjects. She speaks French, English, Spanish, and German. But, really, just an ordinary girl, changing the world, one passion at a time.

71

Passionate Engagement: The Key to Competing in Today's Job Market

❧

Karen Tax

"One sees clearly only with the heart. What is essential is invisible to the eye." Antoine de Saint-Exupéry, *The Little Prince*

The results you have achieved may be the ticket that opens the door to your next career opportunity. But what lands the deal will be something less tangible and more essential: your passion for your work. Strong and compelling feelings and a sense of career purpose will set you apart from others, provide the energy needed for ongoing and sustainable success, and allow you to emotionally connect with potential colleagues—required for making a sale. Stories and concrete examples come easily when you passionately talk about your work; these are the behavioral examples and inspiration needed to convince others you can do the job.

However, continued economic woes have worn away at the hopes of many, and excitement about work has given way to overwhelm and burnout. The good news is that your ability to maintain energy and enthusiasm for your work can be a distinct competitive advantage!

Your heartfelt emotional connection with your work must be your guiding light in making career choices, whether you are just entering the workforce or you are a veteran with years of experience. The biggest threat to loving your work is fear, which may cause you to make career choices where you sell your soul. For example, you may make decisions based primarily on money, the need to please others, or in an effort to create certainty and safety. Fear-based career steps result in aversion to risk and settling for the status quo—the opposite of passionate engagement. I call this a "slippery slope to disengagement" that starts with saying, "I shouldn't care so much" or "I need to separate work from my personal feelings." Take several steps along this path and you end up feeling numb just to survive.

You are the only one who can control the level of passion you feel for your work. It is not useful to focus on your boss, your environment, or your industry as an excuse. You must take your power back from other people and circumstances and take a stand for being your best at work. You can start by being honest with yourself about how you feel and what you really want.

The IAM Essence Map is a tool you can use to make sure you love your work.

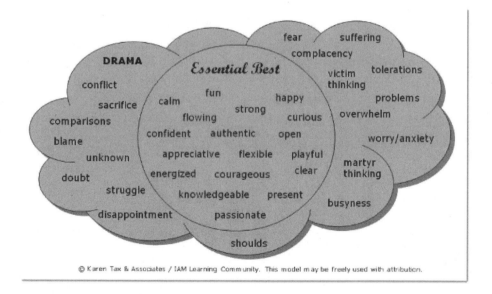

© Karen Tax & Associates / IAM Learning Community. This model may be freely used with attribution.

The words on the IAM Essence Map are the most common I've collected in using this tool with thousands of people.

The center of the map, your "Essential Best," is what it looks like and feels like when you are at your best. It is when you are shining brightly like the sun, energized, confident, and enjoying your work. "Drama" is what I affectionately call the challenges that get in the way of your being your best. It is like the dark gray skies that block the sun, when you feel doubt, worry, or confusion.

When you think about your school or work experiences, how much time do you spend being your essential best? How much time do you spend in drama? Be honest and assess. Is it 60 percent at your essential best and 40 percent in drama? Or is the opposite closer to the truth? How do you really feel about your work?

You need to do two things to sustain or reclaim your passion for work:

1. *Focus on your essential best.* Know your values, strengths, and motivations. Make sure you are aware of when you feel alive and passionate about your work. Make choices that increase the amount of time you feel this way!
2. *Understand drama.* You must face how you really feel and deal with it. Use the challenge of drama to uncork your emotions and tap into the energy of your passions. Use it to learn, heal, grow, and change.

"If we want to reclaim our emotional part of our lives and reignite our passion and purpose, we have to learn how to own and engage with our vulnerability and how to feel the emotions that come with it." —Brené Brown, *Daring Greatly*

It's ironic that the less you feel of negative emotions, the less you feel in general, including passion. You must be vulnerable to the full range of human experience, including feelings, if you are to access the most potent competitive edge there is: being fully alive.

From this perspective, drama is extremely useful. If you are not experiencing drama, you are not risking enough, and you are not discovering new depths of aliveness. Ignoring personal drama leads to problems in the workplace that can look like controlling, micromanagement, overwhelm, keeping busy to avoid feeling, and unethical behavior.

Learn how to focus and align with your essential best and understand and deal with drama, and you have the keys to passionate engagement at work, for yourself and others. Five career factors can guide this process.

1. *Soul alignment*: To what extent are you able to connect with your essential best energy and integrate it into your work and life activities?

2. *Fit*: How well do you align your essential best with your work tasks and work context, setting boundaries to maintain fit over time?
3. *Focus*: How well do you connect your authentic path with a direction that inspires you to overcome the difficulties of drama and meet the needs of others?
4. *Relevance*: How well do you align your essential best with a path of life-long learning while you turn change into opportunity, create impact, and generate results?
5. *Environment*: How well does your work environment support your functioning at your essential best?

To increase your passionate engagement with your work, assess yourself against these five career factors so you can have a realistic view of your situation. You will want to know where you are strongly aligned with your essential best and where you might have some drama to overcome, including obstacles such as feeling as though you have limited choices, difficult colleagues, or not enough time.

The fear eroding passionate engagement is caused by an old paradigm of work based on scarcity thinking and an imbalance of power. This old paradigm is not sustainable; a new paradigm based on authentic power and passion is emerging! Passion is accessed by balancing thinking and feeling, doing and being, and masculine and feminine energies. The five career factors anchor you in your passionate whole self so you can hold steady during the death throes of the old paradigm.

You deserve to love your work. You can be happy and fulfilled in your career by following the steps outlined here. Assess your situation by responding to the questions earlier or by taking the free IAM Career Alignment assessment at http://iamlearningcommunity.com to develop a clearer picture of what's going on. Once you have accurate data, you can adjust.

Passion, purpose, and your sense of being alive are essential in work. The person who brings balanced energy fully to her or his life is the person who will lead the way to the new paradigm of work *and* have the competitive advantage.

B<small>IO</small>

Karen is an Internet entrepreneur, corporate refugee, mentor coach, and strategy/change expert who guides people in aligning their soul, career path, and work environment. The shift from work that is a daily grind to a livelihood that nourishes your spirit is one of the most important you can make. It impacts your finances, your health, your family—every aspect of your life. Karen has developed a proven and simple approach she calls "the IAM Way." It maps out how you can be true to your authentic self, create healthy work situations, and have abundant wealth without sacrifice, overwhelm, burnout, or selling your soul. Check out Karen's free IAM Career Alignment assessment at http://iamlearningcommunity.com to get started.

72

PERSONAL/PROFESSIONAL BRAND

Your Personal Brand: Advantage or Achilles' Heel for Your Career?

❦

Lauren Still

Most people have never given a second thought to their personal or professional brand. Even if you're not aware of what your brand is, you *do have one*. If you're not managing your brand, it is being created by accident, by default, according to how you're perceived by those around you. How comfortable are you with that?

Do you trust your coworkers, your boss, even your friends to be able to describe you completely accurately? Do your career materials and online profiles clearly communicate your greatest strengths, your inherent talents, where you can be most effective and valuable? Are you known for the accomplishments and skills that will cause others to seek you out for your ideal job, opportunity, or promotion?

The risk involved when you allow your own brand to be created by default is that others may not view you the same way you perceive yourself and want to be seen. That disconnect affects your ability to reach your career goals. In the worst case scenario, if you have a negative or uninspired brand in the workplace, it is most likely an *Achilles' heel* in your career progression, preventing you from moving forward the way you wish to.

If, on the other hand, you realize the importance of taking your own image, brand, and what you're known for into your own hands, you have the ability to proactively shift what people think of you. It may take time and some effort, but you gain control over your image. You also gain a tremendous *advantage* over most of your colleagues and contemporaries, who are likely to be unaware of their own brand image and may be inconsistent, disconnected, or simply not showcasing their best strengths.

Managing your personal brand is critical throughout a career, not just when making a career or job transition. It is simply smart career management that can help you position yourself for a promotion, broaden your scope of influence, or stand out in a job search.

What Is a Personal/Professional Brand?

(I use the term *personal brand*, but you can interchange *professional brand* throughout.)

Ultimately, your brand must be an accurate reflection of who you are at your core, and when it is, the brand will be consistent whether or not you are in a work situation. Your personal brand is a *lasting impression about what you do and what it means* for others or the organization. It is *the essence of who you are and what you offer.*

A brand encompasses the features that identify a product or service (or a person) as distinct from others like it. A strong brand is an expectation, a confidence that you know what you're going to get. Consider some brands that you've probably heard of, and an image immediately comes to mind of what you can expect from that brand: Volvo, Apple, Walmart, Coca-Cola.

Just as with a product brand, your personal brand can have positive or negative connotations. For example, consider the personal brand of Oprah Winfrey compared to that of Charlie Sheen. Although both are famous and successful, which one has a brand that is an advantage, and which one has a brand that is an Achilles' heel?

Forget Your Experience; It's the Experience of You

Although your experience shapes who you are and the skills you bring to your career, don't mistake your experience for your brand. *Your brand is the*

293

experience others have of you. Their experience with you forms that expectation of what they will get from you in any given situation.

Consider also that the experience of something creates an emotion around it. When you think of someone you admire, it evokes positive emotions in you (inspiration, affinity, trust). However, when you think of someone you dislike intensely, negative emotions likely emerge (anger, frustration, suspicion). An advantageous brand evokes positive emotions and expectation of positive experiences. A brand that may be an Achilles' heel can bring up negative or conflicted emotions and an expectation of challenging experiences.

Managing Your Brand

Hopefully, by now, you have concluded that clarifying your brand and managing it proactively is an opportunity to manage your career positively and proactively in the direction you want it to go. The following techniques will help you get a grasp of your current and desired brand, and how to go about managing it effectively:

- *Do a personal brand audit.* Clarify what you believe your brand to be today, and verify it with people you trust to give you honest feedback.
- *Define your desired brand.* Based on your career vision and goals, is there a gap between your current brand and how you wish to be perceived? What does your brand need to reflect you going forward?
- *Make it real.* Your brand must be authentically you and reflect who you are at your core, what is meaningful to you, and your inherent talents. If you try to portray an image or brand that is not really you, your brand will be unconvincing or inconsistent; your credibility will suffer; and you will find the task of defining your brand harder, more stressful.
- *Consistently create the experience of your brand.* Align your decisions, actions, communications, and career strategies to create the expectation of your brand every time someone interacts with you.
- *Market your brand.* Your bio, online profiles, résumé, email tag line, public comments and posts, and anything else that markets you to the world should reflect your brand positively. You don't need to trumpet your skills from the rooftops, but remember that no one else is as invested in sharing your unique brand, skills, and potential as you are. Look for opportunities to (appropriately) make your brand known.

Complete, Consistent, and Credible

Your brand is everywhere. It is everything you do, say, and communicate. Once you've determined your positive brand message, every contact people have with you must consistently support that brand.

If your résumé presents you with a certain brand and skill set, but your LinkedIn profile reflects a different brand or experience that isn't consistent with your résumé, your brand will suffer. If you've branded yourself as a straight-arrow professional, but an online search turns up social profiles or posts that give the impression you'd fit right in at a wild frat party at the local university, you have lost credibility. Over time, a disconnected brand leads people to feel underappreciated, misunderstood, and uninspired.

Don't let your accidental brand drive your career success. Brand management = career management. It takes awareness, strategy, consistency, and work, but the benefits are many.

A strong and well-managed brand opens opportunities and positions for you as a great candidate for the right roles and promotions. An authentic brand also allows you to be yourself at work. When you play to your strengths and best attributes and showcase those consistently through your branding, you create a *career advantage* that feels genuine and meaningful and leads to greater success and enjoyment of work.

Bio

Lauren Still helps professionals increase their visibility, confidence, personal branding, and next-level skills to be more successful at work without sacrificing their values. She truly believes that work (even corporate work) can be fulfilling, meaningful, and fun when one is using one's inherent talents and a strategic plan. Lauren has been listed as one of 50 Personal Branding Experts to Work With, writes a career-management blog, has been published and been quoted as an expert in numerous articles on career advice topics (including in *Money* magazine and the *Wall Street Journal*), and is the creator of the Rock Your Role™ proprietary system for on-the-job success. Lauren holds an MBA from the University of Colorado's Executive Program and is a certified coach and a social and emotional intelligence coach. Her work experience spans communications, HR, consulting, employee engagement, and management, and has been gained in small businesses and large multinationals on several continents. She brings this breadth of experience and her style of practical, heart-centered advice to her coaching and consulting. You can contact her by phone at (303) 325-5765; by email at lauren@careerevolutiongroup.com; or at her Web site, http://www.careerevolutiongroup.com.

73

Personal Branding for Career Success

❧

Paige Arnof-Fenn

You do not need to be Oprah, Donald Trump, or LeBron James to start thinking of yourself as a brand. In my experience, the most successful job seekers create and, in fact, *become* brands. Their brands are based on the experience they promise and the values they live by and share.

On the job market, you have to find ways to stand out and be remembered. What will it take to make the recruiter or hiring manager call you back? Here are a few tips that, in my experience, will help you succeed in finding a job that is a great fit for you.

- *Be original.* What makes you unique or special? Is it your voice? Height? Eye color? Athletic ability? Fluency in foreign languages? An invention or patent? Whatever it is, use it to your advantage. Can you imagine Barbra Streisand with a different nose, Jay Leno with a new chin, or Cindy Crawford without her mole? Everyone remembers the original, but the copycats start blending together after a while, so differentiate yourself to stand out from the pack. Be remarkable and extraordinary to grab attention and get noticed. Good is not good enough. Where are you great? When you exploit what makes you unique, people will remember your authentic brand.

- *Be creative.* How do you want people to think, feel, act, or react after interacting with you versus another candidate? What are four words that come to mind when people describe you? Is that how you want to be

297

described? As George Washington Carver said, "When you can do the common things of life in an uncommon way, you will command the attention of the world."

- *Be honest.* Turns out that telling the truth about what you are and are not, what you can and can't do is very refreshing. Who would have thought that, in 2013, brutal honesty would be the killer application? Because many qualified candidates are on the market, companies tend to choose the people they like and trust most. Let your brand be known for speaking the truth. People don't always want to hear the truth, but they'll respect you for telling it, and they'll remember you for it.

- *Be relevant.* Brands aren't created in a vacuum. They require lots of attention, care, and feeding. The process of creating a brand for yourself isn't unlike what you'd do for a product or service —developing a mission, vision, unique positioning, and so on. You must define your brand, communicate it, and review it periodically so your brand stays current. Look at Madonna, circa 1985 (leather, hair, wild child) and today (yoga, family, spiritual). The branding basics still apply when the brand is you—having a core message, a brand promise, visual and verbal identification, and fully integrating all components. You'll need brand positioning, brand architecture, and a brand strategy to develop a promise that resonates clearly with employers.

- *Be consistent.* Develop a cohesive message, and live it every day. The repetition reinforces your key points so people will remember them. It takes time to build great brands—no one wins Olympic gold medals, Grammy awards, Oscars, or anything of importance overnight. These things require an investment of your time and energy. Everything communicates—your voicemail message, signature on your email, your email address—so every touch point is an opportunity to build trust in your brand. You might want to think twice about the pictures you post on social media sites or using partygirl@gmail as an address online. It might leave the wrong impression!

- *Be passionate.* If you remember nothing else, remember this suggestion—it makes up for any shortfalls mentioned earlier. Everyone loves to work with people who are passionate about what they do; it makes life much more fun and interesting. So build your brand around what you enjoy, and remember the words of John Ruskin: "When love and skill work together, expect a masterpiece."

I hope I've convinced you that successful job seekers do, in fact, start with great personal brands. Your brand is a compass that should provide a foundation to help you connect with potential employers. The goal is to find a job where you can bring your whole self to work every day so when you meet with a company and there is a strong fit between your personal brand, your core values, and the company's culture, you will have the key ingredients for career happiness and success.

Bio

Paige Arnof-Fenn is founder and CEO of Mavens & Moguls, a global marketing strategy consulting firm. She was formerly VP marketing at Zipcar & Inc.com (sold to Bertelsmann); SVP marketing and key member of IPO team at Launch Media (now Yahoo Music); and worked at Procter & Gamble, Coca-Cola, and the Department of the Treasury. She is the appointed director for Harvard Business School on the Harvard Alumni Association Board and chairs the Board of Trustees of the Sports Museum at the Boston Garden. She holds an undergraduate degree from Stanford and an MBA from Harvard Business School. She can be reached at info@mavensandmoguls.com.

74

Create Your Power Schedule for Success

~

Andrew Horton

My research and my personal experience have shown me that we operate best when we schedule time every day to carry out our VIPs (very important priorities)—those activities, when performed daily, that bring the most value to our experience.

Identifying the Right Priorities

Your Power Schedule can be effective only if you ensure that you first discover the right activities to include in it. Choosing the right activities depends 100 percent on what you want to achieve. Explore your vision and goals, and identify a few crucial daily activities, when performed daily, that will deliver the results you want. These are the crucial activities you must include in your Power Schedule. Once you have the right activities, all that is left to do is to schedule time every day to perform them.

Example: Say you work as a sales professional and you need to achieve your sales target for the year. Certain activities are crucial to your success. Crucial activities could include prospecting; visiting existing customers; researching your customers, prospects, and markets; completing your administrative tasks; and working on your personal and professional development. If you want to achieve your sales targets as a sales professional, you will need to include all five of these crucial elements into your Power Schedule.

Schedule Your VIPs

Most people remain trapped in average, not because they lack the talent or the ability to achieve greatness, but because they don't make time every day to carry out the crucial tasks needed to succeed. Commit to adding worthwhile items, crucial priority, goal-specific tasks to your schedule every day. Make time available to perform these tasks. Don't allow anything to get in the way of your actually doing them. The compounding of these activities, over time, will add up to remarkable results for you.

Creating Your Power Schedule

Having sufficient energy to successfully complete all your VIPs every day means that you need to be getting sufficient sleep and rest. So when creating your Power Schedule, use sleep and rest as your starting point.

I find it most effective to plan my upcoming week on Sunday evening. Your circumstances may dictate that you choose a different day. The first thing I put into my schedule is a minimum of twenty-four hours of uninterrupted rest time. For me, this time is from 12:00 on Saturday afternoon to 12:00 the following afternoon. During this time, I switch off completely, do not think about work, and just focus on resting and investing quality time with my family.

Secondly, I decide on a time when I am done for the day, every day. This is a time I schedule into my calendar every week to guide me to stop working and to switch off and rest. The time I choose for this is 8 p.m. every day. As soon as I get to 8 p.m., I do two things. First, I review my day, learning all the lessons my day had to offer, filing these away to use the next time I encounter a similar challenge or obstacle. Second, I check to see if there are any tasks that I had scheduled for that day that I didn't manage to get done. I then transfer these to my schedule for the next day during my planning session.

Once I have finished reviewing my day, which takes no longer than five minutes, I move into a quick-planning process, where I plan my day for tomorrow. This process is a quick review of my daily priorities and commitments for the next day, ensuring that I have time available to perform them. I also review my appointments and to-dos. This daily commitment to review and plan for the next day allows me to leave my day content, satisfied that everything is in place. This allows me to switch off, rest, and recover, ready to make the most of the next day.

The reviewing and planning process takes only about fifteen minutes every day. Yet it gives me a huge advantage in the form of a head start every morning. I also wake up every day with an organized schedule, with scheduled time to carry out my VIPs. I am in complete control of my day.

Schedule Time to Carry out VIPs Every Day

The next crucial element when creating your Power Schedule is to time every day to carry out your VIPs. We operate and live according to our circadian rhythms, which means we sleep when it's dark and work when it's light. According to these rhythms, our energy levels are at their highest first thing in the morning. So it makes the most sense to choose this time of day to perform the most important tasks for the day, namely your VIPs.

Another rhythm that affects your daily performance is the ultradian rhythm. This ninety-minute rhythm repeats throughout the day. You are not designed as a marathon runner, where you can keep slogging away relentlessly all day. Your body works best when you work at high intensity for about ninety minutes, followed by rest. When designing your Power Schedule, build these ninety-minute cycles into your plan.

Creating the Perfect Day

- Start creating your perfect day by planning the time you will go to sleep and the time you will wake up. Research shows that if you sleep fewer than seven hours a night, there is only a 1-in-80 chance you are getting enough sleep.
- Next, put your first ninety-minute segment into your day. This is the time to complete your VIPs. I refer to this time as meeting my future. Calling it something as important as a meeting with your future gives it the priority attention it needs every day and ensures that you never cancel or postpone it.
- After each ninety-minute segment, schedule time to rest. To operate optimally, you need to change your sprint rhythm to one in which you slow

down and relax. This allows you to rest and prepare for the next sprint during the next ninety-minute cycle. During these rest periods, you can do some light exercise, mediate, call a friend to discuss something unimportant, or anything to allow your mind time to rest and relax. This rest can be as short as five minutes but should be no longer than ten minutes.

- Working from the first ninety-minute segment and scheduled rest periods, build the rest of your day, in ninety-minute segments.
- Next, schedule breakfast, lunch, and dinner into your schedule. Schedule meal times to coincide with your ultradian rhythm.

The secret to making this Power Schedule work for you is to ensure that you have sufficient time available, every day, to perform all the tasks you identify as crucial to your success. As long as you make enough time available to perform these tasks, and you use this time effectively to carry them out, you will succeed at anything.

Bio

Andrew is an international expert inspirational speaker, successful entrepreneur, and expert in positive behavioral shift. He specializes in sales training. As a doctoral student, he is researching how a few small shifts in personal daily habits and the development of a success habit set can result in massive improvement to the outcomes a team will enjoy. His purpose is to empower exceptional people, winning teams, and authentic leaders, and to inspire them to shift their behavior, attitude, and philosophy, thereby encouraging sustainable and on-going success. Visit his Web site at http://www.andrewhorton.co.za, or contact him by email at Andrew@andrewhorton.co.za.

75

PROCRASTINATION

Need to Stop Procrastinating to Compete in Today's Job Market? Find out Which Type of Procrastinator You Are

❦

Sharon Melnick, PhD

Do you know what you should be doing to be world class in your position, in your business, in your job search? But you aren't doing it? If so, you're procrastinating, getting in your own way. Many of us have been there. Indeed, 70 percent of North Americans report procrastinating from time to time, and 20 percent of us are chronic procrastinators regularly and habitually putting important job-related tasks off for the utopian tomorrow.

If you haven't acted on an important task, project, or job-search strategy that will make you competitive in the job market, it's only for one reason (and it's not because you are lazy): you haven't identified the specific type (or types) of procrastinator you are and then been shown the right solution for your type.

After working with hundreds of businesspeople, I have identified 10 types of action blockers. You can see from reading the following list that there are different reasons that set you up to put things off. And the skills you need to become an action taker are accordingly different. (You can take the quiz to see what type of action blocker you are at http://www.sharonmelnick.com/actionquiz.)

10 Types of Procrastinators

1. *Avoider*: You don't feel like doing it; you think that tomorrow you'll be more motivated. You're great at making excuses why it's too complex, too boring, too____ (fill in the blank).

2. *Pressure seeker*: You are motivated only by last minute pressure such as a presentation or an interview; you stay up late and create a crisis for all around you.

3. *Spinner*: You are going in too many directions. You don't know how to decide what is most important in your role or specifically which kinds of roles would fit you best, so you can't get started. You move quickly from one project or idea onto the next shiny new penny or idea of the week.

4. *Protector*: You expend a lot of worry and hold yourself back to protect yourself from others' perceptions of you, particularly their disapproval: "What if I fail or others criticize? What will the other person think of me?"

5. *Perfectionist*: You keep redoing it to get all details right. For you, the work never gets to the point of good enough to send.

6. *Learner*: You are chronically in a state of information overload. You generally think you need more research to get started instead of getting started in draft form with what you have, and then learning just in time rather than wasting time scouring the Internet just in case you might someday need the information.

7. *Dreamer*: You have great ideas but are all talk, no action. You can't break down your vision into the first step to get started.

8. *Prioritizer*: You are good at putting efforts into short-term priorities of the moment but don't tend to other longer-term priorities. You might do currently important projects at work but neglect expense reports, strategic plans, health checkups, networking follow-ups, or garage cleaning.

9. *Distracted*: You tend to be disorganized, prone to distraction. You are a little ADD; you can't focus and think systematically.

10. *Starter*: It's easy for you get started, but you get distracted with new projects, and it's hard to maintain motivation. You don't know how to finish.

Most conventional wisdom offers generic advice to act such as start with the hardest task first thing in the morning. But if you are an avoider, you know you should get started, but you don't know how to motivate yourself or get yourself into the mental or physical energy state that gives you the willpower to get it done. If you are a perfectionist, you have already been working on the hardest task first thing in the morning and driving others crazy doing the details over and over again! That's why all the advice you've tried to follow may not have helped you make any more than small incremental changes, or why you may have started to make some changes but then fallen back to your old ways within days.

Knowing your type of action blocker will guide you to know the specific tweaks you need to make to become an action taker. For example, if you identify you are a pressure seeker, then you want to learn to create your own urgency, impose external deadlines, or create a start-by deadline instead of only a finish-by deadline. If you are an avoider, you want to know how to get yourself to feel like doing it (even when you don't), solve problems to overcome tasks being too complex or too boring, and figure out if there are other ways to get it done without your being the bottleneck. If you are a spinner, you want to learn how to figure out your priorities and discipline yourself to follow one project until it gives you results before you allow yourself to start another. If you are a perfectionist, then you want to develop objectivity so you can determine when you have done enough that your deliverable fulfills its intended purpose, learn to put out a first draft and test the results (or get feedback) rather than waste a lot of time redoing your work over and over, and become a better DJ of your own mental iPod so you can change your inner soundtrack from self-critical to self-confident. (Learn to do this with a free audio training at http://www.sharonmelnick.com/60kgift.)

Well-meaning friends and coaches can be cheerleaders for you by asking, "How many sales calls did you make this week?" But you can take charge of your own behavior once and for all if you know the missing piece: what type of action blocker you are (http://www.sharonmelnick.com/actionquiz). Imagine how much further along you will be when you do those tasks that will move the needle for you in your career. Get out of your own way so that you can become an action taker and a rock star in your career!

Bio

Sharon Melnick, PhD, is a business psychologist and stress resilience expert who helps talented businesspeople accelerate promotion into their next role while experiencing less stress. Her practical tools are informed by 10 years of research at Harvard Medical School and field tested by more than 7,000 training participants at organizations such as P&G, GE, Merck, Moody's, Bloomberg, Coldwell Banker, the American Management Association, Women Presidents Organization, Working Mother Media, and CEO clubs. She is the author of the recently released *Success under Stress: Powerful Tools for Staying Calm, Confident, and Productive When the Pressure's On.* Discover more at http://sharonmelnick.com.

76

RECESSION-PROOF YOUR CAREER

10 Steps to Recession-Proof Your Career

❦

William Arruda

Some experts say we're recovering from the recession; others say we could fall back into an economic downturn. Who is right? I don't know. What I do know is that you must be regularly building your brand to build a recession-proof career. Here are 10 steps.

Step 1: Unearth and Build Your Brand

During a challenging economic period, highly differentiated branding becomes even more important. To thrive, your company needs innovation. Innovation comes from creativity. Creativity derives from a diverse workforce of individuals. And when we talk about diversity in the world of personal branding, we are talking about each individual delivering an ingredient that is not available from anyone else. So unearthing and living your brand will give your company what it needs—making you an indispensable resource. Personal branding is the most effective way to clarify and communicate what makes you differentiated and valuable. It allows you to articulate why your company needs you. Unclear about your brand? Uncover it here: www.reachcc.com/360v5register (a complimentary tool from my company).

Step 2: Build Bridges

In a recession, you may have to cross them. Reach out to former managers, employees, and colleagues. Strengthen relationships with peers, customers, and business partners. Take a former boss or business partner to lunch. Build those bridges so they are solid, should you have to cross them. Schedule time in your daily agenda to build and cultivate your network. Are you a power networker? Find out with this quiz: www.reachcc.com/networkquiz.

Step 3: Know Your GQ (Google Quotient)

Whether you're looking for work or you want to be the best passive job candidate, you need a strong virtual brand. Today, a Google search is as standard as a reference check. If your online identity doesn't impress recruiters or hiring managers, you'll be eliminated from the short list. Virtual brands are not built overnight, so investing now will reap rewards in the future. To start, first understand where your brand stands on the Web with this complimentary tool: http://www.onlineidcalculator.com.

Step 4: Get out of Your Office

If those around you don't know who you are or what you do, management will think they don't need you when it is time to start preparing the layoff list. You must consistently make others aware of the value that you bring to your team or project. And you need to know what's going on beyond the project you are working on. Don't underestimate the value of networking with your peers, team, and colleagues in other departments. So visit the coffee machine or water cooler, go to the cafeteria for lunch, and connect with those around you. It's part of your job!

Step 5: Associate

Professional associations provide the greatest opportunity to demonstrate your value outside the company. If you find yourself looking for a new job or just want to do your job better, the connections you make at your local PMI chapter or AMA group will help. Belonging to fewer organizations and taking on a leadership position or volunteer role that enables you to get to know the entire membership is the best way to build your brand.

Step 6: Create Career Karma

Now is not the time for a "me, me, me" attitude (as if there is ever a time for total selfishness). Helping others recession-proof their careers is one of the greatest karma-building actions you can take. Remember, what goes around comes around. If you build great karma now, goodness will come back to you at some point when you truly need it. Pen these activities into your to-do list.

Step 7: Establish Metrics

Measure the value you bring to your employer. Whether it's increased revenue, reduced expenses, improved efficiency, increased sales leads, reduced attrition—find a way to quantify your contribution to your organization and to the company overall. And be sure your manager is abundantly aware of this. Don't wait until your performance review to start measuring the value you deliver!

Step 8: Refine Your Career Marketing Tools

The time to get your résumé, bio, and cover letters in order is at least six months before you hear you have been put on the layoff list. And to make sure yours stand out (from the stack of others touting similar credentials and experience), hire a professional résumé writer. It will be well worth your investment.

Step 9: Get Coached

Every great athlete has a coach; you should too. From helping you excel in your current position to enabling you to find the ideal next role, a career coach is critical to turning a good career into a stellar one. Invest in a career coach now to keep your career on course.

Step 10: Reconnect with Recruiters

You don't have to be in active job search to be in touch with an executive recruiter. Remind recruiters you have worked with of who you are and what you do. And seek their advice on what's happening in your industry or job function. They work with many different clients daily and have their fingers on the pulse. They can give you a perspective you can't find anywhere else.

BIO

Dubbed the "Personal Branding Guru" by *Entrepreneur*, William Arruda is credited with turning the concept of personal branding into a global industry. Founder of Reach Personal Branding and author of *Ditch. Dare. Do!,* he has delivered more personal branding keynotes, in more countries, than anyone else on Earth. He inspires top talent in Fortune 100 and respected global brands with optimism, enthusiasm, creativity, boundless energy, and genuine belief in the power of the individual to achieve great things. Learn more at http://www.williamarruda.com or http://www.ditchdaredo.com.

77

Assess and Focus on Building Your Reputation

David K. Rehr, PhD

If you are in marketing or sales or hold a leadership position in an enterprise, you spend your entire day helping create positive perceptions for your company and your clients. You help build and manage brands, communicate value, and monitor social media to see how people are experiencing your client online. But how much attention do you pay to your own reputation? Have you looked at how people perceive you, beyond setting up a Google Alert every time you are mentioned on the Web? And what are you doing to enhance your personal reputation?

We live and work in a hypercompetitive global economy. You know this because you live it daily. And in the years ahead, we can expect every sector of the economy to grow. That means even more smart, savvy individuals will join you in your sector, intensifying competition for future projects, clients, and positions. The time to start paying attention to your personal reputation is now.

In any industry, personal reputation increasingly matters. As technology and instantaneous communication permeate the global business world, potential companies and clients have many options from which to choose. More and more often, hiring decisions are turning on subjective judgments about character and values. And research has shown that companies and clients don't just hire enterprises. They hire the individuals who work for companies. They hire you.

Volatility also plays a role. Companies, customers, or clients want as much certainty as possible; they don't have resources to pay for mistakes. To close the deal and get the order, the customer has to have confidence that you, personally, can deliver. And the only way to develop such confidence is to learn about your prior performance, as conveyed through your reputation.

Recently a close friend asked me over lunch what I thought of a professional who someone wanted to "poach" from a competitor and offer a more senior position. I knew this professional but not extremely well. But I was aware of her reputation. Although she never knew it, the decision to hire her was finalized in that moment, solely on the basis of my subjective perception of her character.

Reputation is tough to define. We know it when we see it. Words like *honesty, integrity, thoughtful, successful,* and *character* come to mind. I believe reputation is the culmination of what you have done in your life, demonstrating that you know how to deliver meaningful value and results to those who interact with you.

Great reputations don't just happen. They result from deliberate actions. Here are five ideas for building on work you may have already done on to build a great reputation for yourself:

1. Google your name regularly.

Sounds obvious—but how many people actually do it? We all should. A September 2012 Harris Interactive study for BrandYourself found that 86 percent of adults use a search engine to look up information about another individual; 42 percent have searched an individual's name before doing business with that person; and 45 percent have found something that resulted in the person using the search engine to decide not to do business with the individual. If you find unflattering comments or articles, in particular, you will need a strategy to remove the citations or have them get lost in the vast World Wide Web. (To see the study, go to www.scribd.com/doc/110029755/JUST-GOOGLE-ME-BrandYourself-Harris-National-Study.)

2. During the coming year, repeatedly ask your inner circle of confidants to honesty describe your reputation.

Our reputation is not stagnant. It ebbs and flows with our performance, the challenges we face, our personal interactions with those we work with, and even visibility we might obtain from speeches, columns, articles, or TV appearances. To track shifts, we need to hear the truth about our reputation on a regular basis from people we respect. Getting external feedback is especially important because we often view ourselves as different than we really are. Our best confidants come from our profession. Choose colleagues who themselves have great reputations. Be sure they hold positions equivalent or more senior to yours. Keep the group small but not too small—five or six people, both men and women. And be sure to have the conversation in a nonthreatening location.

3. Determine centers of influence revolving around your social media.

Unfortunately, there are no universally accepted tools to measure reputation online. Still, it's worth monitoring over time those individuals you connect with. The old adage "You are judged by the company you keep" applies in the digital world. We are way beyond the experimental phase where you would accept or confirm everyone who asks to be your "friend"; we now must be selective and discrete. Build an audience of people who will have a positive effect on your reputation or who you want to emulate. Avoid carelessly building your list of contacts.

4. Commit to three specific actions to build your reputation.

We are all busy going the extra mile to drive value for our customers or clients. We work late. We miss important family events. But we need to proactively and deliberately build our reputations. Whether it's 3 or 10, choose specific actions you will take that focus on making your reputation better and stronger. Use your PR skills to draw attention to your efforts: produce a white paper on a timely industry issue; appear in the media with valuable tips for struggling companies or individuals; write a column helping a nonprofit gain support or visibility. Three actions are easily doable in a year.

5. Ask someone to hold you accountable.

Business is about results. So is building a great reputation. Share with a colleague or friend your reputation plan for the coming year. Ask that person to hold you accountable to your actions; it could be someone from your inner circle who already knows what you are trying to achieve. The person will probably be delighted to help you (and it might help her or him focus on building a reputation as well). Positive reminders and assessments of activities give those asking for accountability an extra dose of "can do" encouragement, even after a long day of public relations efforts for others.

6. Don't ask a member of your immediate family to assess or build your reputation.

Family members can't be objective. They know you too well and often have specific goals for you that differ radically from your dreams. Accepting or hearing unsolicited advice could confuse or adversely affect your perception of yourself and your reputation. My late mother, who loved me very much, never could understand why I wanted to advocate before the U.S. Congress. She put lobbyists right behind used car dealers (and slightly above politicians). So with her, I purposely stayed away from conversations about my work and the reputation I was building. Bottom line: keep the family out of determining what your reputation is or can become.

Use the coming year to build a great reputation. It will give you an edge in the marketplace and in life.

B<small>IO</small>

Washington Life magazine named Dr. David Rehr to its list of the Power 100 in the nation's capital. David is CEO of TransparaGov, Inc., and an adjunct professor at the Graduate School of Political Management at George Washington University, where he teaches principled leadership. He holds a PhD from George Mason University and is the former president and CEO of the National Association of Broadcasters. Please share your stories and experiences on reputation or connect with David at DavidRehr@gwu.edu or by calling (202) 510-2148.

78

ROLE-BASED JOB PROFILING

How to Improve Your Chances in the Job Market: The Art of Role-Based Job Profiling

ஃ✥

Tony Deblauwe

With unemployment rates high in the United States, finding a stable job can be extremely challenging. Although the economic situation is a convenient excuse for throwing up your hands and giving up, the reality is that right now is the time to take a different approach to the traditional one-dimensional résumé model. It's time to think of *role-based job profiling*.

Role-based job profiling can be the advantage you need to stand above the crowd. Many headhunters and human resource professionals employ this technique to attract and retain talent for long-term results, and it's a strategy that you can integrate into your job-hunting efforts.

Role-Based Job Profiling Versus Achievement-Based Job Seeking

Most résumés tend to follow the same pattern—a checklist of accomplishments and past work experience. Though this chronological methodology is one way to interpret your career history, it's an incomplete representation of both your skills and experiences as a professional.

The same could be said about the way you present yourself in job interviews, your social media profile, or the job title on your business cards. Incorporating a role-based profiling approach to every aspect of your job search puts your career history in a context that is more beneficial for employers and, in turn, more advantageous for you. This is because role-based profiling adds a story to your achievements and properly emphasizes your unique specializations.

In his book *A Handbook of Human Resource Management Practice*, Michael Armstrong describes the "role" as "the part people play in their work—the emphasis is on their behavior. ... A role can be distinguished from a job, which consists of a group of prescribed tasks/activities to be carried out or duties to be performed."

As a result, role-based profiling is a more flexible and versatile approach to traditional job-seeking techniques. It highlights you as goal oriented rather than task oriented. It showcases your experiences in a way that highlights potential rather than history. It is a more holistic and precise picture of who you are as a professional.

Applying Role-Based Profiling into Your Job Search

When scanning through job postings, it's tempting to look through the list of requirements as a way of estimating qualifications. Unfortunately, recruiters and employers may not see things the same way. They are looking for something more—something that calls out cultural fit, adaptability, flexibility—not just tasks. As a result, it is imperative to communicate a clear picture of your professional abilities in all aspects and elements of your job search, including your résumé, social media profile, networking etiquette, and interview techniques. To help you apply role-based profiling to your job search, try incorporating the following tips.

* *Understand the role you are applying for.* Don't attempt to make a "one-size-fits-all" résumé. Emphasize how your profile aligns to the kind of role the job is really about. You can get a sense of this from the words used in the job posting/description, such as "must have strong project management skills" or "international experience preferred." Such language tells a broader picture of what the employer wants to see in potential candidates beyond the specific technical skills required. By reading between the lines, you can hone your résumé in a way that emphasizes your experiences as a story and that highlights your relevant background in a way that is more functional for prospective employers. When you construct

résumé statements, talk about the challenge you faced up front and how your contribution made an impactful change.

- *Use your résumé as a road map instead of a timetable.* Most people make the mistake of turning their résumé into a chronological history lesson of their professional life, complete with the requisite bullet list. What's missing in this approach is context; it doesn't capture you in terms of what was involved to achieve your goals. Your résumé is, most import-ant, an ad about you. It's meant to be a road map of where you have been, where you are, and where you could go. Employers want to get a sense of your personality, not just your abilities through your résumé. Instead of the checklist approach, give employers insight into what kind of roles you had to fulfill to get the job done. Describe the company, the environment, how it grew, and how you were right in the middle of both strategic and tactical needs that added value. Rather than rely on titles or designations to explain your experience, describe the skills you utilized and what level of influence you had.

- *Communicate the same role online and offline.* The world of job hunting has completely changed, and it is no longer an option to have an incon-sistent online or offline profile. Prospective employers are always on the lookout for great talent, whether you're aware of it. Because of that, your professional profile must be clear, whether it's during social gatherings, networking events, or on social media. A role-based approach to your online presence can build a better story. Whereas you are restricted for space on a résumé, you can elaborate more on social media sites. Talk about what you like in your current or past roles, inject some relevant anecdotes of achievements you feel most proud of, and then highlight a few industry-relevant skills. Recruiters scan LinkedIn and Facebook pro-files even faster than a résumé; consequently, you have an opportunity to stand out and get people interested in you long before they contact you.

- *Interview for fit.* The role-based profiling approach comes full circle as you now have a chance to weave your story in a compelling way that excites a potential employer as well as demonstrates your capabilities to perform the job at hand. In the interview, elaborate on peripheral areas of how you get work done, such as how you collaborate with others in dif-ferent teams, your ability to influence others and manage upwards, your problem solving ability, and willingness to take on new challenges to see how new ways of doing things benefits the company.

Finding a Job That's Right for You

Role-based profiling paints a clearer picture of your abilities as a skilled employee, and it better matches you with a job you are specialized for. In the end, a role-oriented profile becomes a fundamentally more productive method of linking employer and employee that traditional job-matching techniques normally miss out on.

Resources

Armstrong, M. 2006. *A Handbook of Human Resource Management Practice.* London: Kogan Page.

Bio

Tony is the founder of HR4Change and has over 15 years' experience in human resources management and organizational development. He is an award-winning author and app developer and holds a master's degree in human resources and organizational development from the University of San Francisco. He is also a certified executive coach and master career director. Tony has contributed to several blogs and Web sites, including ExpertBeacon (http://expertbeacon.com) and Examiner (http://www.examiner.com). He has been quoted in several career media sources such as CareerBuilder, Monster, TheLadders.com, and CBS Moneywatch. Contact him at (800) 601-6930 or at tony@hr4change.com.

79

Use the Power of Your Routines to Get the Most out of Yourself in Your Interviews

≈⌒≋

Maria Caterina Capurro

What do you do when the day of your interview or your assessment arrives? You have been waiting for it for days. You have prepared for it. You have written a perfect CV and are ready to deal with any technical and motivational questions that might be asked. But when the day arrives, how you perform depends on your state during the interview. This, in turn, will be influenced directly by your routine.

Both my studies and my coaching practice have shown that just before an important performance, a delicate phase kicks in when your technical preparation ends and the actual performance begins. Here the difference is made by the routine you initiate.

Even though we may not be aware of it, many of our actions are routines. This makes our life easier in many ways. Think about when you wake up, for example: you do not have to start your day over and over again thinking about the actions you need to brush your teeth or to make a cup of coffee. In fact, as with many other daily actions, you do these things automatically with no conscious thought. The characteristic of a routine is precisely that—it is a sequence of repeated actions carried out automatically while our attention is left free to deal with new or more urgent decisions.

But this is not the only power that routines have. They also bring us to states. This is because we are made of states: every thought, word, gesture, action—or a combination of these—produces a state. The term *state* comes from Neuro-Linguistic Programming and refers to the mental and physical processes we experience at any moment that make us feel a certain way.

States and routines are essential parts of dealing with an important performance such as an interview. Without deliberately choosing a powerful state, we may not be able to perform at our best and reach the desired result. In other words, learning to manage your state is the secret to a successful performance. It makes the difference between using your internal resources to lead you to your goal and letting external events dominate you.

The first step is to choose your routine. If you do not do this, your usual routine will automatically prevail and start up. And this is not necessarily the routine that will lead you to empowering states. To interrupt the automatism, you need to make a conscious choice that involves asking yourself three questions:

1. What state (or states) will ease me toward my desired result?
2. What state (or states) will highlight my preparation/skills/abilities/ experience?
3. What state (or states) will allow me to perform at my best?

In this light, your states become resources you can access when you need them. The basic principle is: empowering states will favor your best performance and this, in turn, will lead you to your goal.

state → performance → goal

Now, imagine that tomorrow you have your interview. When does your performance begin? Does it start when you enter the room where your assessment or interview takes place? No!

Your performance starts before that. This means that you need to access the state you need for that particular event before the event itself takes place. To do this, you need to learn what leads to states to be able to choose them. Our states are influenced by our thoughts, our words, and our bodies.

Thoughts

If I ask you to think of something funny, what happens in your mind? An image, a picture, or a film of something funny you have experienced comes up. Immediately after that, you smile, and you feel that same level of amusement. This means that in a few seconds, just by remembering something funny, your state has changed and you feel how you felt that day. Why is this useful for your interview? Here is a short exercise:

- If you answered the three questions earlier, you will have decided what state you need for your interview. Let's say you answered self-confidence.
- Think of a time when you experienced a state of total self-confidence.
- An image, picture, or film of that event will have formed in your mind. And while you see what you saw that time, associate with this picture and increase its qualities, enhancing the brightness, the focus, the colors, the size, the shape, the proximity, and do this up to the point that makes you feel self-confident at a peak.
- You may also note sounds and words. Increase their volume, tone, pitch, clearness up to a point that is right for you. You will know by sensing that you have reached the peak level of your self-confidence.
- Now, locate this feeling and again become aware of its qualities, and adjust them until you feel your self-confidence is at a peak. You may change its temperature, make it move more quickly in your body, or make it still. Sense its weight, intensity, and rhythm, and want to change it to the level that is best for you.
- Now, fix this moment by making a gesture, saying a keyword, or visualizing an image or symbol. This will be your secret access to your self-confidence in the future, when you need it again.
- Proof: Try to use your secret access and check whether your self-confidence switches on. If not, repeat this exercise over and over again until it does.

Words

You may have realized from the exercise that sounds and words are just as important as images are because they too may be ingredients of your thoughts. The words we say to ourselves have an impact on our state and, therefore, need to be considered. When going to an interview, it is of the utmost importance to be aware of what you say to yourself. Try this exercise:

- How do you describe/talk about your interview? If you find you are describing it as a gallows, how do you think this will make you feel? I bet stressed or even frightened!
- How do you describe/talk about yourself as an interviewee?
- If you realize that you are putting yourself down, consider choosing something more empowering to say to yourself.

Body

Our body is both a vehicle to our internal states and an expression of them. Just think about yourself when you are tense. What happens to your posture? To your breathing? To the expression on your face? And what kind of impact will this have on your interviewer?

Now, think about yourself when you are at ease, relaxed, and self-confident. How is your posture? The rhythm of your breathing? Your facial expression? What impression do you convey?

If you want to have a strong impact on your interviewers, start off on the right foot: learn to be aware of your body. As a quick exercise:

- Check your posture from time to time, especially when you feel a bit nervous or tense. You will notice that you are breathing fast, you have a closed posture, you may be swinging your leg when sitting, your jaw will be tightened, and you may be frowning.
- Quickly change. Slow your breathing down. If you are sitting, stand up and take a short walk. Relax your shoulders and neck by slowly moving your elbows back; slightly tilt your chin up, keeping it centered; and then open your palms and point them downward, feeling that all your tension is flowing away through your palms.
- And now that you feel refreshed, reinforce this feeling with powerful images and words. You are ready for your interview!
- If, during the interview, you sense that your tension is coming back, change your posture and breathing, and remember to switch on your powerful state.

You can do it. Why I am so sure? Simply because you are the one who thinks your thoughts and chooses your posture.

<u>Bio</u>

Maria Caterina Capurro is a professional coach, trainer, consultant, and author. Apart from her native Italian, she speaks fluent English and understands Spanish and French. She is a graduate in psychology, a Licensed NLP Coach™, and a CfPAC coaching-for-performance accredited coach. She also holds clean language certification for coaches. She works throughout Europe with international and national organizations, as well as with private individuals. Her mission is to "facilitate her clients in developing their potential, achieving their self-actualization, maximizing their performance, and accomplishing their goals through a process that helps them to be more self-aware, focused, and effective." You can log on to http://www.coachingservices.it or contact her at mariacaterina.capurro@coachingservices.it.

80

Selling Yourself into a Job

❦

Tom Hopkins

If you're currently without a job or need to upgrade your job, it's time to exercise your selling skills. What are you selling? Yourself. This should be the easiest sale you'll ever make. Who other than you has more in-depth knowledge about your talents, abilities, and desires than you do?

The first thing is to look at an employment situation as a selling situation. You'll play two roles. In a job interview, you are both the salesperson and the product. Your goal is to match your particular features and benefits (skills and talents) with the needs of a qualified employer. Here are six steps to help you.

Step 1: Begin by Prospecting

Prospecting means finding the right potential buyer for what you're selling. When you're selling yourself into a new job, it means finding the right potential employer.

You should already know what type of work you most enjoy. That word *enjoy* is key here: if you don't firmly believe that you would enjoy the type of job you're seeking, you'll have trouble being enthusiastic about job hunting. It's a lot easier to be excited about a job that interests you than about one that happens to have the biggest ad in the Sunday paper or has the salary range you need to have an enjoyable lifestyle.

You may send out literature on your product. Product literature in this case is called a *résumé*. Have your résumé professionally prepared. Chances are good that it will be competing with quite a few others that have been professionally prepared. You don't want yours to look like a poor relation.

Be different. Use only what may be appropriate for your particular employment situation. Enclose a photograph of yourself, dressed appropriately for the position. Having a face on the résumé to put with the attributes of the candidate establishes a certain familiarity. Add a clever quote to the bottom of your cover letter. Taking a few moments to research this attention getter could make your résumé stand out.

To ensure that your name gets in front of the interviewers more than once, send a thank-you note the day after you send your résumé. Thank-you notes are always read. If they haven't had the time to review your résumé when they receive it, don't you think they'll go looking for your name among the stacks of others? You will have made a positive first impression that will bring you closer to getting that precious interview.

Step 2: Stand out at the Original Contact

When in doubt about what to wear to an interview, err on the side of conservatism. You want to look your best, but also remember to be comfortable. If your clothing is uncomfortable, you'll be distracted and won't put all of your concentration into the interview.

Because this is a business situation, be prepared to shake hands, make eye contact, and build rapport. Building rapport is the getting-to-know-you stage that comes with any interview. The person doing the hiring doesn't just want someone competent for the position: she or he needs someone who has *people* skills. Be prepared to talk about previous work and civic experiences that show your ability to communicate and work as part of a team.

Step 3: Prequalify Yourself and the Company

Determine if you are qualified to work for the company and if it is qualified to be your employer. For you, *qualification* means finding out who the company is, what it does, how it treats employees. Doing so will save both you and the company a lot of time.

If you haven't prequalified the company, take a few moments during your interview to ask questions that would tell you whether you and the employer would make a good match. Interviewers respect proactive potential employees. Go in with a list of at least five questions whose answers will help you decide whether a prospective employer has an ideal work environment for you.

Here's a valuable hint: *Don't just ask about salary and benefits.* These two topics are most important to you, but when you're selling yourself, you need to show interviewers how having you on staff benefits them. If you focus on what you can do for the company, what the company can do for you will follow.

- Ask questions specific to the position as well as about the company.
- Ask about the company's future plans for growth.
- Ask about the product line.
- Ask about the position.

It doesn't matter if you're applying for a job in sales, accounting, or shipping. You'll eventually have to know a lot of information about the company, if you get the job. So if you're truly convinced this is the right job for you, you might as well ask these questions now. The more specific your questions, the more impressed your interviewers will be with your expertise. Asking pertinent questions now shows that you're interested in more than just a paycheck.

It may turn out that you are not comfortable taking a job. If it's offered and it's really not what you're looking for, be honest with them, thank them for their time, and decline the job.

Step 4: Prepare Your Presentation

Your presentation of your product requires the most preparation. Practice your answers to common interview questions with a family member or close friend. Make a list of the qualities you think are your strongest. Then try to figure a way to work those points into responses to common questions.

To demonstrate dependability, tell the interviewers an anecdote from a previous job or even from an outside activity. If you were an Eagle Scout as a kid, that tells a lot about you, doesn't it? Find a way to bring it up. You may want to mention long-term friendships that evolved from past employment experiences.

Step 5: Address Concerns

How do you handle any negative qualifications that might come up? If any objections arise, explain yourself in as simple, unemotional terms as possible. If you're the primary caregiver for your 95-year-old grandmother and you have to arrange nursing care in advance on weekends, let them know.

If you sidestep obstacles in an interview, there's a good chance they'll come back to haunt you if you do get the job. Find a way to bring up and elaborate on any concerns about fulfilling the needs of the "buyer" as early in the presentation as is appropriate.

Step 6: Close the Sale

If you do want the job and it hasn't been offered, you may have to ask for it. Don't panic. This isn't where you have to turn into Joe Typical Salesperson and apply pressure to get what you want. Getting the job can be as simple as saying, "How soon do I start?" At this point, if you're confident about being able to give the company what it needs, you should begin taking verbal ownership of the position with assumptive statements and questions.

Immediately upon leaving the premises, drop a thank-you note in the mail to the interviewers. This will guarantee your interview will stay fresh in their minds for at least a few days while they're deciding on whom to offer the job to.

Bio

Tom Hopkins is recognized as "America's No. 1 Sales Trainer." His sales training books, audios, and videos have launched the careers of millions of sales professionals worldwide. His how-to selling skills are proven effective in all types of industries and economic times. Tom has authored 17 books on selling, salesmanship, and success. To learn more about how his nuances of selling can make a positive impact on your career, read his blog: http://www.tomhopkins.com/blog.

81

SELF-CARE

Compete in Today's Job Market by Starting with You

≈≈≈

Shari Beaudette, MBA

How do you foster your energy and ability to show up and deliver each day? Do you proudly and intentionally incorporate self-care and renewal into your daily routine? Or are you tired, overwhelmed, and unable to juggle everything?

Your well-being is the foundation for everything you do. If you're feeling broken and unstable, you're just not effective. Neglecting sleep, recovery, and renewal puts you in a state of chronic stress and affects your energy, your relationships, and your productivity. It's time to stop the vicious, unhealthy cycle of stress.

Integrating a New Approach: SPA Time Living

SPA time living is a new mindful approach to living that balances daily stressors and energy expenditure with renewal and recovery. The SPA approach has two goals: to optimize your productivity, your health, and your happiness, and to build renewal and self-care into your life to counteract and release the body's fight/flight/freeze response to daily stressors.

Creating this space is not a luxury but a necessity to keep you strong, resilient, engaged, and productive. Here are 10 tips you can implement today to stand out and thrive.

1. Make a Commitment

Tip: Take a deep breath and proclaim, "I take full responsibility for being the best I can be. I commit to starting with my own mind-set and health. I will nurture my mind, body, and spirit and create a nonnegotiable, guilt-free self-care strategy. I will learn to create space and boundaries to keep me on my 'no matter what' list so that I can thrive and serve from a place of strength and positivity."

2. Know Your "What" and "Why"

To know your purpose and values is essential to nurturing your mind, body, and spirit. Awareness will help you stay aligned with what matters most to you, allowing you to up your game.

Tip: Take a few minutes to write out or reflect on the answers to each of these questions.

- What are your most important lifestyle/career values? Why?
- What motivates you? Why?
- What inspires you? Why?
- What energizes you? Why?
- What renews you? Why?

What's most important to you in your career? Why?

3. Identify What Gets in the Way of Your Self-Care

- Self-esteem? Do you struggle to feel valuable enough to be a priority?
- Fear of what others think, being rejected, or not having support?
- Think you don't have enough time?
- Feel guilty taking time out when there's so much to do?

Tip: pause and release. Take a deep breath in and release these limiting fears and beliefs while saying or writing the following statement: "Taking this time will help me get my work done more effectively and efficiently. I'll be more patient, more energetic, and more focused. I'll be able to share my strengths and gifts with the world from a place of energy and abundance. Staying connected to my values, goals, and purpose while renewing and reviving regularly allows me to show up and be my best!"

4. Develop a Self-Care Strategy

You need a strategy for self-care to plan what, when, why, and how. Creating a plan will help you make self-care nonnegotiable, making it easier to keep you on your "no matter what list" each and every day.

A quick walk or few minutes of focused, mindful breathing can exponentially improve your willpower, your ability to concentrate, your problem-solving ability, and your stress levels.

Tip: Your ability to set clear specific meaningful goals will put you in control. Grab a pen and paper right now and answer the following two questions: What does self-care mean to you? What helps you recover, relax, renew, or restore? List at least 10 things, and schedule them now.

5. Create Boundaries

To honor yourself as the foundation for your growth, change, and potential, you must protect and claim your downtime and self-care habits with pride.

Tip: Feeling guilty? Reread your commitment statement about why self-care matters. If it supports you, create an "elevator pitch" that explains and in-spires. This small act will help your confidence, protect your boundaries, *and* support others to carve out their own space.

6. Create Healthy Habits and Success Rituals

Habits are developed so that your mind doesn't have to work so hard. They can be developed proactively or reactively, consciously or unconsciously. Become aware!

Tip: Choose to develop your habits consciously to serve you. Think about this: What do you do right when you wake up each day? Chances are it's the same thing. It's a habit or ritual. The morning is an amazing time to create a personal success ritual. Maybe a big glass of water, five minutes of mindful breathing, and writing your top three goals for the day. Contrast this with what many do: immediately check email and live by who needs them most.

7. Practice Chaos Cleansing

"Chaos cleansing" is my term for clearing both your physical and mental space. It's important to have a clean, clear work space and mind space.

- Make sure you have a trusted system for capturing all the clutter in your head, or your mind will try to remember it all, creating stress. One of my favorites is David Allen's Getting Things Done.
- Have a place for everything and have everything in its place. You'll eliminate the stress of not finding what you need when you need it.
- Nourish, cleanse, and optimize your mind, body, and spirit with nutritious, whole foods (veggies, fruits, grains, and lean proteins), plenty of water, movement, and renewal.

8. Practice Mindfulness

When you're at work, do you feel guilty about all the things that need to be done at home? When you're at home, do you feel like you need to be working? Notice when this happens and shift your focus back to the present—from a place of nonjudgment and self-compassion. Being hard on yourself is the worst thing you can do. The more you practice, the better you'll get!

Tip: If you're struggling to stay focused, try what I call a distraction catcher to capture open to-dos that pop into your head.

- Use either a notebook or piece of paper, ideally organized by context (@ computer, @home, and so on).
- Capture items as they pop into your head. Then quickly but gently return your focus to the present.
- Make sure you have a trusted system and process to review the recorded distractions later.

9. Keep Growing

All the cells in your body keep regenerating and changing. It's time to learn to love and embrace change. The latest research in neuroscience introduces us to neural plasticity, showing that we can even move beyond past programming and literally rewire our thoughts.

Tip: Embrace a growth mind-set to keep growing, learning, and taking on new challenges. This will help you reframe negative events to find lessons learned, inspiring forward growth and positive change.

10. Quit Waiting for the Right Time

There is no right time. Your life will never be less busy, unless you create space.

Tip: Add in what supports you now. The less important things will fall away as you step into your greatness.

Bio

Shari Beaudette, MBA, is a busy mother of two, yoga and spa aficionado, founder of SpaTimeLiving.com, and creator of Chaos Cleanse(TM) conscious living programs.

As a self-care, renewal, and mindfulness coach, Shari is on a mission to inspire meaning, positive change, and overwhelm resilience.

After a traumatic childhood and path to motherhood, Shari discovered several powerful secrets that helped her re-write her story, which she now shares through her FREE Weekly Retreat and five minute mindfulness meditations at http://www.spatimeliving.com/weekly-retreat and FREE six minute a day Chaos Cleanse Audio series at http://chaoscleanse.com/now

Shari lives with her family in Denver, Colorado, and online at http://www.SpaTimeLiving.com. You can also find her on Facebook and Twitter @SpaTimeLiving.

82

Help Yourself: How to Create a Whole New You, More Income, and a Better Life

≈⌒≈

Becky A. Davis

How often do you invest in developing yourself? Sounds like a simple question, right? Chances are good that you want to achieve something in your life. It could be fame and fortune. You may just want to maintain your job and move up in the ranks. That's a goal and that's good.

All of the big names in the world, people you would recognize if you heard their name, have done more that others have to achieve their success. They didn't just land in the right situation at the right time. They made it happen by working on themselves.

They didn't just rely on schools. They didn't rely on a boss to teach them the skills, They didn't wait around for an opportunity to come to them. They went out and learned everything they could to become the people they are. In other words, people like Oprah Winfrey, one of the wealthiest women in the world; Russell Simmons, a millionaire mogul; Jim Carrey, a successful comedian; and John Mackey of Whole Foods all became who they are because of the work they put into the process of improving and helping others.

I want to share with you a few actions you can take to grow your skills and compete in today's job market. These actions will excel and propel you forward faster. Here we go.

Grow Through Reading and Learning

There are books on everything. Select a book in the area you want to grow. You can search the Internet and put in what you want to learn, and I guarantee a book is written about it. Subscribe to trade magazines to learn more about your industry. Keep up on news and newspaper reports that impact your company and job. Read blogs. There are so many experts who write blogs that will keep you in the know of other perspectives. Do a search for blogs with your area of interest, and you will find several.

Webinars and teleseminars are great ways to learn new information, and they are widely available. Some are free; some ask for a fee. Go to www.findtutorials.com to find a wide range of tutorials. Go to www.teach-nology.com to see classroom-like tutorials for technology and money managing. And www.entrepreneurshiplife.com/online-media-grow-business has plenty of options to teach you how to run your own business. Another good option is www.leadershiptrainingtutorials.com to help you manage and lead better.

Grow Through Wisdom of Others

There are so many benefits to using a mastermind group. Namely, it is an opportunity for people to come together who have the same pursuits or different pursuits but all in the same field to talk through issues and problems and to celebrate successes. You can go to www.meetup.com to find a wide variety of professionals who get together locally. You can create your own mastermind or Google-specific mastermind groups to find one that will work for you.

So many leaders today use life/executive/career coaches to help them navigate through their career. There is nothing more important than working toward your life goals. Find a coach who can help you improve your life, your business, or your job role. You can go to www.lifecoach.com to help you find a life coach for any needs, including relationship, personal development, and business coaching. You can also go to http://findyourcoach.com to select a coach who will help you compete in the marketplace.

Seminars, workshops, and conferences, as components of transformation, can help you. Every city hosts different public training events. You can find seminars on business, spiritual healing, improving relationships, goal setting, time management, interview skills, and so many more topics. If you want to compete, find a seminar, workshop, or conference in your city or nearest city to attend to expand your knowledge. You can go to www.trainingmag.com for business-related seminars.

Go to www.podcastawards.com for numerous options for podcasts. You can also check out iTunes or Google Play to download podcasts to your smartphone, with some of the most influential speakers.

Grow Through Experiences

Learn from good and bad experiences. Your experiences are very valuable because they are teachers. If you do something very well, make sure you know exactly what you did to get that outcome so you know how to repeat it. When you have bad experiences, they are better teachers because you need to look at the lesson of the experience so you know what to do next time. This is used by so many celebrities to propel them forward in their career. Don't keep repeating the same actions that don't work. It will keep you stuck.

Learn through trial and error. This just means you have to take chances and try new things. You will get things wrong, but that's OK if you learn from it. Don't stay in the safe zone. People you compete with will be outside of the box so they can stand out. J.K. Rowling, the author of the Harry Potter series, had her manuscript turned down more than 15 times, but each time she worked on improving the book—and look at what she has created!

Learn from others' mistakes. You don't have to experience everything to learn. You can watch the mistakes of others to know what not to do. If you have a mentor, ask that person some of the mistakes she or he made and what she or he did differently to correct it. This will help you not make the same mistake of others.

Now it's time for you to take some action. Determine what's your next move and which move will help you be more competitive in today's job market.

One of the hardest parts of any learning is to take the information you've gathered and to use it to achieve something you want to accomplish. Here is a success formula that works every time, IAT: Information + Application = Transformation. You have been given a great deal of information; it is up to you to apply it. When you do, I guarantee there will be a transformation. Dream big because it's possible if you do the work.

Bio

Leadership transformation coach Becky A. Davis is a former VP of the world's largest global optical company. Becky uses her 20 years of leadership experience to equip entrepreneurs with leadership tools to drive profits by effectively leading and engaging employees. Becky is a speaker, trainer, coach, and author of *The Leadership Transformation Blueprint* book and workbook; *10 Things Managers Should Know That Employees Hate: How It's Costing You Profits*; and *Help Yourself: How to Create a Whole New You, More Income and a Better Life*. To learn more about her services of for more information, go to http://www.mvpwork.com, or call (678) 265-8076.

83

Self Directed Leadership© to Ensure Your Career Success

Diane Lange

Hard work, outstanding skills, leading-edge competencies, industry knowledge, and an ability to navigate office politics will all set you on the road to career success. But none is guaranteed to ensure your career success as developing the essential and fundamental leadership skills that will set you apart, get you noticed, and catapult you up the career ladder.

According to recent news media, America is in a leadership crisis. Organizational leaders fear that future employees won't have the leadership abilities with the advanced skills and knowledge necessary to lead our organizations into a competitive global marketplace.

But what does being a leader mean? Does position or title make one a leader? Is leadership only for those with charisma or only for those with money who can buy position or an Ivy League education? Is a leader someone who is promoted into a managerial track at work? And does that person's title guarantee that he or she will be effective in that position? Or do actions define leadership? If so, what are they? These are important questions and you must know the answers if you want to successfully compete in today's job market.

By virtue of the definition of the word *leader*, one must have followers. How, then, does one get others to follow? Students of leadership learn the essential functions of leadership to become successful and effective leaders. There is good news; the basic tenets of leadership are the steps in Self Directed Leadership© that will walk you through the fundamentals of leadership development. Self Directed Leadership© offers you a simple step-by-step action plan that will show you how to launch your leadership career.

Self Directed Leadership© is based on the following important assumptions: anyone can be a leader; effective leadership can be taught; and leadership is independent of a title. If you want to be a leader and don't have a leadership work history or leadership title, this plan is for you. If you do have a leadership history and title, but you don't feel that you inspire or influence those whom you lead, then this is for you too. I encourage you to work through each of these steps and commit yourself to the actions necessary for your leadership and career success.

Self Directed Leadership© Action Plan

Vision: The first step of your plan is to develop your vision. What do you see yourself doing in your career? What is your ultimate goal? Where do you see yourself working and living? How do you define career success? A vision is essential because without it, you may lack direction or waste time, energy, and money by going in directions that won't deliver you to your career destination.

Values: Next, look at what you value. In determining your values, reflect on the good things that you want to bring to the world. This is essential because people who may be your followers must know what you value; no one wants to follow someone whose values are different from their own. The 2012 presidential election exemplified how people decide whom to follow based on values. What do you value? To find lists of values, search online for "list of values"; review them and make a list of your top 10 values upon which you will base your actions and career.

Actions: Your next step is to decide how you are going to act as a leader. You may have heard the old adage "Actions speak louder than words." Indeed, our words can be empty if they aren't followed up by actions that support our words. As a matter of fact, people who espouse one thing and do something different are not respected by those who know them. Our actions tell others what we believe in, how we choose to live our life, and whether we respect ourselves and others. Our actions tell others what we think and what we value. How do you think leaders should act? What kinds of things should they say and do? How should leaders treat coworkers, people in power, strangers, and people who are less fortunate? As a future leader, you must be clear about how you will act because others will *always* be observing you!

Skills and knowledge: Leaders must have knowledge of many things: the industry that they lead, policies, procedures, technology, and where to go to learn what they need. Think about it—if you are in an organization and you don't think the leader knows what he or she is doing, will you respect his or her decisions? Would you trust that person's leadership? Continually develop yourself, your education, your knowledge, and your skills. It *will* pay off.

Relationships: Good relationships are our most important resource and cannot be underestimated. Having supportive, encouraging, and trusting relationships is nothing short of a survival tool. Everyone has heard the phrase "It's not what you know, but who you know." This is often true because people like to work with those with whom they have good relationships. As a result, those who are well liked and respected often move into positions of ever-increasing responsibility and prestige. Those who do not establish and maintain positive relationships at work are often overlooked and sometimes ostracized, despite their quality or quantity of work.

Influence and inspire: Dwight D. Eisenhower's famous leadership quote conveys the essence of effective leadership: "Leadership is the art of getting someone else to do something you want done because he (or she) wants to do it." This definition is powerful because it implies a leader must inspire and influence others to do what must be done. Your ability to influence and inspire is predicated on your vision, values, actions, behaviors, and relationships because they all must be *consistent* to inspire others. The ability to influence and inspire is the ultimate test of leadership because to be a leader, you must have people who are willing to follow you. If you don't or can't inspire or influence them, you will not be able to lead them.

Trust: Trust cannot be mandated or bought. It is a by-product of your actions and behaviors. Many people fail to understand that their actions and attitudes are *always* noticed by those with whom they live and work. Think about the actions that build trust. Do your coworkers gossip about others in the organization? Do they say one thing and then do something else? Does that build trust? How do you act? Are you trustworthy?

If you follow these steps, you will lay the foundation for a powerful leadership platform. As you develop your leadership abilities, you will then, by default, become a role model for all you meet. Becoming a leader and a role model will be the culmination of a successful career that you have carefully and intentionally built.

I wish you much success to that end!

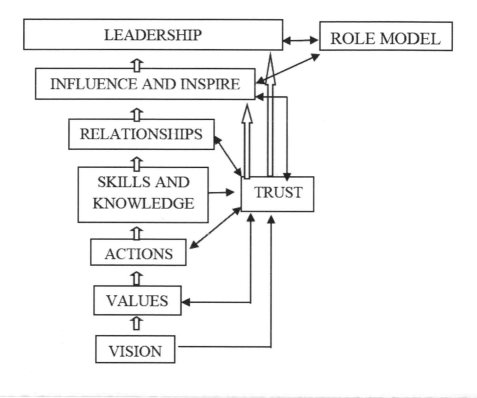

Bio

Diane Lange, founder of Proclivity LLC, developed Self Directed Leadership© to develop leaders in the fundamentals of leadership. She also trains managers and consults on performance management, change management, conflict resolution, and team building. Self Directed Leadership© is also included in the internationally published edited leadership book Tapping into Your Inner CEO—Self Leadership. Self Directed Leadership© will be available as an e-book in 2013. Diane is a doctoral candidate in education, organizational leadership, and communication from Northeastern University and a certified leadership coach from George Washington University's Department of Organizational Sciences and Communication. She can be reached at diane@proclivityllc.com; http://www.proclivityllc.com; https://www.facebook.com/ProclivitlLlc; https://twitter.com/prodiane; or http://www.linkedin.com/in/dianelange.

84

How to Motivate the Most Important Person in Your Life—You!

Charlie Silva

My favorite motivating question is, "Loving life … are you loving yours?" If so, wonderful! If not, why not? If something is stopping you from loving your life, what is it? Let's find ways to overcome it.

Not loving your life indicates you are not controlling it; if you controlled your life, you would obviously love it, wouldn't you? And when you truly love your life, you know you are able to achieve any goal you desire, including finding your passion in your professional life as well as your personal life.

When you are in control, that control enables you to find ways to motivate yourself to achieve your goals. But how do you take control and stay in control? It really is simple: choose to stay positive rather than negative. Staying positive enables you to take back the control that for whatever reason you gave away. You can't control everything that happens in your life. However—and this is very important—you can control, in every situation, *how* you choose to react to that situation. Choose to react negatively, and you give up control; choose to react positively, and you keep control. It's really that simple.

A shorter version of the motivating question is, "How are you feeling *right now*?" If you answer that question with any sort of negative emotion—negative emotions such as stress, anger, frustration, sadness, fear—then you are not in control of whatever is happening in your life at this moment. On the other hand, if you can answer in a positive way, with positive emotions such as happiness, joy, love, then you *are* in control.

You need to realize that negative emotions give you nothing; positive emotions give you power. You can always choose how you react to whatever is happening in your life. I was watching a television news broadcast recently that truly illustrated this point.

It was right after several tornadoes had almost completely demolished an entire town. A news reporter was walking through a neighborhood that had been destroyed by one of the tornadoes. He stopped in front of one home that was completely gone and asked the owners how they were dealing with the situation. The owners were crying, saying although no one in their family was hurt, it was the "end of the world" for them, and they didn't know what they would do. The reporter then moved over to the house next door, which was completely gone also. He asked those owners how they were dealing with the situation. Those owners looked at the reporter and told him the situation was obviously challenging, but that they were grateful that they were all alive and that they would rebuild and go on with their life.

Imagine that! The same situation, both homes utterly destroyed. One family allowing themselves to be devastated by the ordeal, while their neighbors, who experienced the same ordeal, looking at it and saying they'll rebuild and go on with their life. Remembering you can't control everything, but what you can control every time is how you react to everything. Who would you say is in control of the situation? The members of that first family, crying and choosing to be negative, were definitely not in control. The members of that second family, grateful they survived and choosing to be positive, were definitely in control. And by being in control, I have no doubt, they were motivated to achieve their goal of rebuilding and moving on with their lives.

Unfortunately, we live in what can be viewed as a very negative world. We are constantly bombarded by negative stories and reports about wars, natural disasters, and financial disasters. When we see and hear these negative stories constantly and choose to allow them to impact us in a negative way, we're giving away our control and love of life to the stories or politicians or whatever it is that is making us feel negative. We need to take back that control, and we can do it by staying positive. By staying positive and in control, we choose to be happy and love our life, and we easily find ways to stay motivated and achieve our goals.

To achieve anything, including finding the perfect job, you need to ask yourself why you've made that particular thing your goal. Why did you decide to lose weight or stop smoking or look for a better job or buy that particular car or … ; fill in the blank. If the answer to the "why" is anything other than "because I desire to be happy," you may want to rethink that particular goal. Too often we give ourselves several "ifs" as a condition of being happy and loving our life. If I had more money … If I lost weight … If I stopped smoking … If I reduced my stress … If I had a different job … ; you get the picture.

The usual problem with the "ifs" is that, once you have more money, you'll realize it doesn't necessarily make you happy and love your life. Sure, money can facilitate some happiness, but it doesn't guarantee it. Just listen to the stories about people who have won major lottery jackpots, and within a short time, they've lost it all and are as unhappy, if not more so, than before. You might say those people just didn't know how to deal with it. But are you confident you'd be able to deal with it to ensure your happiness?

Once you lose the excess weight, it doesn't necessarily make you happy and love your life. Once you stop smoking, it doesn't necessarily make you happy and love your life. And so on. Staying motivated and achieving goals is important, and always giving ourselves more goals to achieve helps us grow. But goals in and of themselves don't necessarily make us happy and love our life. It actually depends on the type of goals we pursue and why we're pursuing them.

Many times our goals or resolutions are more to impress other people rather than to improve ourselves, and in those cases, we are pursuing the goals for reasons other than desiring to be happy; therefore, we seldom achieve them. Or if we do achieve them, they don't satisfy us in the way we expected. If we're not satisfied and truly happy after achieving a goal, we begin feeling negative in some way. When we're feeling negative, we're not in control of our life; we've chosen to allow someone or something else to be in control. We do choose how we react to everything (remember the two families' choices after their homes were destroyed by a tornado).

I don't suggest putting on rose-colored glasses and disregarding the negative. That would not be reasonable. What I am suggesting is that, when given a choice (and realize you always have choices), choose to be positive rather than negative. Positive emotions keep you motivated and on track toward achieving any goal you set for yourself.

And always remember to answer the question, "Loving life … are you loving yours?" If so, wonderful! If not, why not? If there is something that is stopping you from loving your life, what is it? Let's find ways to overcome it.

Bio

Charlie earned a bachelor's degree in political science from the University of Massachusetts and a master's degree in computer information systems from the University of Phoenix. He also earned certification from the Fowler Wainwright International Institute of Professional Coaching as a certified professional coach. He is a board-certified hypnotist and member of the National Guild of Hypnotists. Charlie's professional experience has included a combined total of over 35 years in major corporations and academic environments (including AT&T, Sprint, University of Phoenix, and VCI Group, Inc.), where he has coached and motivated highly successful employees and students in various areas.

85

The Art of Self-Promotion

≈⌒≈

Regina Barr

In today's job market (or any other job market for that matter), it's critical to be able to effectively promote yourself. But something about the combination of the words *self* and *promotion* makes most people cringe.

Research has shown that people must overcome a number of barriers with the concept of self-promotion. Men typically have a leg up compared to women simply because they are more comfortable talking about themselves. Unfortunately, most women are socialized as children to not talk about themselves. Regardless of gender, most people are reluctant to talk about themselves and their accomplishments, or they go about it in the wrong way. Most people feel that this is—dare I say it?—bragging.

Of course, there are exceptions to the rule, and some of us—given time to think about it—could identify one or two people who handle self-promotion extremely well and do it with a grace and style to be admired. However, I guarantee that almost all of us could immediately identify some people who have gone over the top in promoting themselves, and it's these people who make us feel queasy when we think about doing it for ourselves.

In our adult lives, many people often feel that their work should speak for itself. Although that sounds good on paper, this strategy simply doesn't work very well for most of us. That's why—even though you may be working hard and doing good work—you may be passed over for plum assignments or, worse, for that coveted pay raise or promotion.

It's critical for you to develop a comfort level with talking about yourself and your accomplishments. Self-promotion can make you visible, help you realize your goals and dreams, establish you as an expert in your field, and—perhaps most important—lay the groundwork for future opportunities.

Effective self-promotion requires preparation. Here are a few simple steps to get you started.

Step 1: Take Inventory

You need to have a sense of what is worth promoting about yourself and why it's important. Not sure where to start? Look at previous performance reviews. Take note of what people say you are good at. And when all else fails, ask people who you have worked with in the past for feedback. I suspect you'll be pleasantly surprised by what you hear.

Step 2: Identify Your Key Accomplishments

These should be quantifiable and showcase your most important contributions. What have you done that has made a significant impact on your organization? Think quality, not quantity, but do have a few examples in your back pocket at all times. You just never know when they'll come in handy.

Step 3: Describe Your Accomplishments

This is where most people trip up. I like to keep it pithy but with some substance to it. Think in terms of telling a story. A simple technique you can use is the "CAR" method: describe the challenge, the actions, and the results. Using this technique will help you organize the details of what you want to say and provide a framework to help ensure you don't forget any critical components. Remember, it's not just what you say, but how you say it.

Step 4: Craft a Vision for Your Self-Promotion

Start by answering these questions: What is the outcome you want to achieve? By when? What will success look like, and how will you measure your success? What is your time frame for getting started? Who will you ask to help you and why? How will you communicate your vision? Where will you track your progress, including successes and key learnings?

Step 5: Identify Individuals to Help You

Who in your sphere of influence could be helpful in promoting you? Your list should include individuals both inside and outside your organization. Don't forget people you've interacted with outside of work such as former professors and classmates, your pastor, attorney, financial planner, or even your mother in-law or father in-law. Don't forget those with whom you may have volunteered with or served on a board with, or members from your industry or professional association. When someone else is your champion, it doesn't feel like bragging as much, so don't be afraid to ask for help!

Step 6: Implement Your Strategy

It's never too early to get a jump-start on self-promotion. Done right, self-promotion can take time, especially if you don't want to appear to be too self-serving. Begin promoting yourself now because if you wait to start until you need to promote yourself, it will often be too late.

Of course, as with anything, it's critical that you feel comfortable with whatever steps you choose to take in your quest for self-promotion. One piece of advice: start small and discuss your approach with a trusted colleague or coach. Keep telling yourself that there is nothing wrong with self-promotion. And remember, success doesn't usually come to those who wait for it. It comes to those who have taken the time to get their accomplishments noticed and are prepared to leverage opportunities when they arise.

Here's a personal example. While working in a corporate marketing position, I sent an email to the president of my division (whom I barely knew at the time) about his hosting a series of educational programs. I told him how much I appreciated the programs and what I had gotten out of them. A few days later, I got a call from his secretary asking to schedule a time for the two of us to meet. I had already forgotten my email, so I was a bit confused by this and immediately assumed that something was wrong. When we finally met he said, "I bet you're wondering why I asked to meet with you." Of course, that was an understatement. He then said, "Well, I wanted to meet the one person in my division of more than 100 employees that took the time to thank me, and I wanted to find out more about who she is, what she does, and how I can help her going forward." From a visibility standpoint, it doesn't get better than this.

Here's another example. A client of mine was in transition and working hard to land another position. He was getting frustrated because his networking had become stale and his contacts were overutilized. In talking with him, I realized he wasn't engaged in any volunteer or board activities. I suggested that he strategically select a professional association or nonprofit organization to get involved with, and to join a committee that would showcase his skills and experience while broadening his network. He did such a great job for one organization that the president was singing his praises to several senior-level executives he knew, which landed my client his next position.

Keep in mind that it doesn't have to be hard or complicated to promote yourself. Sometimes it can even happen organically (as it did for me). And, if you've done your part in sharing your accomplishments, others will often take the lead in doing the rest for you.

Still not feeling completely comfortable with self-promotion? When all else fails, remember this: if it's fact, it's not bragging. So share away.

Bio

Regina Barr is a former financial marketing executive and founder/CEO of Red Ladder, Inc. Regina brings over two decades of corporate experience to her consulting, coaching, and speaking practice where she helps women scale the barriers—both internal and external—that prevent them from achieving the career success they deserve. A nationally recognized authority on women and leadership, she is frequently quoted in local and national publications. Regina's Women at the Top® blog was recognized as one of 25 career and businesswomen blogs to read by BlogHer. Contact Regina directly at regina.barr@redladder.com or (651) 453-1007. Learn more at http://www.redladder.com.

86

SELF-PROMOTION STRATEGIES

How to Self-Promote Without Losing Self-Respect

Christine Brown-Quinn
Jacqueline Frost

Using your network should always be one of your top strategies for making your next career move, whether that be entering or reentering the job market or making a move internally or externally from your current position. But *how* do you leverage your network to improve your chances of getting that juicy role? You do this by letting others know what projects you're involved in, what you're good at, and what you're looking for. The secret is doing it in a way that doesn't look or feel like self-promotion.

As is often the case, there's an easy way and a hard way. There's a big downside in doing self-promotion the hard way. It is not only less enjoyable but can also actually backfire. On the other hand, self-promotion done the easy way—and the way that's most effective—will not only protect you from losing self-respect, but better yet, it will actually increase both your self-respect and self-belief.

Self-promotion is not about you. It's about the other person. It sounds counterintuitive. Here's how it works. You're looking for a new role. Just think about how much time you're saving the person who's looking to make the hire. He or she can avoid sifting through hundreds of résumés and poorly written cover letters because you've highlighted how you're a perfect fit for the role. If you want people to listen and be interested in what you have to say, make it relevant to *them*. In this instance, the hiring manager is focused on filling a role. Think about how you can relate your specific experience to what the company needs.

Be aware of your current reputation. We refer to this as the "water cooler moment." Do you know what people are saying about you around the water cooler? If you're not sure, then think of someone whom you can trust (business can be like war; you need to be aware of your enemies; proceed with caution). Whom can you trust and who will tell you straight? It's time to meet that person for coffee and get some honest feedback.

Self-promotion isn't extra; it's part of your job; it's part of being a professional. We are all busier than ever. In the current economic climate, fewer people are doing more things. Their job responsibilities are expanding. Your colleagues are incredibly busy, which is why it would help them to hear about the successes you're having. Your manager and other more senior staff in your organization need to manage upward. Think about sharing those key pieces of information about what's happening on the ground—that project running ahead of schedule or that new client in the new strategic region the company's been looking to develop. One of our clients, Jane (IT manager in financial services), is such a believer in this motto she's set each of her team members a goal of spending 20 percent of their time doing self-promotion. This way all the key stakeholders know what's going on.

Think of yourself as a business. Just as with successful consumer brands, it's helpful to think of ourselves as business owners. Thinking of ourselves as business owners shifts control into our own hands (and, boy, does that feel great!). We're not waiting for others to do our self-promotion for us. We're now in the driver's seat. The best type of self-promotion is when others are talking about us. Think about feeding others exciting, positive information so they can pass it on and people can start talking about you. A consumer brand such as Apple offers a good example of this concept. At almost every new product launch, customers line up outside the Apple stores to be one of the first through the door. This kind of publicity is much more effective than any advertisements Apple itself might run.

Be strategic with your messaging. What's your goal? Is it positioning yourself for a role in a new area? Is it moving up a level? Is it going into a new industry? Effective self-promotion is targeted, intentional, and strategic. Who are the key people you need to be interacting with? What are the key messages you want to deliver? Remember, it's business and we're all busy, so make it short and sharp yet interesting. Think back to the water cooler moment. Now that you have your specific goal in mind, who's saying what about you that facilitates the career path you want to take?

Louise, a talented accountant, came to us distressed after she had recently been passed over for promotion. She was a senior manager at the time with clear aspirations to becoming a director. We asked Louise about her self-promotion campaign. Who did she get feedback from about her aspirations to become a director? Were there any development points outstanding? Who were the key people involved in the promotion decisions, and how had she ensured that they knew about her work and contribution to the business? You guessed it—outside of friends and family, absolutely no one knew about Louise's aspirations. She thought she would simply be recognized for the fantastic work she was doing.

This is the great myth of one-dimensional meritocracy. Doing a good job is only one part of how to compete. Competing requires communication. The irony is when we don't speak up and we don't let others know how we're moving things forward, we can actually be perceived as not ambitious or not committed. It's time to think about your own strategic self-promotion campaign to make sure your name is at the top of the list when that next opportunity comes up.

Now that you know what you know, work through your *Self Promotion Circle,* followed by the questions you want to be aware of (and perhaps change) that are being asked about you around the water cooler.

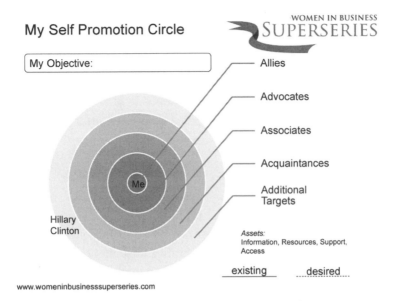

My Self Promotion Circle

WOMEN IN BUSINESS
SUPERSERIES

My Objective:

Allies

Advocates

Associates

Acquaintances

Additional
Targets

Me

Hillary
Clinton

Assets:
Information, Resources, Support,
Access

existing   desired

www.womeninbusinesssuperseries.com

Questions that will be asked about you by those talking about you:

- **Do I know what they've done or accomplished?**
- **Have I interacted with them directly?**
- **Have I seen them do presentations?**
- **Have I read things they've written?**
- **Have I heard others talk about them?**
- **In a nutshell, are they visible?**

How do you change this perception?

BIO

As cofounders and managing directors of Women in Business Superseries, Jacqueline Frost and Christine Brown-Quinn share their practical and hands-on career strategies through their global online professional development club, workshops, corporate programs, and coaching. Following their 40+ years combined experience in business, they are well versed in what it takes to forge a thriving career in demanding corporate environments, working with more than 5,000 women from global companies such as Accenture, Barclays, Cisco, KPMG, Microsoft, and Norton Rose. To receive your complimentary career checklist, log onto http://www.womeninbusinesssuperseries.com

87

What's the Value in Developing "Soft Skills" in the Workplace?

Genevieve Roberts, MBA, PHR

A recent article published in the *Wall Street Journal* caught my attention because it talked about how many top business schools in the United States are beginning to revamp their curriculum to focus on building the "soft skills" of their graduates. Soft skills are personal attributes that enhance an individual's interactions, job performance, and career prospects. Unlike hard skills, which are about a person's technical skill set and ability to perform a certain type of task or activity, soft skills relate to a person's ability to interact effectively with coworkers and customers and are broadly applicable both in and outside the workplace. Sure finance, accounting, and marketing courses are still important; however, these disciplines are realizing something that I have been preaching for more than 10 years, which is that successful employees and job hunters need to be as strong in the areas of soft skills as they are in hard skills.

When you hear the term *soft skills*, it often conjures up the image of something touchy-feely, but what does it really refer to? I have assembled a sample list that I think reflects what my clients tell me are the most relevant soft skills for people seeking to be hired or to succeed once hired. Each employer is likely to have unique cultural or environmental demands that would add soft skills to the list. So don't take this as *the* list but only as a good general statement of what is needed in almost any workplace.

- *Communication*: This involves active listening, the ability to present ideas to others in a coherent and understandable way, as well as excellent writing capabilities. A good example is the ability to explain technical concepts to an audience that isn't tech savvy.
- *Collaboration*: The ability to relate to people and work well with others is a valuable asset in the workplace. Knowing how to tactfully disagree with others or seek out others opinions is valuable.
- *Change tolerant*: Few organizations are static. The ability to adapt to change and manage multiple tasks is critical in today's technology-driven and rapidly evolving business environment.
- *Problem solving*: Managers seek employees who are skilled at assessing situations and able to seek multiple perspectives and gather more in-depth information. The ability to use creativity, reasoning, past experience, information, and available resources to resolve issues saves everyone at the organization valuable time.
- *Organization*: Organization, planning, and effectively implementing projects and tasks is important because many companies expect all of their employees to possess the ability to deliver results.
- *Strong work ethic*: Employers are looking for employees who take initiative, are reliable, get the job done, and can do the job right without having to "babysit" them.
- *Emotional intelligence*: Being attuned to the situation and its impact on people's emotions and possible reactions includes self-awareness, empathy, self-confidence, and self-control. Knowing when to speak or be quiet, when to challenge and when not, when to continue the argument and when to stop are part of what leads to success.

Managers can lead by positional power in the short term, but when they actually learn and apply skills related to building relationships, emotional intelligence, communication, and active listening, their performance and the performance of their team increases over the long term. As you think about how well you are competing for the best jobs in today's market, whether you are currently employed or looking for that next great opportunity, consider conducting a self-assessment of your soft skills. Identify where you are strong and, more important, what are your growing edges? Where could you stand to improve a bit? Reflect on performance feedback a supervisor gave you or take an assessment tool such as a 360-degree or skills assessment to gain valuable insight on how others perceive you. Then try some of these suggestions:

- *Get feedback.* Assessment tools and coaches can work with you to figure out your strengths and weaknesses. Consciously reflect on what you are doing and saying. You can even have someone videorecord you in a group setting. Learn, reflect, practice, and try again. If you don't know where you are, it is hard to get someplace else.
- *Get coaching.* It is hard to break old habits and learn new ones. Get a coach. More than likely, this professional can assess your soft skills and provide the feedback and examples to improve your skill set.
- *Read and take classes.* Local universities may offer classes that focus on this topic. The best books and classes have solid examples, stories, and cases you can learn from.

I am proud that at Titan Group, we have had the opportunity to develop hundreds of clients through our coaching and leadership programs. By learning the soft skills that are relevant to the job, you will know that others will respect what you have to say, appreciate that you have listened to them, and trust you will get the job done. This will get those significant breakthroughs you want as you seek the next job up the ladder.

One of my clients attended a breakthrough management development program and shared that as a result of the learnings in the program, he and his employee had one of the best meetings ever. The manager struggled with reaching this employee. But after completing a self-assessment tool, he gained an understanding of his own leadership and communication style. Armed with this knowledge, he took a new approach to communicating with his employee that was so much more effective. His employee responded more positively. These techniques and tools also weren't anything he ever learned in school or on the job.

Although I have been successful and even built the business acumen side of the leadership equation, I was not the most effective leader. It was only through participating in a 360-degree feedback tool and being open to hearing feedback from my managers over the years that I learned I needed to become more emotionally intelligent and to stop acting like "Business Gen." That indeed was a nickname I was given. Although it was hard to hear at the time, I was lucky enough to engage a business coach and took a couple of developmental classes that helped me tremendously. It was certainly my blind spot; however, I feel fortunate to have received the feedback to identify where my shortcomings were and, just as important, to have the chance to work on them. I am conscious when I meet with people to focus on making a strong connection on a personal level first, before we dive into the business part of the conversation. It has paid off for me as I have learned how to remain relevant and integral in the market with both my clients and my employees.

So the next time you have a chance to get feedback and take a class or program focused on building your repertoire of soft skills, I challenge you to take it and watch your relationships with and value to your organization and others bloom.

Bio

Genevieve has over 20 years of diversified experience in human resources. She is the cofounder and partner of Titan Group LLC, a consulting firm that loves to partner with leaders who want to create great places to work. She has performed as a business partner with varied industries, including technology, health care, manufacturing, retail, financial services, nonprofit, and professional services. She has specialized experience in executive coaching, leadership and organizational development, selection and recruiting, and assessments. Besides serving on the boards of several local charities, she also is a regular columnist for Virginia Business.com. She is married with two wonderful kids and loves to play golf and travel. Email: genevieve@titanhr.com; blog: http://www.titanhr.com/blog; Web site: http://www.titanhr.com.

88

5 Steps to Stand out From the Crowd and Get the Job

≈⌒≈

Darshan Shanti

One reason that competing in today's job market is tougher than ever is there are more people vying for fewer positions. So if an employer has dozens of candidates (or more) to interview, you have to stand out. You have to differentiate yourself from everyone else. You have to be memorable. Why? Because if you're just like everyone else, you'll get lost in the crowd. For example, just think of Simon Cowell from *American Idol* and *X Factor*. He would say to some contestants after they've auditioned, "You're absolutely forgettable. I won't remember you." Do you want a potential employer thinking that about you? I don't think so.

Read these five quick, but powerful, tips and strategies and apply what they say, and you'll be well on your way to landing the perfect job for you.

Step 1. Be Yourself

Be genuine. Be authentic. Just be real. People can sense if you're faking it because you're trying to impress them. There's no need for that. There's only one you. If you try to be a carbon copy of someone else, even if you get the job, it won't last because you can't keep faking it. When you're asked questions in the interview, answer them honestly. Don't make stuff up or tell interviewers what you think they want to hear. If you don't know something, just say you don't know. If you are unsure of what their question is, ask what they mean. They will see you're not just a robot and that you can think for yourself and not just spitting out answers that sound good.

Step 2. Be Confident

You know you can do the job, don't you? You know you would be extremely effective at whatever you're assigned to do, don't you? You sure had better be. If you're not, what do you think an employer is going to sense in you? A lack of confidence is a surefire way to make sure that your application goes into the "no" pile. On the other hand, strength and confidence are very powerful and send a message to the people interviewing you that you're more than capable.

By the way, don't worry about the other candidates applying for the job. They've got certain skills, talents, and abilities; and so do you. So whether they've got more education or experience or more of something else, it doesn't matter because you can't do anything about the other people interviewing. It only matters that you are confident, sure, and certain and that you communicate that you are the best candidate for the job.

Step 3. Be Present

When you're being interviewed, be completely focused on the interview; don't become attached to the outcome. Don't be desperate. Don't be needy.

To illustrate my point, think of a pushy salesperson who is trying to sell you something you don't want. No matter what you say, he keeps pushing and pushing. Why is that? One reason may be because he has to make the sale. It's all about his need; it's not about you. He's attached to the outcome, and you can sense that. And it actually pushes you away.

The bottom line is this: even if you need the job, don't worry about the result because if you do, the interviewers will sense it, and you'll push them away. It's not the end of the world if you don't get that job. There are more out there. That's what you have to keep in mind. You'll be OK no matter what. And when one door closes, another one always opens, and you could find an even better opportunity than the one you're interviewing for.

Step 4. Have a Great Attitude

Attitude is altitude. The better your attitude, the higher you'll go. When you're around happy people, you feel better; you feel happier; and your energy goes up. On the other hand, when you're around negative, sad, or angry people, you feel those emotions too. You want to leave the best impression you can. Having a great attitude sends an unconscious signal to the interviewers that when you're around, people are going to feel better.

How do you do that? Here are two possible ways. Just look in the mirror before you go to the interview and put a smile on your face and tell yourself at least 10 times something like, "I can do it. I've got this handled. This is my job." On your way to the interview, listen to music that pumps you up and makes you feel good and gets you in the right, positive frame of mind.

Step 5. Relax

Let your shoulders drop. You've done everything you can to prepare for the interview. You know your stuff. There's no need to be anxious. Sometimes people work themselves into a frenzy trying to think of everything that they might get asked in an interview. Well, you can't know everything. The truth is that you can't say the right things to the wrong people and you can't say the wrong things to the right people. So, if you're not a fit, you're not a fit, and there's nothing that you can do about it. If you are the right fit, you can bumble practically everything and you'll still get the job.

These simple and easy tips will prepare you, relax you, and give you a great game plan to go in and truly impress your potential employers. Take them to heart and put them into practice, and pretty soon you'll be starting your new career.

Bio

Darshan is the founder and president of Freedom Incorporated, Inc. He is a personal and professional development leadership speaker, coach, and author of the book *The 24 Hour Champion: Discovering AND Living Your Priceless Life*. Across North America, he has worked with more than 30,000 people and spoken to more than 1,100 audiences from many diverse industries and backgrounds to help them find their hidden potential, purpose, passions, dreams, and desires so they may experience true freedom in their lives and big success in their business.

89

Mastering the Business of Staying Employed

※◡～౩⁓

Barbara Wainwright

In 1986, I founded J.F. Positive Systems, Inc., a software development company, which I ran for 23 years. As a consultant, I was never out of work, not even for a day. I attribute this to three things.

- Networking: I constantly kept in touch with recruiters, coworkers, hiring authorities, and other consultants.
- Providing excellence: When I consulted, I did my utmost to provide excellence in all areas of my work.
- Opportunity seeking: I was always on the lookout for ways to be of service.

Networking

Staying in touch with people who you can help and people who can help you is so important. You never know who is going to be in an authority position to hire you one day. Your coworkers today may be the hiring authority of tomorrow. Colleagues can be great sources for job referrals. Employment agents and recruiters can be your best friends.

Something that many job seekers don't realize is the difference between human resource personnel and agency recruiters (headhunters). The difference is that recruiters are connected to the hiring authority and know exactly what that hiring authority is looking for. Human resource personnel are primarily responsible for making sure that you are capable of being a great employee, that your previous employers didn't fire you for incompetence, and that you are not a troublemaker.

Think about it. Part of HR's function is to keep out the riffraff. The consequence of hiring someone who has a poor work ethic, or a shady past, is huge for employers. In addition, HR personnel are inundated with résumés. You are lucky if your résumé makes it to the hiring authority's desk.

Agency recruiters are primarily responsible for making sure you fit the detailed criteria for the job and that you can competently fulfill the requirements of the position. Recruiters typically have long-term relationships with the hiring authorities they serve. Recruiters are specialists in finding the right person to fit the job requirements. Placing people in jobs is the way recruiters make their living.

Think about it. Agents are there to find candidates who are perfect for the job. They will promote you directly to the hiring authority, sometimes without even submitting your résumé to them. They are your advocates. They are specialists in their field. For instance, some agents specifically recruit for CEOs or doctors or attorneys. That's all they do. Their job is to know who is looking for a job and who is looking for a new employee. That's it. They are in the business of matchmaking.

Providing Excellence

Providing excellence in everything you do will take you far when it comes to looking for work. By providing excellent work, you will get great references, which is a huge plus. Always get your references written on letterhead from the company that you were working for. People change jobs and sometime are unavailable to give a "live" reference for you.

Be outgoing and friendly while you work. The more friends you make while working, the more referrals you will get and the more people you will know who could potentially hire you in the future.

Opportunity Seeking

Going above and beyond in your work efforts will bring plenty of rewards. Be social. Get to know everyone, and always find out how you can be of service.

I'll give you an example here. I was working for a software company (I'll call it Company X) that created a customer management and mobile phone billing system. The billing process was very complex, as were the programs that calculated the billing, created the invoices, and performed other functions. Company X outsourced the billing system maintenance to another company that, unfortunately for Company X, was going out of business.

The in-house programmers of Company X knew the billing system was complicated and didn't want to touch it. They had good reason. The system was complex, with a long learning curve to understand it and little documentation on how it worked. It was a critical piece to the entire system, and if an error was made, there would be undesirable consequences. (No one likes an error on an invoice!)

Naturally, I saw this as a golden opportunity. I decided that I would learn the system by digging into the code. Eventually, I became known in Company X as the "Billing Queen." And because no one else wanted to learn the system, I was consulting for Company X for a very long time.

Networking, providing excellence, and always being on the lookout for opportunities to be of service are great ways to stay out of the job-seeking market!

Bio

Barbara Wainwright, CEO and founder of Wainwright Global—Institute of Professional Coaching, has dedicated her life to helping others. Barbara's life experiences led her on a path of self-discovery and higher learning in her personal quest to make the world a better place for her family, friends, and clients. As an author, speaker, and master coach, Barbara's dream is for each person to live a life of divine purpose, which she believes leads to an experience of authentic inner peace, which leads to outer peace, resulting in peace on Earth. You can contact Barbara at (800) 711-4346;
http://www.LifeCoachTainingOnline.com;
http://www.bestofcoaching.com;
http://www.twitter.com/bwainwright;
http://www.facebook.com/barbara.g.wainwright;
http://www.barbara.trustedteam.com; and
http://www.linkedin.com/in/barbarawainwright.

90

Healthy Eating for the People on the Run

≈⌇≈

Kathy O'Keeffe, MS, RD/LD, CDE

In today's job market, it's tough to be competitive if your energy is low. Everyone knows it's important to eat healthy, but how can you do this when you're a busy parent, business owner, professional constantly on the go?

Typically, busy people skip meals or run into a convenience store and grab chips and a soda for a quick pick-me-up. The meal skippers end up overeating more high-fat, high-calorie foods later in the day and exceed their calorie needs. The desperate consumption of quick pick-me-ups usually results in feeling less satisfied and more exhausted later in the day.

Ask yourself, "What are my overall personal and professional health goals?" Do you want to maintain higher energy levels and greater productivity? Poor eating habits can negatively impact both energy and productivity. Would you include better food choices if it took minimal effort on your part? You can if you start with a strategy and the essential ideas that work: *thinking ahead* and *keeping track*.

To begin, dispel all the negative myths you've heard yourself say about healthy eating. ("I don't have time." "I do better if I skip breakfasts or lunches.") Next, develop a plan or a strategic approach, whatever you want to call this. Thinking ahead will enable you to consume healthy foods when you're too busy or too distracted.

These suggestions can ensure nutritious eating when you're on the go.

Go for the Color

No, jellybeans won't count! Include a variety of food with colors—greens, reds, oranges, yellows, purples. Almost all of these colored foods, primarily fruits and vegetables, are excellent choices for a variety of vitamins and minerals and tend to be lower in calorie content. Even if you take a vitamin/mineral tablet, unidentified food substances, known as phytochemicals, seem to have health benefits. These phytochemicals are more prevalent in brightly pigmented foods. Ideas for increasing your diet's color palette:

- Use romaine lettuce and other dark green leafy vegetables as the basis for a salad.
- Add carrots, red and green peppers, and purple onions.
- Add slices of peaches or blueberries to yogurts or cereals.
- Eat an orange.

Choose Whole Grains

Whole-grain foods typically contain various types of dietary fiber that provide wonderful health benefits: satiety (the full after-meal feeling), slower digestion of foods, improved cholesterol levels, and lower risks for colon cancer. The key: *read the label*! Just because a label states "whole grain" does not necessarily mean high-fiber content. Look for food items that contain at least 3 grams of fiber per serving. Choosing higher-fiber foods throughout the day can enable you to consume the recommended 25 to 40 grams of fiber per day.

The Benefits of Breakfast

Lots of folks know that breakfast is the most important meal of the day but balk at having one. ("It takes too much time." "I'm not hungry in the morning." "If I eat breakfast, I'm hungrier later in the day.") However, study data are consistent: skipping that morning meal compromises physical and mental performance. To be a more productive worker, eat your breakfast! (Just as your mom always told you.)

Be Restaurant Wary

Avoid the all-you-can-eat restaurants. People always try to consume their money's worth but then exceed their daily calorie needs. In general, you may need to fear fast-food restaurants. But some of the popular chains offer good choices if you know what to look for. Following are some examples. (*Note*: None of these suggestions is an endorsement for any of these restaurants. The items listed are merely *suggestions*.)

- Taco Bell: Bean Burrito = 370 calories, 960 milligrams of sodium, 9 grams of fiber; Fresco Soft Taco = 340 calories, 530 milligrams sodium, 3 grams fiber.
- McDonald's: Grilled Chicken Sandwich (hold the mayo) = 350 calories, 530 milligrams sodium, 3 grams of fiber.
- Hardee's: Look for Low-Carb It, Trim It, Veg-It as options.

Overall, you may want to forget the fries. (Sorry, but it's true!) When choosing fast foods, look for calories listed and other nutrition information. Omit the condiments such as mayonnaise, guacamole, sour cream, butter. Ask for other condiments to be included on the side so you can control the amount you eat. (You can find additional information at the resources listing at the end of this chapter.)

Pack It Yourself

Follow the ideas presented previously: colors, whole grains, lower fat. Suggestions include:

- ¼ cup hummus + ½ cup sliced carrot chips + 1 whole wheat bagel (frozen grocery store size) + ½ slice of low-fat Swiss cheese + 1 teaspoon mustard + water or cal-free drink = about 495 calories, 595 milligrams sodium, 10 grams fiber, and a full tummy.
- ¼ cup roasted, lightly salted cashew + 1 cup raw veggies (broccoli, carrots, cauliflower) + 1 cereal bar + 1 small apple = about 410 calories, 210 milligrams sodium, 12 grams fiber, and another satisfied luncher.

Meal Replacements

Some people do better with having an item ready to replace the choices and preparation of other options. Suggestions include power or energy bars, frozen meals, and smoothies. Look for lower sugar content, approximately 10 grams of protein, lower fat content, and approximately 300 to 400 calories.

Mind Your Meals

Mindfulness—paying attention to what is currently taking place— can have great pay-offs if you want a healthy lifestyle. Some recent research studies have reported that the less we pay attention to what we're eating, the more we eat. So, "inhaling" food while working at your desk may save you a few minutes, but you'll find that the "meal" you just ate won't be filling or satisfying. So take 5! Take 10! Go ahead, take 15! (That's minutes, not servings of food!) And then really savor the food! Appreciate the flavors, tastes, aromas, textures—really enjoy it all. You will find that you'll feel fuller and more satisfied with your meal.

Keeping Track

Nothing works better to ensure healthy eating than documenting the foods consumed. Keeping track allows you to be more aware and more mindful of your food intake. Regardless of the method you use (your own Excel spreadsheet, written records, or a point system), *do it*! Research studies have reported that keeping track for three days, one of which is a weekend day, is sufficient recording to stay on track.

Additional Ideas and Resources

Short of hiring your own personal registered dietitian to analyze, prepare, and provide you with food throughout the day, here's a summary of what you can do.

- Plan ahead.
- Keep a record.

- Generally, avoid fried foods; omit the sauces; ask for salad dressings on the side. Try to consume at least 300 to 500 calories for those meals on the go.
- Include a variety of food with colors (dark green vegetables, red tomatoes, orange carrots, green cabbage, purple onions).
- Overall, know yourself. If you do better with fewer choices, do that. If you need a variety of foods to stay on track, follow that approach.

With minimal effort and thinking ahead, keeping track, and making these ideas part of your lifestyle, you can successfully eat healthy on the run.

For additional and more specific information, the following resources provide sound, quality nutrition advice, as well as sample menus, suggestions for healthy eating, and calorie and nutrient content of many foods:

- Academy of Nutrition and Dietetics (http://www.eatright.org)
- American Diabetes Association (http://www.diabetes.org and http://www.ShopDiabetes.org)
- American Heart Association (http://www.heart.org)
- *Guide to Healthy Fast Food Eating*, by Hope Warsaw (available at www.Amazon.com)

Bio

Kathy has worked as a registered dietitian and certified diabetes educator for over 25 years, teaching, training, mentoring, and now coaching students, patients, and clients. She actively participates in various professional organizations, including the Academy of Nutrition and Dietetics, American Diabetes Association, American Heart Association, Wellcoaches, and Dietitians in Business and Communications. She is the founder and owner of KOK Consulting & Coaching, which partners with businesses and individuals to achieve their professional goals. Kathy's mission is to enable people to make healthier choices that improve personal performance and business outcomes. Contact Kathy at http://www.koksolutions.com; she can also be found on Facebook and LinkedIn.

91

Strengths: A Great Way to Compete in Today's Job Market

Julie Hickton

If you knew that you would enjoy and be energized by what you did and were generally more productive than others around you, how great would that be? It's possible through connecting with your strengths. A strength is something that you are good at, that you enjoy doing, that energizes you. It brings together your natural talents, your skills, and your knowledge naturally, producing high performance in this area.

Often we don't recognize our strengths because they feel so normal that we think everyone can do it. This is not the case. It's also important to understand what a strength is not. We may be good at something that we have learnt how to do. And, over time as we have used this skill, we have become skilled at it. However, you notice it drains you. It seems to take energy to motivate yourself to do it. Just because you are good at something does not mean it's a strength.

Understanding your strengths helps you to compete into today's job market. Knowing who you are and what you are good at enables you to find a role that better suits your natural talents and strengths, which will enhance your performance in the role and your enjoyment. This is beneficial for you and the organization. If you seem to be dissatisfied with your current role, working with your strengths to redesign it could bring back more energy and enjoyment.

For example: I was coaching a lady who was, on first meeting, truly dissatis-fied with what she was doing. She felt tired. She didn't feel she was using her talents and was starting to think it was time to find another role. We worked on identifying her strengths and relooked at her role in connection with these. She was not using her strengths as often as she had been in a previous role but hadn't realized it. Through a bit of redesigning and change of emphasis, she managed to shift what and how she was delivering in her role to utilize more of her strengths. As time evolved and she used more of her strengths, she realized she didn't need to leave her job. The changes she had made enabled her to feel more energized, and she was enjoying what she did.

We often focus on our weaknesses. They can't be ignored if they are required for the role, but it's about being imaginative in how we mitigate for them. Rather than spending huge amounts of time trying to become good at them, find a partner or another member of the team who has it as a strength.

A while back, I did a job share as a training manager for a large retail company in the United Kingdom. At the time, I didn't fully understand the strengths concept and wondered why our boss had put us together. Initially, there was some tension around our joint working. We were lucky enough to come across the strengths concept and got ourselves assessed through an online assessment. Once we shared our profiles and redesigned how we worked the role to harness our individual strengths, we transformed our performance and how we felt about working together.

Redesign Your Current Role

- Is it that you really don't enjoy your role, or is it about redesigning it so you can utilize more of your strengths?
- What is it that really deenergizes you? Be clear so you can look at what else you can do with those tasks.
- Whom can you delegate these to?
- Whom can you pair up with to redistribute, based on your different strengths?
- If you work within a team, how can you work on distribution of tasks based on strengths rather than traditional job roles?
- Can you do the task differently so that the outcome will still need to be achieved but can you do it in a different way that utilizes your strengths?

371

- Finally, if none of the above is possible, what can you do to learn how to do that task more effectively so that you minimize the weakness so it no longer impacts on your performance negatively?

Future Role

The first step to ensure that your future role connects with your strengths is to know what your strengths are. Once you know what they are, understand how you currently use them or how in the past you have used them. Being able to describe what and how you achieve things helps you draw up a CV that reflects your strengths and will enable you at interviews to describe your strength-based successes. When you are looking for roles, having a clearer understanding of your strengths will enable you to better match yourself to potential roles. If you don't have an idea of what type of role will bring out your best performance, then you potentially will find a role that doesn't tap into your strengths and deenergizes you.

Another client I did career coaching with was in the situation where she knew that in eight months her role was going to be eliminated. The great thing about this is that we had time to really explore what she wanted to do, as well as identify the key ingredients she needed to ensure she performed at her best. We identified her strengths ensuring any role she considered would enable her to use her strengths when she delivered it. She was able to articulate at interviews her strengths-based successes and ensure that the role she chose enabled her to use her strengths.

Tapping into Your Strengths

You can explore your strengths through asking yourself a number of questions.

- As a child what did you find yourself spending your time doing?
- What is it you enjoy doing?
- What do you find yourself gravitating toward doing when you have free time?
- When you are performing at your best, what are you doing?
- What are you doing when you feel invigorated?
- What are doing when you feel energized?
- What are you doing when you feel it's the real you?
- What are you doing when you lose track of time and are fully absorbed?

Another way is take one of the online assessments available.

- The Clifton Strengths Finder measures the presence of 34 talent themes and is supported by the book *Now Develop Your Strengths* by Marcus Buckingham (https://www.gallupstrengthscenter.com).
- The Via Strengths Inventory measures 24 character strengths and is supported by positive psychologists Christopher Peterson and Martin Seligman (http://www.viacharacter.org).
- The Reaslie2 model looks at realized and unrealized strengths, as well as weaknesses and learned behavior, and is supported by Alex Linley's book *The Strengths Book* (http://www.cappeu.com).
- Strengths Scope looks at strengths in four categories: relational, execution, emotional, and thinking (http://www.strengthscope.com).

Enjoy being energized by what you do. Harness your strengths and continue to develop them. One note of caution: be aware that you don't overplay them so they have a negative impact on your performance.

Bio

Julie's passion for assisting individuals and businesses to achieve their potential is a real inspiration. Her positive motivational personality is infectious, creating a real sense of purpose, focus, and enjoyment for all those who work with her. Julie uses her previous business experience and people understanding, along with her coaching talents, to assist businesses and individuals to understand their key people-related issues and how to harness their talents to achieve both business and individual success. She is a real believer in positive psychology, utilizing one's strengths and emotional intelligence, and ensuring one's well-being is in balance before starting to work on other aspects. Visit her Web site, http://www.naturescoaching.co.uk. Visit her on LinkedIn http://www.linkedin.com/in/juliehickton. Join her on Twitter JulieHickton@NaturesCoaching.

92

How to Use Targeted Selection to Stand out From the Crowd When Interviewing for a Job

Bob Kantor

Note: Although this chapter refers specifically to the IT industry, it applies just as readily to all job markets and to all types of jobs within those markets.

The IT industry prides itself on using structured methodologies to dramatically improve process quality and efficiency. We create and apply these methodologies even to creative processes that seem not to lend themselves to such structured approaches, for example, bringing engineering discipline to the art of coding.

One such process that is critical to the success of all IT organizations, and to optimizing the development of our careers, is the job-interview process. Yet many job seekers and hiring managers still practice this key process as an art form rather than as a process structured for repeatable successful outcomes.

I hear from the hundreds of IT managers with whom I do leadership coaching that they struggle with making the job-interview process an effective tool for finding the right candidates. I also hear from the dozens of search firms with whom I collaborate that both candidates and hiring managers constantly sub-optimize this critical business process.

The good news is that a simple process has been successfully used by firms as a best practice for the interview process. The better news is that IT job seekers can also use this same tool to stand out from the crowd. Understanding how to make the most of this process will significantly enhance your chances for a successful interview, whether or not the interviewer uses the same technique. That is, if your interviewers use it, you will be much better prepared to address their questions. If your interviewers don't use it, then your use of the technique will improve the quality of the interview process and give you more control of the conversation.

This simple process is called targeted selection (TS). It's based upon the premise that past performance in work situations is often a good indicator of future performance in similar situations. Even though the financial services industry is quick to advise us that this is not the case for financial investments, the HR industry has many studies to prove that it is the case for on-the-job performance.

The TS process is a behavior-based approach to collect job-related behavior from your past experience. As such, the basic structure of a TS interview question includes the phrase, "Tell me about a time when ..." or "Tell me about a situation where ... ." Contrast this to these more typical interview questions:

- Do you know ... ?
- What is ... ?
- What would you do if ... ?
- How would you handle ... ?

How and Why Targeted Selection Works for the Hiring Company

Targeted selection works so well and is so highly valued by the companies that use it for several reasons. A person's past behavior *is* a good predictor of future behavior in similar circumstances. This is why financial institutions place so much emphasis on your credit history, which is a reflection of your past behavior related to managing your money.

Additionally, TS brings a repeatable structure to what is too often an unstructured process. When a company applies targeted selection to its job openings, managers specify all the critical requirements of the job. This includes skills, qualities, knowledge, and behaviors most important for succeeding in the job. They then create a list of questions specifically designed to uncover how well your experience matches their requirements. (This is actually similar to the process of designing test cases for a project's test-case register.)

The specificity needed to answer such experiential-based questions quickly weeds out people with insufficient experience and makes it much harder for candidates to bluff their way through the questions. It's relatively easy for anyone to give a good answer to, "How would you handle a client who demanded an unreasonable project completion date?" It's more of a challenge—and better indicator of what you would do in the future—to answer, "Tell me about a time when a client demanded an unreasonable project completion date. What were the circumstances? What did you do? How did they react? What was the final outcome?"

How to Use Targeted Selection as a Job Seeker

The same properties that make TS so valuable for hiring companies make it a potent tool for the job seeker as well. Planning for a TS-interview process prepares you to provide much higher quality answers to any interview question, whether or not is based on the behavioral approach.

Suppose, for example, you were asked a typical interview question like, "What do you know about pivot tables?" Anyone could provide a fairly generic answer to the question, whether or not he or she had extensive hands-on experience. For example: "A pivot table is a data summarization tool in data visualization programs like Excel and BI software. It can sort, count, total, or give the average of the data stored in one table and display the results in a second table showing the summarized data."

Compare that to providing a brief story of how you addressed an actual business situation by using a pivot table. For example: "Several months ago one of our sales managers came to us with a request for a program to analyze data on a recent campaign. He was in a hurry for the results and was not quite sure what he wanted. It was one of those 'I'll know it when I see it situations' we so often face. So I suggested we sit down and play with his data in Excel to get a sense of what trends they might contain. We imported a representative extract from the sales system into Excel and then used the Pivot Table functions to slice and dice the data. By working interactively with him, he quickly saw what he wanted to know, and within half an hour had the answer to his questions. In fact, he had figured out a useful set of questions around which he could do further analysis on his own."

How much more compelling is this second approach than the first one? Look at what you've communicated by answering the question this way:

- I've actually done this hands-on.
- I was creative and responsive to my client's needs.
- I was effective at helping the client clarify those needs and showed up as part of the solution. (How often do IT staff stumble when clients aren't sure what they need?)
- I'm comfortable in situations of ambiguity.
- I can communicate well and collaborate with colleagues.
- I get things done.
- I'm credible!

Another benefit for the job seeker in this latter scenario is that we are often more comfortable and articulate when we describe a situation that actually occurred than we are with answering to a more conceptual question.

Here are some tips for applying TS and preparing for an interview:

- Identify the key skills, qualities, knowledge, and behaviors most important for succeeding in the job.
- Identify one to three experiences you have in applying or using those behaviors. You may want to use some different examples with different interviewers. This way when they compare notes after the interviews, they get an even more impressive picture.
- Practice telling your story for each experience a few times, until you can describe it easily and briefly. Give a short version as your initial answer and allow the interviewers to ask for more detail if they want it.

Once you have your arsenal of stories, keep an open mind during the interview and be flexible. If you are asked a question for which you don't have a perfect fit, respond along the lines of, "I was in a situation somewhat like that one once where … ."

<u>B</u>io

Bob Kantor is an IT management coach and consultant, specializing in improving IT leadership effectiveness. He also provides career-development coaching to all levels of executives across multiple industries. You can reach him at Bob.Kantor@KantorConsultingGroup.com.

93

Telephonic Appearance

They Can Hear You in Your Pajamas (And Taking the Job Search Seriously)

Michelle A. Riklan, ACRW, CPRW, CEIC

We live in a world today that brings a completely new meaning to multitasking. Potential employers call about our résumé while we're driving to the soccer field; deals are negotiated in the supermarket produce section. With virtual offices, teleconferences, e-summits, and Skype, we need to be aware of the types of messages that we are sending and their appropriateness.

- Nonverbal body language makes up for 55 percent of communication.
- Our tone, speed, and volume of voice make up 38 percent.
- Our words equal 7 percent.

Communication

Nonverbal body language: 55%

Tone, speed, and volume of voice: 38%

Words: 7%

If you think that the person on the other end of the phone is not getting a message from your nonverbal communication, simply because they cannot see you, you would be incorrect. Your voice becomes the "telephonic appearance," and how you sound on the phone is affected by your appearance and surrounding.

For example, let's say you have sent your résumé to several places. You just get out of the shower. You're in your bathrobe with wet hair. You run down to the kitchen to grab a piece of toast and are swallowing your last bite as the phone rings with an unrecognizable number. You answer and someone asks for you. Assuming it's a telemarketer, you ask, "Who is this?"

It was a hiring manager calling about the résumé that you recently sent. What was the first impression that you gave? Did you sound rushed? Annoyed? Inconvenienced? Curt? It would have been better to have let the call go to voicemail and returned it when you had your professional hat on your dry hair! Remember, you only have one shot to make a positive, lasting first impression. If that impression is going to be by phone, then you need to control the situation and set it up to your advantage.

Here are some crucial tips for acing during the phone interview and tackling your job search.

- It's easy to get comfortable during a job search. On the other hand, maybe the job search has gotten you down, and you are losing motivation. If you are in job-search mode, get up early, get showered and dressed, and attack your search feeling and looking professional, even if you are not planning to meet with anyone for the day. The reason is simple: they can hear you in your pajamas. Your appearance is important.
- If you are making calls regarding your job search or scheduling a phone interview, take the calls seriously. Place yourself in a professional setting (a home office, quiet room and *not* the car, the mall, the supermarket, or the soccer field). And you certainly don't want anyone to hear any flushing or sinks running! Get yourself comfortable and compose yourself in a professional manner. Take a deep breath and smile before making your calls. You will sound more professional and project a positive image over the phone. Preparation and location matter.
- Call people when you are prepared to do so, not distracted, so you can give the call the attention it warrants. Let unknown calls or calls clearly

from people calling to discuss your résumé go to voicemail if you are not best prepared to answer professionally. Don't get caught with other people talking (or crying) in the background. Set the stage for yourself to project a positive, professional image over the phone. Timing counts.

Remember, they can hear you in your pajamas!

Bio

Michelle A. Riklan is a career expert, speaker, author, certified professional résumé writer, career coach, and employment interview consultant. She is cofounder of Self Improvement Online. She can be reached by phone at (800) 540-3609; by email at Michelle@riklanresources.com; at her Web site at http://www.riklanresources.com; and at http://www.linkedin.com/in/michelleriklan.

94

The 10 Commandments for Competing in Today's Job Market

❧～❧

David Riklan

Finding a new job in today's job market is one of the most challenging things to do. The world is changing rapidly, as is the way we communicate and interact. But with all of these rapid changes, some key rules remain for making changes in your life, including finding a satisfying high-paying job in your field.

I call these key rules the 10 Commandments for Competing in Today's Job Market.

1. Take Responsibility for Your Career

So many experts talk about taking responsibility. When I think about taking responsibility, the question for me is not who is responsible for your current situation but who will take responsibility for where you'll be tomorrow.

The answer for each of us has to be, "I will." It's time to take responsibility for your future job and career growth.

2. Take Action

If you want to make changes in your career, you'll need to take the necessary actions required to advance in your field, to change fields, or to find your next successful position.

We fail to take action for several reasons. The first step is to understand the reasons stopping you. Is it fear? Fear of failure, fear of rejection, fear of success? Is it plain laziness, complacency, bad habits, or despair? Once you understand what is stopping you from taking action, figure out the steps necessary to overcome it. In many cases, that first step of awareness will help propel you forward.

3. Have Desire

"Desire is the starting point of all achievement." — Napoleon Hill

You have to figure out what your passions are to help you discover your desires and dreams. Take a moment to sit back and think. Remember what you dreamt of being when you were a child. Did you want to be an astronaut? The president of the United States? A firefighter?

As we grow older, our dreams start to seem more and more unattainable. But that's only because certain things seem more important to us as we grow up—paying our bills, taking care of our spouse, or making sure the kids are safely tucked in bed. It doesn't give us much time to think about our dreams, our desires, or our passions.

But it isn't just about these lofty dreams that we pursue. We might desire to be more assertive in our personal or professional lives, or we might want to simply be more outgoing. It's just a matter of identifying *what* we want then making it happen.

4. Set Goals

Everyone, no matter who they are, sets goals. The best approach is to create SMART goals: specific, measurable, achievable, relevant, and time framed.

Make your goals specific. Define the exact type of job you want, the job responsibilities, the location. The more specific the goal is, the greater the likelihood that it will be achieved. That goal should also be measurable. "I want to get two job offers with a salary of $85,000." It should be achievable. Are you goals achievable in this time frame?

Make sure they are relevant. Are these goals that truly apply to your life? And make sure they are time framed. When are you going to start and when are you going to finish? For example, "I'll start sending out résumés next Monday, and I want to get a position in three months."

5. Create a Plan

"If you fail to plan, you plan to fail." — Anonymous

This is one of my favorite quotes, most often attributed to Ben Franklin. A well-developed plan includes several practical steps, all leading you toward accomplishing your goal. This plan should include specifics on how to create an effective résumé, how to find the job you want, how to network, how to interview well, how to follow up, and how to move toward getting the job offer you desire. It should include the resources, connections, time, and capital required to get the position you want.

6. Pay the Price

"The price of success is hard work, dedication to the job at hand, and the determination that whether we win or lose, we have applied the best of ourselves to the task at hand." — Vince Lombardi

Finding a new ideal job isn't easy. Sometimes you have to make a sacrifice and "pay the price" to get the position you want. You might need to send out 100 résumés, go to 50 networking meetings, and have 15 interviews.

If you want to get your master's degree, you'll need to pay tuition fees, and you'll need to free up your schedule to find the necessary time to attend classes. But that's not all. You'll have to pay the price as far as your social life goes because it's likely you'll be spending a lot of time studying.

7. Be Persistent

"Nothing in the world can take the place of persistence. Talent will not; nothing is more common than unsuccessful men with talent. Genius will not; unrewarded genius is almost a proverb. Education will not; the world is full of educated derelicts. Persistence and determination alone are omnipotent." — Calvin Coolidge

Setbacks are inevitable. But when a setback or roadblock to your goal shows up, don't let it stop you. One thing to keep in mind about being persistent is that you should try to be as prepared as you possibly can before attempting something. If the trials associated with staying persistent are getting you down, find a buddy to help motivate you. And remember to keep your overall goal in mind. It'll help you keep things in perspective when accomplishing your goal starts getting tougher than you had first anticipated.

8. Believe

"If you believe you can, you probably can. If you believe you won't, you most assuredly won't. Belief is the ignition switch that gets you off the launching pad." — Denis Waitley

You'll need to believe in yourself and your own ability to find the job you want. Positive self-talk also helps. When you go to do something challenging, it's crucial to maintain a positive internal dialogue with yourself. Don't immediately think, "There's no way that I could solve this" or "I'm not good enough for that company to hire me."

What you should be thinking is, "If I apply myself, I can solve this problem" or "I'm qualified, intelligent, charismatic, and hard working. If these guys don't hire me, it's their loss, not mine."

9. Learn from Your Mistakes

"All men make mistakes, but only wise men learn from their mistakes." — Winston Churchill

You work and work and work at something, putting in the proper amount of planning and effort. But you fail anyway. It's not the end of the world. And it's going to happen again. It's all a matter of perspective. Instead of seeing a failure just as something you messed up, start seeing failure as a learning experience. Think about what went wrong, and identify mistakes you made along the way. If you don't usually think of an alternate plan before trying to do something, I recommend that you start doing exactly that. And be positive about it. Try to have a sense of humor about your failure. Don't beat yourself up. That's only going to delay the chance of your reaching your goal.

10. Create a Clear Picture of Your Future and Visualize It

"Picture yourself in your mind's eye as having already achieved this goal. See yourself doing the things you'll he doing when you've reached your goal." — Earl Nightingale

Another important method that can help you accomplish anything—be it a minor job change or a full-blown career change—is the art of visualization. Simply picture the result of all of your efforts to fulfill your personal vision. If your vision is to get a position as director of operations, picture it clearly in your mind's eye.

These are the 10 Commandments for Competing in Today's Job Market. If you can implement these 10 commandments, you'll be on your way to getting the career you want.

Bio

David Riklan is the founder and president of Self Improvement Online, Inc. His company specializes in publishing information on self-improvement and natural health on the Internet. The company manages multiple Web sites, including SelfGrowth.com, the No. 1 ranked Web site for self-improvement on the Internet. His Web sites get more than 2 million visitors a month. His company also publishes four different email newsletters (ezines) going out to more than 950,000 subscribers weekly. David has published eight print books on self-improvement, natural health, marketing, and sales. David's first book, *Self-Improvement: The Top 101 Experts Who Help Us Improve Our Lives,* has been praised by leading industry experts as the "encyclopedia of self-improvement." His most recent books include *Mastering the World of Marketing* and *Mastering the World of Selling*. David has also created four powerful Internet marketing and training programs on e-book marketing, search engine optimization, email marketing, and social media.

95

Muse Methods: Why It's Secretly Great That Times Are Bad

Jennifer Sebesta-Gligoric

My muse ability is showing people their truth and then helping them act. It means that you look around you and don't deny the reality. Ask yourself: "Is gas higher than milk? Do the majority of your friends have full-time jobs that support them?" Describe the activity at your town's business district and mall.

When I read *Who Moved My Cheese?* by Spencer Johnson, a book with a very large message, my take-away (as with countless others) was the nine-word query: "What would I do if I were not afraid?"

Fear has struck us all as the recession has turned into depression. The silver lining is that all the richest, most accomplished, and most successful Americans created their wealth during depressed times. It's the best time for those of us who believe heart and soul in the American Dream. Thankfully, the rags-to-riches aspiration is still very much alive and hasn't been ground into dust by the *über* rich whose communistic ideals of utopia involve making everyone else feel guilty for wanting to have the same luxuries they enjoy. I realize that you might be one of the people who can't sleep at night because some goat herder in a country I can't pronounce can't sell his goat milk. But that is *his* government's problem. What about *our* goat herders whose milk gets mixed with stem cells for my antiaging cream? That last part is something I just made up, but there you go.

I am not so obtuse as to not realize that there are many who believe the idea of America as the shining golden society where all citizens feel a global duty to live as incredibly well as possible, thus lifting up the whole world, can't be achieved, despite its previous success doing just that. They feel that America is too happy, too prosperous, and this joy somehow hurts all the other countries and peoples of the world when they listen to our music and drink our soda because our prosperity comes at some invisible cost to all.

I'm here to tell you that's not so. There is more than enough in the universe for everyone to be completely and totally fulfilled because what fulfills you does not fulfill that goat herder. So let's get started on how you can more than just survive the next 10 years but really prosper by following, what I call, my six Jenness rules.

Rule 1: Get up Early

Get up earlier than you normally do, get dressed, and leave your "lazy zone." This lazy zone could be your entire home or just your couch, and only you know where it is. The clothing is clean, work casual, and something you wouldn't mind being caught in should you run into someone you haven't seen since high school.

Rule 2: Don't Waste Time at Local Workforce or Governmental Job-Search Sites to Find a Job

This rule is sure to be controversial, especially with those who have no clue about reality. All the government-hosted application sites are overcoded with *zero* human reviews of submissions. The only way your résumé will make it through the filters is if you paste the proffered job description straight off the work order. This means you will have to create a new résumé for every job you apply and delete any experience that goes over and above the stated needs or that might be seen as conflicting by the filters. It's worthless.

Rule 3: Think Twice About Working for Free

Never work for free for someone more than four hours a day, four days a week, and take what you can get in barter or future work. Work for free only if you have a reasonable chance of making important contacts or learning something valuable. I got paid by a client once in fine china. Did I need that? No, I needed money; however, the experience I gained doing that technically difficult job was priceless. I am still in contact with them and respect them, and we'll work together in more lucrative ways in the future. I also have come to absolutely adore that china.

Rule 4: The Key to Working Is by Working

Avoid stating you are unemployed on cover letters, emails, voice mail, or to friends. Pay the $35 filing fee for a DBA and put your current "company" on your résumé and in your mind-set during the earlier mentioned free work. The only entities you must reveal your true abysmal income to during the hardest times are the government agencies you may be getting benefits from. Employers, investors, and real friends are not impressed when you admit, "I'm unemployed and spent yesterday in a screaming match while playing Call of Duty with some 10-year-old over voice."

Rule 5: Don't Stay in Situations That Don't Make You Feel Good About Yourself

Don't get involved with shady ventures, and especially don't do anything you'll later be ashamed to admit. You'll never know how important it is for you to be able to look yourself in the mirror until the one day you can't.

Rule 6: Stop Hanging out with Losers

This is the most important Jenness rule. If you want to be a success, you need to say bye-bye to three main people.

The easiest to spot are the *it's-really-about-me's*. The moment you tell them about your job loss or unhappiness, they freak and make it all about them. And when you are down, they curb stomp you. If you come home after a pink slip to a five-hour interrogation designed solely for you to admit to being a failure, and you are expected to comfort them, then pack your stuff and leave because they are the definition of takers.

Second on my list are *passive-aggressive-supporters* who annoyingly "help" by enumerating reasons why any offer you are considering strongly isn't right in the most buzz-kill way possible. There is a big difference between solicited dialogues of "let me play devil's advocate" designed to support your decision and unhealthy, unsolicited deconstructions of potential opportunities designed for you to deflate, feel hopeless, and stagnate. Learn to trust your instincts, and don't be afraid to fail if the opportunity to succeed is high.

Last are the *shame-and-blamers*, who force five-minute conversations into two hours and then have the nerve to complain that you never spend time with them. You feel drained and guilted into not wanting to be drained more. Your conversations consist of you lifelessly muttering, "You're right," ad nauseum. Don't allow people who need more than you feel able to give make you feel bad about focusing on aligning your life with your dreams. The only *S&Ts* you must have a plan for dealing with on a daily basis are your school-aged children. All others need to be put into permanent time-out unless they can learn to be a healthy and supportive part of your life.

Good luck, have fun, and be thankfully excited that you live in times meant for those who believe that hard work and ambition really do pay off.

Bio

Jennifer "Jenness" Sebesta-Gligoric is a muse, conservative, and capitalist business consultant for small to medium-sized American sole proprietors. "In a nutshell, I help start-ups get off the ground and established businesses with new project implementation, expansion, and change. My greatest talent is helping owners of broken ventures stop the decay and take back control of their dreams by actually working by their side to dig into the knots that have prevented them from achieving true growth." To learn more about what a muse offers and to make contact, visit her at http://www.JenniferMarketing.com.

96

How Twitter Can Help You Land a Job

Miriam Salpeter

Maybe you've heard that Google is the new résumé and that your online presence is the most important thing hiring managers will consider when you apply for jobs. In reality, most companies are not abandoning the résumé, and hiring is still done using traditional methods in most companies. However, social media should still be a key component of your job search. What many people forget is that the most time-honored way to get a job is via networking, and social media is just the latest and greatest way to tap and grow your network. Twitter is one of the best online tools to help you network well online.

When used well, Twitter can be a real door opener for job seekers who are willing to try a new strategy to reach out and connect with people who may be able to refer them for jobs. If you're not convinced Twitter can help you, consider this: CareerXroads, a consulting practice, conducts annual studies about how organizations source and hire employees. Their most recent study showed that nearly half of all companies make at least one hire for every five referrals they get.

Even if you're not good at math, it's clear that you'll have a better chance to land an interview (and a job) if you can increase the number of contacts who know, like, and trust you. Luckily, Twitter is a terrific way to improve your chances in all of those areas.

How Twitter Can Help You Compete in Today's Job Market

Provide a mechanism to help you demonstrate your expertise: Job seekers don't always spend time thinking about how to showcase their expertise, but it's an important strategy everyone should keep in mind. If you're an expert in your field, but you don't make an effort to let people know, it's difficult to attract opportunities, and it's unlikely anyone will approach you with an opportunity for a job. When you use Twitter to share information and news about your industry, you make it clear that you have your finger on the pulse of what's going on in your field, even if you're not currently employed.

In addition to highlighting what you know by posting status updates to appeal to people in your field, Twitter gives you a chance to demonstrate skills employers like to see. For example, if you say you're a great, efficient, and effective communicator on your résumé, you can prove it by having a useful and well-written stream of information on Twitter. If you're touting your skills as a great team builder, you can show how you built a community on Twitter as proof.

Allow you to meet and connect with people beyond your normal circle of friends and colleagues: There's a logical limit to how many people you can meet, even if you go to every networking event in your area. When statistics show how important referrals are for job seekers, it becomes a numbers game in addition to a skills issue. How many people know about you, and how many of them would be willing to pass along your name for an opportunity or introduce you to a key contact?

You may be surprised by how generous people on Twitter can be. Even if they have not met you in person, many people who connect with you online and see a useful and intelligent stream of information via your Twitter handle may be willing to connect you with someone who could change your job-search trajectory dramatically! Don't think of Twitter as frivolous; it can help provide some important contacts and potential access to people you'd never otherwise easily access, including CEOs, hiring managers, and colleagues at target companies.

Teach you new information: It's important to keep abreast of what's new in your field, but there's so much to do every day that it's easy to get out of the loop. Once you follow a well-connected, informed group on Twitter, you'll

393

never need much more than to sign into your Twitter account to learn what's new and what's hot in your industry. Ideally, you'll become one of those go-to people to follow. And on your way there, you'll learn a lot about what's going on in your field by following other people who care about the same topics as you and tweet about them.

Help people find you: When you take the time to demonstrate your expertise and expand your network, the next logical step is that you'll make it easier to find you. One of the best things about social media is the opportunity to reverse the job-search process. Instead of always applying for jobs (pushing your résumé and application into a position), social media allows you to be out in the media sphere so hiring managers have a chance to find you. Wouldn't it be great to be recruited to your next job, without even needing to apply? That's more of an option when you hop on Twitter and other social media sites to showcase what you know and engage with potential colleagues.

Don't discount the social media tool with the bird logo. You could be 140 characters away from connecting with someone with the power to change your career!

Bio

Miriam Salpeter, owner of Keppie Careers, is an in-demand coach, writer, and speaker regarding job-search and small business marketing strategies. She is author of *Social Networking for Career Success* and coauthor of *100 Conversations for Career Success* and *Social Networking for Business Success*. CNN named Miriam a top 10 job tweeter, and she's been featured on CNN and quoted in outlets such as the *Wall Street Journal* and the *New York Times* for her cutting-edge advice. Miriam teaches job seekers and entrepreneurs how to take advantage of social media tools and creates and optimizes social media profiles. Learn about Miriam via her website: http://www.keppiecareers.com.

97

Winning in the Résumé-Saturated Job Market

꿏꿏꿏

Adam Maggio

Most people cannot compete in today's job market. Why? Simply because they do not *understand* today's job market. The days of showing up in a shiny suit with a smile on your face and a résumé are long gone. And, truthfully, there has never been more opportunity than there is now.

Back in the day, our parents sought out good employers that made a promise to "take care" of them. This made sense. After all, Dad retired from the factory after 25 years and more than likely met Mom there. In the old days, before career fairs and access to Monster.com, we were often hired at a job because Mom and Dad worked there previously.

The Résumé for Today

Then came along infinite means of global communication: the Internet. As the Internet became more prominent, Web sites such as Monster.com and Careerbuilder.com grew to be incredibly popular. Through use of these Web sites, job seekers simply posted a résumé and waited for potential employers to contact them. As a result of the simplicity, people seeking employment flooded the Web sites' job boards, and the quality of the résumé suffered considerably.

Because there are so many applicants for a given job nowadays, employers have the upper hand. An incredibly large pool of individuals is seeking the same jobs as you are. To put it lightly—and to get my point across—*you* need to *stand out*. Résumés just don't cut it in today's job market. It's your responsibility to differentiate yourself from the competition.

We live in a "what have you done for me lately?" society. Potential employers need to know what *you* can bring to the table that *someone else cannot*. They need to see and feel that you're a quality hire, not just have it written on a piece of paper.

The Internet has increased our efficiency dramatically. You're no longer competing locally for employment. You're competing globally. Internet bandwidth has made outsourcing almost the norm. As each week passes, online outsourcing increases in prominence and popularity.

Entire books have been written on the idea of the four-hour workweek. People with MBAs in India are working for pennies on the dollar; manufacturing in China is dirt cheap. If you want a design team in London, you have it available at your fingertips.

If you really want to stand out for an employer, you need to take chances. The future economy will be dominated and controlled by risk takers, those who think outside the box and refuse to accept the status quo. When applying for a position, shoot a quick video. This is what it takes to differentiate yourself and catch an employer's eye. Extra effort illustrates an eagerness to work. This can go a long way in the current job market. An employer, particularly a company on the cutting edge, will appreciate your additional effort and creativity.

Introduce You

The steps are actually very simple. And, seriously, don't worry about messing this up. Probably 99 percent of people won't even try this. (In case you haven't noticed, it's tough to get people to follow advice.)

- State which field you are qualified to be in and why.
- State what you can bring to the table.
- Allow the word to spread, and have employers actually seek you out.
- Start networking with people who are going places; attend events; and even ask for pointers.
- Volunteer your time in the field you're interested in.

- Consider an internship. Internships are no longer just for hung-over college students.

Jobs Are for Employees, Not Entrepreneurs

Employees essentially trade their freedom for security. Give up your security for freedom. Seriously, what is so secure about a job anymore? We're living in the 21st century, and stuff moves at the speed of light. Consistent evolution and change lead to huge opportunities.

Remember, there is always some sort of trend going on. On one side of the trend, money is made. On the other side of the trend, money is lost. The trend is to not be an employee, but an *entrepreneur.* If you want to make money and become a better individual in the process, look for entrepreneurial opportunities and make yourself stand out in the crowd. Start actively looking for opportunities, not jobs. They are everywhere.

The truth is, if you want to compete in today's job market, you must create your own opportunities. Luckily, there are plenty of them out there. All you have to do is open your eyes and take advantage of the opportunities. This is precisely why I *always* stress the importance of working for yourself and starting a business.

If you want to compete in today's job market, you need to *create jobs,* not fill them. The global economy is ideal for entrepreneurs. Your unique qualities are in demand. The key is finding out what someone is willing to pay you for. If you want some really good ideas on how to get going, visit Web sites such as fiverr.com, and check updates on my blog at adammaggio.com.

If you find a system where it's "plug and play" and follow the leader's strategies, you will most likely achieve the exact results. This is why I usually recommend direct sales opportunities. In these businesses, you step into a franchise, roll up your sleeves, and go to work. From my own experiences, I can tell you that building a business is not easy, but it is worth it. If I had started out needing a lot of capital, I would not be here today. But because of the unique direct sales model, you can trade equity for sweat.

When you find the right mentor, follow each of his or her steps and make absolutely no excuses. One hint of an excuse, and any mentor worth his or her

397

salt will drop you immediately. All leaders got there by not giving excuses. They will certainly not accept them from you.

Bio

Leading rock star marketer Adam Maggio took the sales force by storm when, at the tender age of 24, he was ranked No. 8 out of more than 68,000 distributors at an Inc. 500 company. Since then, Adam has gone from strength to strength leading his team to generating several million dollars per year. Being successful offline and wanting to help more people, Adam decided to take his business online so he could reach a wider scope of audience and help anyone from any walk of life to wake up to his or her inner entrepreneur. To find out more about Adam Maggio, and see available openings at his agency, visit his Web site and take advantage of the free training available there: http://AdamMaggio.com/davinci.

98

Lifelong Learning as a Practical Solution to Unemployment

George Grant, IMD, PhD

Times have changed. Not that long ago many people stayed in the same job, or at least the same career, from the time they entered the workforce until they retired. Today, the experts tell us, the lifelong career is a thing of the past. In fact, the typical North American can expect to make eight job changes and have as many as five different careers during his or her working life.

Some will have change forced upon them by downsizing, mergers, and re-structuring, as well as by new technology. Others will have it thrust upon them by stress and burnout. And still others will seek career changes because they want something more challenging.

Whatever the reasons for job or career changes, it's obvious that we are going to have to learn new skills and expand our fields of knowledge. No longer is the education we had when we entered the workforce going to sustain us until we retire. In other words, we are all going to have to become lifelong learners to keep up with the changing times. And for many of us, this will mean taking three giant steps.

Lifelong learning means that education is diverse, adapted to the individual, and available throughout our lives. The greatest benefits can be summarized into three categories: coping with the fast-changing world; receiving greater paychecks by having more job opportunities; and—the huge last one—enriching and fulfilling the life.

Lifelong learning is viewed as a strategy to create opportunity for people to learn throughout their life span. Lifelong learning is the continued educational experience that utilizes noncredit academic courses, educational travel, and community service and volunteerism to fully engage the brain, heighten physical activity, and maintain healthy social relationships.

Lifelong learning is a process through which individuals acquire knowledge, skills, and values in a range of formal and informal settings throughout life. It provides formal education, vocational training, and personal development. Lifelong learning enables informed citizens to make positive and rewarding contributions to sustain their environment, their community, and the economy.

This is the most practical solution to unemployment worldwide. When it comes to our working lives, one of the most important benefits of lifelong learning is that it provides us with more choices. In other words, the more skills we have, the more marketable we are, and the more able we are to take advantage of the positive aspects of change.

By adopting lifelong learning through academic learning, educational adventure travel, and our renewed sense of volunteerism, we expand our awareness, embrace self-fulfillment, and truly create an exciting multidimensional life. This can create a new job, career, or self-employment opportunity. It doesn't get any better than that.

The last few decades have been a period of significant change for the higher education industry. Although many programs have had trouble surviving, continuing education, professional development, and other nontraditional programs have managed to thrive, despite steep budget cuts and rapidly advancing technology. Lifelong learning is an essential skill in obtaining an entry-level position or to qualify for future promotion.

There is yet another giant step we must take toward lifelong learning: learning how to learn. And it is especially important and perhaps difficult for those of us who have been out of school for many years.

Lifelong learning is being recognized by traditional colleges and universities as a valid addition to degree attainment. Some learning is accomplished in segments or interest categories and can still be valuable to the individual and community. The economic impact of educational institutions at all levels will continue to be significant in the future as formal courses of study continue and interest-based subjects are pursued.

Whether you attend a brick-and-mortar institution or online schools, there is a great economic impact worldwide from learning, including lifelong learning, for all age groups. The lifelong learners, including persons with academic or professional credentials, tend to find higher-paying occupations, leaving monetary, cultural, and entrepreneurial impressions on communities. E-learning is available at most colleges and universities or to individuals learning independently. Online courses are even being offered for free by many institutions. In recent years, lifelong learning has been adopted in the United Kingdom as an umbrella term for postcompulsory education that falls outside of the higher education system—further education; community education; work-based learning; and similar voluntary, public sector, and commercial settings. Most colleges and universities in the United States encourage lifelong learning to nontraditional students. Professional licensure and certification courses are also offered at many universities, for instance, for teachers, social services providers, and other professionals.

Lifelong learning contributes significant benefits to the economy. It provides individuals with appropriate skills, adaptability, and better access to employment. They contribute to the economy through their labor and personal prosperity. A strategically trained workforce sustains the existing economic base and attracts new growth industries and regional investment. Organizations and communities that embrace a learning culture are more adaptive and resilient, and better able to meet new economic trends.

The social benefits of lifelong learning are equally important. Lifelong learning provides individuals with opportunities to develop self-knowledge, personal mastery, and self-esteem. Community education can foster family cohesion, social inclusion, community building, and civic participation in a democratic society.

Lifelong learning allows us to keep up with the world around us. No longer do we expect to remain in a single job or career for our entire working life. We must be willing to learn new skills, be flexible enough to change direction midstream, and be able to accept and establish new goals. To some people, this reality is frightening and can make things seem uncertain.

But this uncertainty can become your opportunity. If you feel your skills are lagging behind those of coworkers, or if you wish to change the direction of your career, talk things over with a counselor. With a counselor's guidance, you can explore the best ways to update presently needed skills. A counselor can help you to decide on what you need to learn if you are looking to move up from your present position.

We must brush up on basic skills such as taking notes, reading a textbook, and studying. What's more, we must find out how to manage our time so that we can juggle the triple responsibilities that many of us have: a home, a job, and school.

Without a doubt, pursuing personal and professional development enriches the life of those who are lifelong learners. Those relationships built along the way and the opportunities to network and to learn from each other give rise to growth and development. In-class learning is just as essential as the relationship building. Formal training and higher education promote learning new ways to lead and manage organizations, projects, and workloads. Similarly, opportunities for mentorship present themselves to new leaders who crave the guidance and direction of seasoned ones.

If you think that education is expensive, try ignorance. If you think that wellness is expensive, try illness.

Bio

Dr. George Grant is considered Canada's wellness ambassador and champion of integrative medicine, biofeedback, and nutraceuticals. He is the founder and CEO of the International Academy of Wellness. Dr. Grant enjoys a stellar academic and a fascinating career in research. He is a scientist; professor; chemist; toxicologist; nutritionist; and biofeedback, stress management, and pain specialist. He has worked as a senior consultant for Health Canada, FDA, and CDC, as well as in private practice. Dr. Grant has helped Fortune 500 companies and Olympic athletes, along with 5,000 clients worldwide. He has 100 published articles, conference presentations, book reviews, and seven bestselling books. He can be reached at http://www.academyofwellness.com.

99

Become a VIP (Very Important Person) in Your Career

❧

Deborah Brown-Volkman

Competing in today's job market has done two things to job seekers: humbled them and caused them to reinvent themselves. Humbled because people are working harder to find a job, win a job, or keep a job. Reinventing because industries are changing, companies are changing, and priorities are changing, and job seekers need to change with them.

No matter what is going on around you, you have the power to decide where your career is going. No matter what friends or family say about how hard the job market is, you are the driving force that determines your next move. Once you are able to let go of "I can't" or "It won't happen for me" and replace it with "I can" and "I will," your career transforms, and so does your job search.

You can become a VIP (very important person) in your career and take back the power in your job search by following the three steps:

Step 1. The *V*: Create Your Vision

All of life's journeys begin with the phrase *I want*. Think about your career and the times when you said I want. Maybe you said I want go to college—and then enrolled in school and completed your degree. Maybe you said I want to work for a large or a small company—and you are working there now. (Or were working there previously.) Maybe you said I want to lead teams—and that's one of your current or past responsibilities. *I want* is a very powerful phrase. Without it, it's hard to go very far.

Imagine going on a trip without selecting a destination beforehand. What would you pack? How would you get there? Where would you stay? Your trip probably would not end up being much fun. It's the same with your job search. Not being able to visualize your desired result leads to results not happening.

So what's a vision? My definition of a *vision* is a snapshot of what you want your career and life to look like in the future. Ask yourself, "What is my ideal job? What is my dream career? If I could not fail, what would I be doing next in my career?" This picture will be your road map and will give your job search a reachable destination. It will also provide you with focus and direction.

Step 2. The *I*: Get Inspired

I've seen many individuals create amazing careers. Even in this job market, when they are told there are no jobs, they are still securing positions they love. How are they doing it? They are inspired.

Inspiration is that almighty force that arises from the inside. It lights you up and gives you more power than you'd ever expect. Think about a time in your career when you were excited and energized because everything was going your way. Apply that feeling to where you are now.

This step is about letting go of the negative thoughts that are holding you back and creating positive ones that will excite you and move you forward. So what's important to let go of?

Let go of fear. Fear is normal. Who isn't afraid when faced with uncertainty? If you let fear win, fear will kill your creativity and stop your momentum. You will not wake up one day and be magically unafraid. You get over fear when you face it and you take steps forward. That's when you get to see that what you fear is not as bad as you think it is.

Let go of believing your efforts won't make a difference. Or the need to have a guarantee. Do you want to know 100 percent up front that if you go for your goal, it will come out exactly the way you want? Guess what? You will not get that promise. Maybe the road you think you are supposed to take will shift as you take it. You don't know, and maybe you are not supposed to know. The only thing you get up front is a feeling in your gut. If it feels right, that's the direction to follow. If it feels wrong, run the other way.

Let go of believing you can't reach your goal. Why can't you reach your goal? You may have a long list with reasons why you can't. If you've already made up a failure list in your mind, create a success list instead. Write down why you are great at what you do. Detail your accomplishments. Look at what you have written every morning. You may not believe it today, but if you keep looking, you will believe it tomorrow.

Let anger go. The longer you work, or look for work, the greater the chance of being disappointed. When you hold onto an emotion that hurts you, it holds you back. Bitterness and blame are for victims. You are not a victim. You are in charge of your career. Release anger so you can move forward again.

Once you let go of the negative thoughts that are holding you back, you are free—finally. Once you start believing for the best, you get the best. Ideas come to you in the middle of the night. You feel as though you can tackle anything. Your power is returning, and it's time to make what you want, aka your vision, happen.

Step 3. The *P*: Create Your Plan

Once you can see what you want, and you are excited about it, it's time to get moving. Here are three steps to put into your plan:

- What do you want? Example: I want a new job, want to change careers, make more money, or enhance my attitude.
- When will your "what" be achieved? Example: three months from now, six months, a year from now. Be specific.
- How will you get there? These are the specific steps you will take to get what you want.

Goals are reached when you are actively working on them. Mapping out what you are going to do—and then doing it—is your recipe for success.

Then you get into action. Nothing happens without movement. Action is essential to your success. You must work on your plan for it to happen. And you achieve your plan one step at a time.

Then you move forward, no matter what. I've seen many people on the brink of success fail because they stopped right before they reached their goal.

There are no accidents when it comes to goal achievement. If you are working toward your goals on a consistent basis, you will reach them. It might not be in the time frame you want, but you will get there. If you are not working on your goals, or if you just work on them here and there, you probably will not reach them, or it will take a long time.

Move forward, no matter what. Movement will make you a VIP in your career.

Bio

Deborah Brown-Volkman is a professional certified coach (PCC), veteran coach, career expert, and the president of Surpass Your Dreams, Inc., a successful career, life, and mentor coaching company that has been delivering a message of motivation, success, and personal fulfillment since 1998. She provides career coaching for those who want a new job, new career, or a new way to flourish in today's workplace. Deborah has been featured in a number of prestigious publications, including *The Wall Street Journal, The New York Times*, and *Fortune* magazine. Deborah is the author of several best-selling books, including *Coach Yourself to a New Career, Don't Blow It! The Right Words for the Right Job,* and *How to Feel Great at Work Every Day.* She can be reached at (631) 874-2877; at info@surpassyourdreams.com; or at http://www.surpassyourdreams.com.

100

You've Been Fired. Now What?

⁓

Connie D. Henriquez

I know. It seems like the end of the world. Whether you knew it was coming or not, guess what? You're going to be OK. In fact, you're going to be more than OK. Instead, you're going to be just freakin' awesome once you move through this little hurdle called the next very fabulous phase of your life.

Now. I get that you can very quickly line list every possible reason in the world that losing your job is the worst thing ever. I get it. You've lost your job security; you're concerned about money; and you have no clue what to do next. In fact, you don't know what to do at all.

It makes perfect sense that you would be concerned and possibly angry about being fired. But think about this: Will feeling bad or angry get your job back? Will feeling bad or angry pay your bills? Hell, no. If it did, I would say knock yourself out. But knowing what I know about universal law, you can feel angry and discouraged for only so long before you need to move on toward your next step to feel any sense of relief (or hope, for that matter).

Right now you have only two options. That's right, just two. And usually you will need to try out Option 1 for a bit before going to Option 2. But that depends on the individual and how quickly you want to feel better.

Option 1

You can be upset, angry, fearful, and scared to death. Again, these are all normal emotions based on what you have just experienced, and it is very important that you validate these emotions. But the clincher is this: the longer you stay in this angry state of emotion, the longer you will feel bad. And the longer you feel bad, the longer you keep yourself apart from being a vibrational match to the solution you are seeking such as a new exciting position, new opportunities, new business idea, more money. Get it?

All emotions are good and necessary; they indicate what direction in life you are thinking and moving toward. Therefore, if you feel good, you are moving toward good things such as new opportunities, new ideas, new people that can help or inspire you on your way to your next phase in your life.

Or if you feel bad or angry, you are instead moving toward not such great things such as discouraging conversations about a declining economy, no opportunities, or people who will discourage you (unintentionally, of course) thus preventing and moving you away from the next very fabulous phase in your life. Make sense?

Once you have experienced the clarity of Option 1 and have accepted that you no longer want to feel like crap, you will find the only other choice you have to feel better is to surrender to Option 2.

Option 2

Everything is always working out for you. Even if at this time you do not see the bigger picture, you need to know that everything is working out perfectly for you.

How do I know this? Because the universe knows what you want from life. Since you were born, you have been collecting data from all of your life experiences, whether it's been regarding work, career, relationships, health, whatever. Every time you experienced something you did not want, you then, in turn, created a newfound clarity about what you did want! Your then strong wants or preferences were established. As a result, the universe has been knocking itself out sending you the signals necessary to move you in the direction of what you want—but you don't go.

You see, the most common thing people are afraid of—and hence why most people stay in the same mundane career a lot longer than they should—is change. Most people become comfortable far too long and forget that life is supposed to be fun. Life is supposed to be a myriad of new adventures, new careers, and new possibilities.

Because of the fear the news channels love to impose about everyday life, people become disinterested and complacent fearing change of any sort when, in reality, it is the eagerness of change that brings about the excitement of life and our life's purpose.

Although most have become disinterested and complacent and fearful of change, those working in an unfulfilling career have become oblivious to the signals the universe has been sending in regards to inspiring them (and you) to make a change:

- You hated your job. (And you stayed working there anyway!)
- Your job became so easy it was so not inspiring. (And you stayed working there anyway!)
- You were stressed beyond belief. (And you stayed working there anyway!)
- It affected your health. (And you stayed working there anyway!)
- Your boss was a jerk. (And you stayed working there anyway!)
- You did not agree with the management style. (And you stayed working there anyway!)
- You were passed over for numerous promotions. (And you stayed working there anyway!)
- You didn't really care for the people you worked with. (And you stayed working there anyway!)
- You knew you deserved more money. (And you stayed working there anyway!)
- You knew you wanted something different. (And you stayed working there anyway!)

And the list goes on. You get my point.

Many any of us have lived by the same belief that you find a career early on and you stick with it for the rest of your life. Can you imagine one career for an entire life? Now, I know many people have done it, and many people still do stick with one career choice and are perfectly happy.

But I hate to break it to you: you were not born to be like everyone else. You didn't come into this lifetime to do what everyone else was doing. Instead, you came into this lifetime with the knowing you wanted to create a freakin' awesome life full of fun experiences and opportunities that would contribute to your overall growth and evolution while here on this planet.

After several attempts in failed signals, the universe knew it was time for you to make your move. And because you weren't going on your own, the universe released you from where you were to help get you to where you want to be. Even if right now you have no idea where that may be, trust that who you were wanted so much more than what your job was offering and that opportunities lie ahead.

So move forward with the inspiration that all will be great. One day, not far from today, you will look back at this experience and past employer with much appreciation for being the catalyst of change necessary in setting you free to be who you are and for being the force of change needed to get you to where you want to be—moving toward the next very fabulous phase of your life.

Bio

Connie D. Henriquez is an upbeat, chic New York-based beauty executive, certified life coach expert, and founder of the premier lifestyle brand Start Loving Life®, the lifestyle choice of forward thinkers who know they deserve more out of life and settling for less is not an option. Discover how to finally feel secure, cool, and confident. Live your life full throttle. No more BS. Now is the perfect time to *start loving life*. For more information visit, http://www.startlovinglife.com.

You're Hired! Career Secrets from the Mind of Donald Trump

❧

Samantha Etkin

Love him or hate him, Donald Trump has become synonymous with success in the business world. Even if you're not a fan of his public image, it's almost impossible to deny that he knows what he is talking about when it comes to career success. Trump not only has built a massive empire but also has enabled numerous people to accelerate their careers with an opportunity to help run one of his companies via his hit reality show *The Apprentice*, which has been billed as "The Ultimate Job Interview."

Just as Trump's guidance and advice have furthered the career paths of *The Apprentice* contestants, it can assist you on your path. Following are a few of Trump's most motivational quotes that can easily be applied to both your job search and the advancement of your career.

"Get going. Move forward. Aim high. Plan a takeoff. Don't just sit on the runway and hope someone will come along and push the airplane. It simply won't happen."

You don't really expect your dream job to simply land in your lap, do you? It takes a lot of legwork to find the best opportunities and simply get your foot in the door. The more time you invest in the hunt, the more likely it is that you'll secure an interview. If you are looking to advance in your current career, take the first steps toward fostering a conversation with your superiors. Prove to them that you deserve the position you want to hold. In either case, be proactive and take your future into your own hands.

"You can have the most wonderful product in the world, but if people don't know about it, it's not going to be worth much."

You might be the most qualified candidate out there, but your interviewer doesn't necessarily know that. You need to sell yourself the same way you'd sell a product. Advertise your best qualities, and clearly highlight how you can uniquely benefit the company. However, as Trump says, *"Don't brag too much. It can be taken the wrong way. Being confident doesn't have to include too many of your greatest accomplishments."*

"Many people are afraid to fail, so they don't try."

How many times have you decided not to submit your résumé for a position because you didn't think you were qualified? How many times have you passed on an opportunity to suggest something "outside the box" that could potentially have opened up new doors for your company? If that sounds like you, then ask yourself, "What do I really have to lose?" What's the worst that could happen if you apply for a position a bit out of your reach? What is the dreaded result of proposing an idea that gets rejected? Not much, really. You end up where you started. On the flip side, what is the best-case scenario? You land a job you really want or you're seen as a great innovator. If you never put your neck on the line, you can't fail, but you can't succeed either.

"If you're interested in 'balancing' work and pleasure, stop trying to balance them. Instead make your work more pleasurable."

Are you currently "working for the weekend," waiting impatiently until you can finally clock out and really enjoy yourself at home? If so, take some time to figure out what you need to accomplish on a day-to-day basis to feel useful, productive, appreciated, and fulfilled at work. If you can't make that happen, consider a change in career. What are you truly passionate about, and how can you turn it into a profession? Which brings me to Trump's next piece of advice …

"Be passionate about your work. Never let it become just a job."

Most of your time will likely be spent at work, so wouldn't you be better off if you genuinely enjoyed what you do? Furthermore, your boss or prospective employers will—consciously or subconsciously—evaluate you on whether you show enthusiasm for your work. Who would be more likely to receive a promotion, an office drone or a passionate employee? Who would be more likely to land the job, someone who "just needs the work" or someone who exudes interest and excitement about the industry and the position?

"It doesn't hurt to get more education."

If you're currently out of work, or if you are looking to move forward in your current job or company, consider taking some time out of your schedule to further your education. There are multitudes of continuing education programs available for adults who are unable to take on the role of a full-time student. Check out your local community college to see if it is offering any classes that can build your skills to help you progress in your industry.

"It's very important that people aspire to be successful. The only way you can do it is if you look at somebody who is."

Do you have a career mentor? If not, go out and get one! If you're looking for a job, find someone in your industry to speak to. Perhaps a mentor can offer you invaluable insider advice that can help further you in your job search. If you're looking to move up the ladder in your company, find a superior and try to gain some insight into how that person got to where she or he is. One of the best ways to succeed in your career is to find the people who have already gained the kind of success you aspire to and learn as much from them as possible.

"I am no stranger to working hard. I have done it all my life."

You know the old saying, "Nothing worthwhile ever comes easily." Career success is no different. Donald Trump has reportedly said that he works seven days a week, and, clearly, all his hard work and dedication have paid off. If you want to advance in your career, give your current workload the time and effort it truly needs for the finished product to really shine. You will be noticed if you are constantly keeping your nose to the grindstone, surpassing expectations, and producing quality work.

If you're looking for the "magic bullet" that will guarantee your career advancement, you're probably not going to find it. However, advice straight from the mouth of Donald Trump himself should prove to be a pretty reliable means of guiding you on your journey toward a fulfilling and successful career.

<u>B</u>io

Samantha Etkin is managing editor of SelfGrowth.com, the No. 1 resource for self-improvement on the Internet. She has been immersed in the editorial arena since 2006, having previously worked as a scriptwriter for Daytime Emmy Award-winning Discovery Channel and TLC programs at Tapestry International and as an editor for the B2B publication *Applied Clinical Trials*. Her work has also been published in the 2012 and 2013 Stephen King Desk Calendars. Samantha holds a degree in journalism and mass communication from New York University. She can be reached at sametkin@gmail.com.

A PRODUCT OF SELFGROWTH.COM
AND RIKLANRESOURCES.COM

Self Improvement Online, Inc. - Our network is composed of four websites, SelfGrowth.com, NaturalHealthWeb.com, SelfImprovementNewsletters.com and SelfGrowthMarketing.com. Our network of websites receives more than 2,000,000 visitors a month and our email newsletters or e-zines go to more than 950,000 weekly subscribers. Our websites and newsletters are read in more than 100 different countries, with the largest groups of readers and visitors coming from the United States, Canada, Australia, United Kingdom, and New Zealand.

Riklan Resources, LLC. – A career services firm for the individual and corporations.

For individuals: We offer résumé writing and related services, career coaching, interview training, and behavioral profiling.

For corporations and businesses: We offer a wide variety of customized training programs such as customer service, team building, supervisory, leadership, performance management, interviewing, diversity, sexual harassment awareness / hostile work-environment, and more.

ABOUT SELFGROWTH.COM

SelfGrowth.com is an Internet super-site for self-improvement and personal growth. It is part of a network of websites owned and operated by Self Improvement Online, Inc., a privately held New Jersey-based Internet company.

Their websites receives more than 2,000,000 visitors a month and their email newsletters or e-zines go to more than 950,000 weekly subscribers.

The company's mission is to provide their website visitors with high-quality self-improvement and natural health information, with the one simple goal in mind: making their lives better. They provide information on topics ranging from goal setting and stress management to natural health and alternative medicine.

Other Facts About The Site

SelfGrowth.com offers a wealth of information on self-improvement. Our site:

- Publishes three informative newsletters on self-improvement, personal growth, and natural health.
- Offers more than 340,000 unique articles from more than 27,000 experts.
- Links to more than 71,000 websites in an organized directory.
- Gets visitors from more than 100 countries.

Contact Information

ADDRESS: Self Improvement Online, Inc.
            1130 Campus Drive West
            Morganville, New Jersey 07751
PHONE: (732) 617–1030
E-MAIL: webmaster@selfgrowth.com
WEBSITE: www.selfgrowth.com

ABOUT MICHELLE A. RIKLAN, ACRW, CPRW, CEIC

Michelle A. Riklan holds a B.A. in Theatre, English Literature and Speech Communications from Hofstra University. While beginning her corporate career, she pursued and completed a M.A. in Speech and Interpersonal Communications from New York University where she also served as an Instructor in Voice and Diction/Public Speaking. Utilizing her education and presentation skills, she continued a career path in Human Resource Management. Her generalist background is all inclusive, but her areas of expertise include employment, employee relations, and training and development.

With a combined 25 years of in-house corporate and targeted consulting experience, Michelle services large corporations as well as small businesses and individuals in all aspects of organizational development and career management. As a consultant, she has had the opportunity to work in a wide range of industries.

Corporate, Media, and Speaking Engagements

Michelle is a frequent media guest, training/workshop facilitator, and speaker. Topics include leadership development, management, team-building, DISC, social media, marketing tools for job seekers (resumes, cover letters, LinkedIn), job search, interviewing, entering the workforce, changing careers, and more.

Corporate Outplacement

Michelle's firm, Riklan Resources, offers outplacement services to help companies and employees ease the pain of what can be a stressful and sensitive process. With a variety of valuable programs and solutions, Riklan Resources is available for both on-site and remote support.

Certifications/Training

Michelle is an internationally recognized, award winning résumé writer and a member of several prestigious career and résumé writing organizations. The resources and support afforded by being a member of this industry/community are plentiful and allow her clients to reap the benefits of these affiliations. Résumés created at Riklan Resumes are unique, tailored for each individual client and receive the individualized attention that such a service deserves.

As a Certified Professional Résumé Writer (CPRW) and Certified Employment Interview Consultant (CEIC), Michelle has written hundreds of résumés and coached clients through all phases of the job search. Her résumés get results!

Michelle's training as a DISC administrator and Myers-Briggs assessment administrator is a benefit to her clients to gain insight into a person's behavioral style, which impacts a client's chosen career path. She works with her clients to identify specific talents, capitalize on a client's talents and his/her potential and continuing value to an organization, and offer tools to improve interpersonal skills and interviewing performance.

Memberships

- American Society of Training and Development (ASTD)
- Association of Career Professionals International (ACPI)
- Association for the Promotion of Campus Activities (APCA)
- Career Directors International (CDI)
- Career Thought Leaders (CTL)
- National Association of Colleges and Employers (NACE)
- National Career Development Association (NCDA)
- Professional Association of Résumé Writers/Career Coaches (PARW/CC)
- Society of Human Resource Management (SHRM)
- The National Résumé Writers' Association (NRWA)

Self-Improvement Online

Michelle is also a co-founder of Self Improvement Online, Inc. a privately held, New Jersey-based Internet company. The company's mission is to provide informative, quality self-improvement and natural health information to help people improve their lives with information ranging from goal setting and stress management to natural health and alternative medicine. The network is composed of four websites, SelfGrowth.com, NaturalHealthWeb. com, SelfImprovementNewsletters.com and NaturalHealthNewsletters.com. Self-Improvement Online's websites receive more than 2,000,000 unique visitors a month and email newsletters or e-zines go to more than 950,000 weekly subscribers. The websites and newsletters are read in more than 100 different countries, with the largest groups of readers and visitors coming from the United States, Canada, Australia, United Kingdom, and New Zealand.

ABOUT DAVID RIKLAN

David Riklan is the president and co-founder of Self Improvement Online, Inc., the leading provider of self-improvement and personal growth information on the Internet.

His company was founded in 1998 and now maintains four websites on self-improvement and natural health, including:

- www.SelfGrowth.com
- www.SelfImprovementNewsletters.com
- www.SelfGrowthMarketing.com
- www.NaturalHealthWeb.com

His company also publishes four email newsletters going out to more than 950,000 weekly subscribers on the topics of self-improvement, natural health, personal growth, relationships, home business, sales skills, and brain improvement.

David's first book—*Self Improvement: The Top 101 Experts Who Help Us Improve Our Lives*—has been praised by leading industry experts as the "Encyclopedia of Self Improvement." That book's success motivated him to continue publishing books which, like the one you're reading now, seek to improve the lives of others.

He has a degree in chemical engineering from the State University of New York at Buffalo and has 20 years of experience in sales, marketing, management, and training for companies such as Hewlett-Packard and The Memory Training Institute.

His interest in self-improvement and personal growth began more than 20 years ago and was best defined through his work as an instructor for Dale Carnegie Training, a performance-based training company.

David is a self-professed self-improvement junkie—and proud of it. His house is full of self-improvement books, CDs and DVDs. He took his first self-improvement class, an Evelyn Wood speed-reading course, when he was 16 years old, and his interest hasn't ceased yet.

He lives and works in New Jersey with his wife and business partner, Michelle Riklan. Together, they run Self Improvement Online, Inc. and are raising three wonderful children: Joshua, Jonathan, and Rachel.

AUTHOR INDEX

425